Artistic and Rhetorical Patterns in Quechua Legendary Texts

SIL International
Publications in Translation and Textlinguistics
3

Publications in Translation and Textlinguistics is a peer-reviewed series published by SIL International. The series is a venue for works concerned with all aspects of translation and textlinguistics, including translation theory, exegesis, pragmatics, and discourse analysis. While most volumes are authored by members of SIL, suitable works by others will also form part of the series.

Series Editors

Freddy Boswell
Mary Ruth Wise

Volume Editors

Eugene Loos
Mary Ruth Wise
Rhonda Hartell Jones

Production Staff

Bonnie Brown, Managing Editor
Margaret González, Compositor
Barbara Alber, Graphic Artist

Artistic and Rhetorical Patterns in Quechua Legendary Texts

Ågot Bergli

SIL International
Dallas, Texas

© 2010 by SIL International
Library of Congress Catalog Card Number: 2009941810
ISBN: 978-1-55671-244-9
ISSN: 1550-588X

Printed in the United States of America

All rights reserved. No part of this publication may be reproduced, stored in a retrieval system, or transmitted in any form or by any means—electronic, mechanical, photocopy, recording, or otherwise—without the express permission of SIL International. However, short passages, generally understood to be within the limits of fair use, may be quoted without permission.

Copies of this and other publications of the SIL International may be obtained from

International Academic Bookstore
SIL International
7500 W. Camp Wisdom Road
Dallas, TX 75236-5699

Voice: 972-708-7404
Fax: 972-708-7363
Email: academic_books@sil.org
Internet: http://www.ethnologue.com

Contents

List of Figures	ix
Preface	xi
Acknowledgements	xiii
Abbreviations	xv
1 Introduction	1
1.1 A general perspective on the study	1
1.2 About the data	4
1.3 Procedures	5
1.4 Significance of the research	6
1.5 The organization of this work	7
2 Assumptions about Texts	9
2.1 Preliminaries	9
2.2 Text, communication, and context	10
2.2.1 Different orientations	10
2.2.2 Relevance Theory	11
2.2.3 In conclusion	13
2.3 Culture and orality	15
2.4 Linearity, structures and recall	20
2.4.1 The problem of linearity	20
2.4.2 Structures and recall	20
2.4.3 In conclusion	21
2.5 "Text" versus "oral literature"	22
2.6 Poetic versus formula	24
2.6.1 Constancy of form	24

    2.6.2 Is formula art?. 25
    2.6.3 Prose, poetry, and genre 27
  2.7 Linguistics and text analysis. 28
    2.7.1 General assumptions 28
    2.7.2 Linguistic categories and extended functions 29
    2.7.3 An example of extended functions. 31
    2.7.4 In conclusion 33

3 Theory and Methodology 35
  3.1 Preliminaries 35
  3.2 Hymes's approach 36
    3.2.1 Theoretical 36
    3.2.2 Methodological 38
    3.2.3 Other approaches similar to Hymes's 40
    3.2.4 In conclusion 41
  3.3 Literary/folkloric studies 42
    3.3.1 Generalities 42
    3.3.2 Propp's approach 43
    3.3.3 Olrik's approach. 44
    3.3.4 Jakobson's approach 46
    3.3.5 Leech's approach. 49
    3.3.6 In conclusion 52
  3.4 Longacre's approach to text analysis 53
    3.4.1 Preliminaries 53
    3.4.2 The profile and salience scheme of a text 53
  3.5 Other approaches in line with Longacre's salience scheme . 56
    3.5.1 Hopper and Thompson 57
    3.5.2 D. Payne 57
    3.5.3 Jones and Jones 58
    3.5.4 Wallace 59
    3.5.5 Chafe 60
    3.5.6 In conclusion 62

4 Quechua Language and Culture 65
  4.1 Facts about the Quechua languages 65
    4.1.1 Geographical situation 65
    4.1.2 Grammatical features of Quechua 66
  4.2 Some aspects of Quechua culture 74
  4.3 Verbal art forms 76
    4.3.1 Mannheim. 76
    4.3.2 Szemiñski 80
    4.3.3 Carpenter 81

4.3.4 In conclusion	81
5 Textual Patterns (I)—Ayacucho Coracora Quechua	**83**
5.1 The textual data	83
5.2 The basic organization of the *Juan del Oso* text	84
5.3 The presentational form of the story	86
5.3.1 Surface features—artistic patterns?	87
5.3.2 The rhetorical patterns of the text	106
5.3.3 In conclusion	124
6 Textual Patterns (II)—Ayacucho Coracora Quechua	**125**
6.1 Preliminaries	125
6.2 Analysis of smaller texts	126
6.2.1 The presentational forms of *Ampatopa Cuenton*	126
6.2.2 The presentational forms of the *Mankapa Cuenton*	132
6.2.3 The presentational forms of *Watuchi I*	137
6.2.4 The presentational forms of *Watuchi II*	144
6.2.5 Typical features in the texts	148
6.3 Other patterns seen in *Juan del Oso*	149
6.3.1 Acts	149
6.3.2 Complementary halves	154
6.4 Patterns pertaining in general to the texts	155
6.4.1 Specific units	155
6.4.2 Other parallel patterns	157
6.4.3 Numeric patterns	158
6.4.4 In conclusion	158
7 Quechua Textual Patterns—Shausha	**159**
7.1 Preliminaries	159
7.2 Language specifics	160
7.3 Patterns found in the Shausha texts	160
7.3.1 The presentational forms of 'The Fox and the Frog'	161
7.3.2 Patterns of other texts	170
7.3.3 Shausha texts and Coracora texts compared	179
8 Quechua Text Patterns and Their Implications	**185**
8.1 Preliminaries	185
8.2 Structural patterns	185
8.2.1 Generalities	185
8.2.2 The function of the evidential	186
8.2.3 Main event line	194
8.2.4 Which pattern gives rise to the other?	195
8.2.5 Profiles of the texts	197
8.2.6 In conclusion	199

  8.3 Artistic patterns once more 199
    8.3.1 Parallelism 199
    8.3.2 Complementary halves and other patterns 203
    8.3.3 Textual patterns and universality 209
  8.4 Final remarks 211

Appendices
 How to read the appendices 215
 Appendix 1 Okumaripa Watuchin 217
 Appendix 2 Okumaripa Watuchin – Chart 235
 Appendix 3 Mankapa Cuenton 243
 Appendix 4 Watuchi I 247
 Appendix 5 Watuchi II 255
 Appendix 6 El Zorro y la Vizcacha I 263
 Appendix 7 El Zorro y la Vizcacha II 269
 Appendix 8 Hwan Usu 275

Bibliography 289

List of Figures

Figure 1: The profile of the text. 114
Figure 2: Structure of *Ampatopa Cuenton*. 129
Figure 3: Structure of *Mankapa Cuenton* 133
Figure 4: Structure I of *Watuchi I* 140
Figure 5: Structure II of *Watuchi I*. 141
Figure 6: Structure of *Watuchi II* 145
Figure 7: Overall structure of *Juan del Oso*. 149
Figure 8: Act constituting the major part of the stage. 150
Figure 9: Act serving as part of the inciting moment 151
Figure 10: Act containing episodic development 151
Figure 11: Bridging act containing episodic development 152
Figure 12: Act containing climax (and culminating point). . . . 152
Figure 13: Act containing culminating point and denouement . . 153
Figure 14: Act containing final suspense. 153
Figure 15: Parallel patterning at different levels 157
Figure 16: Structure of *The Fox and the Frog* 165
Figure 17: Structure of *El Zorro y la Vizcacha I* 171
Figure 18: Actual structure of *El Zorro y la Vizcacha II* 173
Figure 19: Possible structure of *El Zorro y la Vizcacha II*. 174
Figure 20: Structure of *Juan del Oso*. 176
Figure 21: Hierarchical structure of the city of Cusco. 204

Preface

As a member of the Summer Institute of Linguistics (SIL International) in Peru, I have for years been in an ambience where research within languages and cultures is in focus. The study of text is also an important part of the work done by SIL linguists, and since my initial training with SIL I have had a particular interest in this area. My desire through the present research is to add another dimension to this type of study by approaching it from a somewhat different perspective (as described in the first chapter). On the other hand I also have a desire to contribute something to the Quechua-speaking population in Peru.

During my many years of work in Peru I have acquainted myself with Quechua in various ways. I first spent a short time in the country in 1981–1982 taking an introductory course in Quechua language and culture in Huanuco—a city situated in the central Andean area of Peru. During that time I also had the opportunity to spend a few days in a small Quechua village situated close to 4,000 meters above sea level. The nights were cold but the warm, sunny days with the golden ripe wheat moving in the wind coming down the mountains, and the magnificent view over the valley below, made a lasting impression on my heart. The friendliness and the hospitality of the people only increased an already existing desire to serve the Quechua people in some way or another. Later, during the years of 1985–1996 I acquainted myself with Quechua in various ways. I took a course in Quechua dialectology at the University of Lima, a course given in cooperation with SIL (Instituto Lingüístico de Verano) in Peru. Due to subversive activities in the country it was difficult to do any kind of research or other work in the rural areas, but I had the opportunity to make a few short visits to Quechua-speaking areas as well as to learn more about the Quechua language through my editorial work on academic publications. I worked on several Quechua grammars as well as Quechua texts from different varieties of Quechua, some of them collected by my co-workers for the publication of the book *Juan del Oso* (see below). Most of this time I either worked in Lima or at SIL's linguistic center, Yarinacocha, situated outside the city of Pucallpa in the Amazon rain forest of Peru.

At the end of 1996 I had the opportunity to research Quechua texts for a Ph.D. degree from the Department of Linguistics at the Norwegian University of Science and Technology, Trondheim (NTNU). The present book is a somewhat expanded version of my doctoral dissertation; my analysis is basically the same, but I have chosen to look at it from a few other perspectives by including insights from more authors and some of my other works.

During my editorial work on the collection of the texts in the *Juan del Oso* book (see Weber 1987), I discovered interesting features that convinced me that at least some of the texts were organized in a formulaic/artistic manner. My initial studies concentrated on these texts. However, it became clear that it would be necessary on the one hand to limit the study to only a few varieties of Quechua and on the other hand to expand the study to include more texts from the two varieties I finally decided to include, from the two major branches of Quechua in Peru (see chapter 1 and chapter 4).

In 1999 I again had the opportunity to spend four months in Peru for further research in relation to the present project, which included working through some more text material and interviewing SIL Quechua linguists. A few attempts to interview Quechua speakers in regards to the present study did not prove successful.

However, during this time I had an opportunity to visit the Ayacucho area where I got to know some lovely Quechua people. My trip did not take me as far as the Coracora area where many of my research texts stem from, but the people I got to know in the city of Ayacucho insisted that the Coracora Quechua was roughly equal to their own variety spoken within the city of Ayacucho.

I trust this book will prove useful for linguists and other scholars not only within the realm of Quechua language and culture but in other parts of the world as well.

Acknowledgements

Many people over the years have played a role in my learning more about languages in general and about Quechua in particular, teachers like Stephen Levinsohn and Robert Longacre who have played an important part in prompting my interest in the study of text. The works of many of my SIL colleagues, in Peru in particular, have enhanced this interest. I am specifically indebted to the SIL Peru Editor and Linguistics Coordinator at the time, Mary Ruth Wise, who through my editorial work allowed me to work on several volumes related to both Quechua and to text analysis. As for insights into Quechua language and culture, I am particularly grateful for the courses taught by David Weber, Peter Landerman, and David Coombs.

As for the present work, the following deserve specific mention:

My always positive advisor, Thorstein Fretheim, Professor in linguistics at NTNU Trondheim, who during the writing of my dissertation patiently read my manuscript numerous times, made corrections, and provided useful comments that no doubt helped to improve it a great deal. I am very grateful to him for taking on the task of being my advisor for the project and sharing of his linguistic expertise.

Eugene Loos, Associate Senior Editor of SIL International, who has made corrections and comments and given me numerous valuable suggestions. Working with him has been a very encouraging experience.

David Weber, Quechua scholar that he is, has patiently answered many questions related to this specific research, given numerous comments on my analysis, and provided new insights into Quechua language and culture. I thank him for generously giving of his time.

Mary Ruth Wise, who read my initial analysis as well as the present version, has given many useful suggestions, specifically in regards to literature to read. I want to thank her and the SIL administration in Peru for encouraging me to go ahead with this research.

I also want to thank the many Quechua linguists in SIL Peru for sharing their insights with me.

My home church, Mo Pinsemenighet, and numerous individuals deserve recognition and thanks for the way they have believed in me and supported me, both morally and economically over the years, as well as during the time of my research and the present work.

Last, but not least, I want to thank my loving parents for their support in so many different ways during the years. My father passed away in 2006, but his faith in me and his interest in my work has meant more to me than I can ever fully express.

Now unto the King eternal, immortal, invisible, the only wise God,
be honour and glory for ever and ever!
(1 Timothy 1:17 KJV)

To Him I owe life and the capabilities to reason and to think!

Abbreviations

12	first person plural inclusive
12CND	first person plural inclusive conditional
12FUT	first person plural inclusive future
12P	first person plural inclusive possessive
1FUT	first person future
1FUT2	first person future with second person object
1O	first person object
1P	first person possessive
1PRS2	first person subject with second person object
2	second person subject
2CND	second person conditional
2IMP	second person imperative
2P	second person possessive
3	third person subject
3FUT	third person future
3IMP	third person imperative
3P	third person possessive
ABL	ablative
ABOVE	above/aspectual
ACCOMP	accompany (comitative)
ADV	adverbializer (same subject)/adverbial
ADVDS	adverbializer, different subject
ADVSS	adverbializer, same subject
AFAR	afar
AG	agentive
ALONG	along
ALSO	also
ASP	aspect

BEN	benefactive 2
BELOW	below/aspectual
CAUS	causative
COND	conditional
CONJ	conjecture
CRT	certain
DEF	definite
Den	denouement
DES	desiderative
DIM	diminutive
DIR	direct information
DIRSEC	direct information-for certain (secure)
DOUBT	doubtful
DS	different subject
DUR	duration
EMPH	emphatic
GEN	genitive
GOAL	goal
HAB	habitual
HAVE	have
HERE.AND.THERE	here and there
IMPRF	imperfective
IN	into/with major impact
Inc	inciting
INF	infinitive
INSTL	institutional
INSTRM	instrument
JUST	just
LIM	limitation
LOC	location
MEL	main event line
MOMENT	sudden
MUCH	much
NARPST	narrative past
NEG	negative
NOM	nominalizer
NOW	now
OBJ	object
ONLY	only
OUT	out/aspectual
PL	plural (verbal)
PL2	plural (with second person)
PLIMPFR	plural with imperfective
PLUR	plural
PLDIR	plural with directional suffix
PNT	punctiliar

Abbreviations

PRMC	complement of purpose-motion
PRT	participle
ptcpt(s)	participant(s)
PUR	purpose
QUEST	question
RECIP	reciprocal
REF	reflexive
REL	nominalizer (relativizer)
REPET	repeatedly, various times
RPT	reportative, indirect information
Sc	scene
SIM	simility
SS	same subject
St	stanza
Susp	suspence
THEN	then
TNS	tense
TOP	topic
v	verse
VOC	vocative
VRBL	verbalizer
WITH	with
YET	yet

1
Introduction

1.1 A general perspective on the study

A preliminary study of Peruvian Quechua oral legendary texts[1] a few years ago led me to suspect that at least some legendary narrative texts have a special form where evidential markers[2] and initial connectives, as well as other cohesion features, have a special rhetorical or stylistic function in addition to their strictly grammatical function in the text.

Dell Hymes (1980, 1981, 1984, 1992, 1996, 2003) and William Bright (1982, 1984) both suggest the existence of higher organizational principles in folkloric texts in North-American Indian languages and call them versified narrative texts, not based on metrical rhythm but based on completely different criteria, like repeated initial connectives, evidential markers, direct quotations, and onomatopoeia. Hymes also suggests that cultural patterns, like certain "pattern numbers," play a role as well in the organization of text.

---

[1] For a discussion on the use of the term "text" see chapter 2.
[2] The Peruvian Quechua varieties (languages or dialects depending on the point of view) operate with three main evidential suffixes: -mi, -shi, -chi (the phonological manifestation for these might differ somewhat between varieties). What follows is a general characterization of each of them, based on Weber (1989):
   -mi 'direct information/convinced'
   -shi 'indirect information/unconvinced'
   -chi 'conjecture'
The evidential of interest for this study is the suffix -s(h)i 'indirect information', 'reportative', or 'hearsay'. It is a typical marker in legendary narrative texts.

The present research explores patterns of repeated markers and structures.

Certain linguistic markers and underlying semantic features play a role in forming higher organizational patterns of an artistic nature within Quechua legendary narrative texts. The analysis is partly based on Hymes's somewhat untraditional approach, but several other sources, e.g. Jakobson (1959, 1960, 1966, 1968), Leech 1969, 1973, 1985), Fabb (1997) are consulted as well. Of literature related to Quechua, Carpenter (1985) and Mannheim (1986) have been of most interest but other scholars are also considered in my discussions.[3]

Patterns in the rhetorical structuring of the texts identify concepts like setting, episodes, and conclusion, as well as the marking of the main event line versus events of a more backgrounding nature. This aspect of the study is based on sources like Longacre (1983), D. Payne (1992a), Hopper and Thompson (1982), Jones and Jones (1979), Chafe (1980b), Wallace (1982), as well as literature more directly related to the Quechua varieties: Stewart (1987), Weber (1989), Hintz (1996), Levinsohn (1976, 1991), Shaver (1996), and others.

The study also aims to give some indication about the extent that possible patterns are (a) conventional for Quechua varieties in general, (b) conventional within certain varieties,[4] or (c) based on individual choices.

The study of "text" (a term to be developed in chapter 2) can be approached from many different perspectives as shown by text studies undertaken in various disciplines within the humanities and social sciences, e.g. linguistics, anthropology/ethnography, the study of folklore and other literary studies. In this research I try to keep a global perspective, drawing on ideas from various disciplines to the extent I believe they have something to offer. In more recent years there has been an increasing multidisciplinary integration of the various fields concerned with the study of discourse and text; for example, van Dijk (1985a: Vol 1).

For years within the field of linguistics, study was based on what individual sentences could tell about the language in question. Few linguists stepped beyond sentence level. For example, Wallace (1982:201) remarked: "That linguistic categories contribute significantly to the structure of an extrasentential text, indeed, that one does not truly understand the meaning of a linguistic category until one comprehends its function in a text, are suggestions that mainstream twentieth-century linguistics has all but ignored." In more recent years, the study of text has become more

---

[3]Since the writing of my dissertation more studies related to Quechua oral traditions have been published; I will refer to these when possible, otherwise the publications I am aware of will be listed in the bibliography.

[4]See chapter 4 on the classification of Quechua varieties (languages).

1.1 A general perspective on the study

and more important within the linguistic field as linguists working with languages from various parts of the world have encountered puzzles on the sentence level for which they could find no answer until they expanded their study to include higher levels of text.

The concept of context is very important, but the concept has different contents depending on scholars' perspectives. Although, in the present study I analyze texts mainly from a structural point of view and consider how linguistic markers function within the textual context, I also have a wider perspective in mind and, when possible, I also consider extra-linguistic contexts, such as ethno-historic and cultural factors. Apart from the ethno-sociolinguistic concept of context, I also take into account the more cognitively oriented theories, in particular Chafe's view, as well as ideas from Relevance Theory. The concept of context will be discussed in more detail in chapter 2.

The study of text is not an innovation. Text analysis has been done for more than two thousand years within the discipline of literary studies. I believe that linguists have something to learn from this discipline, for in our studies of language we risk forgetting that language is also a vehicle for artistic expression; the answer to puzzles both on sentence level and on text level may be resolved in the discovery of artistic formulations and patternings. I trust that the present study will demonstrate this point.

On the other hand, one of the problems I contend with in defending my analysis is the matter of judicial elasticity when dealing with verbal art. I also lack a native speaker's intuition about some of the Quechua features I deal with. How can I prove that discovered patterns are artistic?

What makes a poem a poem and a folk story a folk story in general? The criteria are nebulous, but poems and stories exist and are recognized as such. That has to indicate that there are certain universals that narrators adhere to. What enables listeners to recognize them?

The analytical authors that I cite in the first chapters try to cope with identification of the features that a speaker (or writer) either (a) must conform to or (b) can avail himself of, so that the discourse is recognized by listeners as STORY or POEM and achieves the intended effect. These features are based on linguistic structures, as well as extra-linguistic cultural patterns.

The task of defining those features is still rather young in linguistic history. That means that throughout this study I try to push the envelope wider by examining information from unresearched areas (Quechua) against what has been claimed as a set of identifiable patterns in more well-known circuits.

Through my analysis I show that certain connectives, switch-reference markers, and the evidential -*shi*/-*si*, apart from their normally recognized grammatical functions, play important roles in organizing the Quechua texts at hand into regular artistic patternings based on semantic unity corresponding to a smaller episode or scene. In fact, the rotation of subjects even without switch-reference marking is part of forming such a pattern (cf. Wise and Lowe 1996). Moreover, the patterns formed through the mentioned features play a role in the rhetorical structuring of the texts with respect to both plot and main event line marking.

The textual patterns show that the SCENE is a very real cognitive unit to the Quechua speaker's mind. This also applies to the unit referred to as ACT, which is structured according to an underlying principle of duality, where the act is perceived as forming two complementary halves in a mirror image, a pattern observed within other areas of Quechua culture and social organization.

1.2 About the data

The research started with an analysis of different versions of the same story, preserved in different varieties of Quechua spoken within the major language areas referred to as Quechua A and Quechua B. The texts were published in the book *Juan del Oso* (Weber 1987). It was during my editing process of this particular book that the idea about artistic textual patterns was born.

However, as I proceeded in my research, it became necessary to expand my study to include other texts yet keep the volume to manageable proportions by limiting the study to one variety within each of the above mentioned major language areas. The texts of my initial analysis from other varieties of Quechua are only referred to when they aid me in clarifying certain aspects of analysis of the texts presented in this study.

The choice of varieties to be focused on was based on the texts readily available to me. In the case of Quechua A, a number of texts from the Ayacucho Coracora variety were published as early as 1957 (Lauriault 1957, 1958). The fact that the texts were published so early is also significant, because literacy among Quechua speakers (except for those in the larger cities) at that time was rather limited and literate people as yet were not much influenced by Spanish literary styles. A reason to focus on texts from this area, was that the Coracora *Juan del Oso* text gave me the clues to the existing patterns. In the case of Quechua B, the Shausha variety was a natural choice as I had myself helped edit a small book on

Shausha Quechua (Wroughton 1996) including a grammatical sketch as well as several texts.

The texts that I deal with have been written or orally delivered by native Quechua speakers and then recorded by my SIL colleagues in Peru. In the case of the *Juan del Oso* texts, as well as the Shausha texts, they have been analyzed morpheme by morpheme and given a free translation into Spanish by the linguists working with the respective varieties. They are all presented as running texts with paragraph breaks (the linguists' contribution); none of the texts were organized with the intention of displaying any particular patternings that might be of an artistic nature.

In the case of the Ayacucho Coracora texts, only the *Juan del Oso* text, included in the published book of 1987, is analyzed morpheme by morpheme. The presentation of all the other texts in the publications of 1957 and 1958 do not suggest paragraph breaks. The texts have a semiliteral translation into Spanish, as provided by the Quechua speakers themselves, which also often reflects a limited knowledge of Spanish.

1.3 Procedures

I have primarily focused my attention on the *Juan del Oso* text from the Coracora area of Ayacucho. This text is analyzed and discussed in some detail. Based on the analysis, I make some tentative hypotheses and some general observations, which according to good scholarly practices and the notion of empirical verifiability, are then compared and tested with other texts from the same area to see if common textual patterns exist and if my initial hypotheses hold true. These textual patterns are in turn compared with texts from Shausha Quechua. I also take into account other texts from other Quechua varieties where necessary to see if they can be said to support or refute particular conclusions.

Although my study is primarily based on linguistic structures there is a certain subjective intuition involved which applies to the study of poetic material in general. However, a component of subjective intuition is always involved in any kind of scientific research, whether it be within linguistics or some other kind of science. Givón (1984:25–26), in the presentation of his book on syntax, says that the scientist is "bound to act on less-than-complete information and to use liberal amounts of inductive/abductive/probabilistic intuition"; in other words, "a compromise between facts and intuition" seems necessary.

1.4 Significance of the research

From a linguistic point of view, my research will shed new light on some linguistic aspects and add new insights to the study of discourse patterning in general and in the Quechua varieties in particular. I show that the insights gained will also shed light on the relation between language and other cultural manifestations. Although many people have been doing textual analyses in more recent years in the Andean languages (Quechua and Aymara), they have all approached the texts from different perspectives. At the writing of my dissertation I was unaware of some of the textual interest and research going on within anthropological circles.[5] I do, however, believe that my study will bring into focus some perspectives not yet dealt with in much detail; for example, how the switch-reference markers function on text level.

I trust that the research will help the Quechua (and other indigenous groups) value their own mother tongue and their own cultural heritage. Hymes (1996:140) says the following: "Modern society does debase local tradition and creativity but does not succeed in eradicating it." I think this can be said to be true in my own cultural background. Although Norway is now a modern society in every respect and old traditions are losing ground, there are local traditions, artistic handwork, and oral art and/or music that are still very much alive. There is also a lot of initiative to rescue and/or revive old traditions in danger of being lost to younger generations. Viewed from a wider perspective, I believe that in spite of the globalization of the world due to the increasing facilities of communication, there is also a marked trend to put emphasis on the value of cultural diversity. Several organizations, for example, work for the rescue of languages in danger of extinction.[6] Let us hope that, in the case of Quechua, that which is most valuable in their cultural heritage—their mother tongue in all its creativity—will survive along side the use of the Spanish

---

[5] I am especially thinking of the many articles included in the book *Tradición oral andina y amazónica*, which was published in October 1999 (Godenzzi 1999), but brought to my attention only after the finishing of my own dissertation in 2002. In August 1999 I presented a paper "Patrones más altos de organización y su función en textos folklóricos del quechua de Ayacucho" (based on my then ongoing research) at the I Congreso de Lenguas Indígenas de Sudamérica, Universidad Ricardo Palma, Lima, Perú. The paper was published the following year (2000) in the *Actas, I Congreso de Lenguas Indígenas de Sudamérica, Tomo II*, pp. 63–77, Lima, Perú. Reading the published articles in *Tradición oral andina y amazónica* made me aware that many others are thinking along the same lines that I am in regards to certain aspects of my study. One article in particular (Hornberger 1999) has intrigued me as it supports some of my own findings.

[6] Probably the best known of these organizations is The Foundation for Endangered Languages.

language in a modern society that all the time is encroaching on the Quechua-speaking communities.

In conclusion, my more general desire is to stimulate and generate a greater awareness of how linguistic structures function in the creation of artistic narrative patterns that should be taken into account by linguists and educators working in Quechua and other languages.

1.5 The organization of this work

The remaining chapters are organized in the following way:

Chapter 2 presents some general theoretical assumptions that the present work is based on and deals with some issues related to the concept "text," particularly with respect to oral structures and artistic patternings in societies that are basically oral. It also includes a discussion related to linguistic categories and extended functions, as well as the concept of context.

Chapter 3 gives an outline of the work of various scholars and their theoretical and methodological approaches to the study of text; most attention is given to those of Hymes, Jakobson, Leech, Longacre, and Chafe. Many of the issues touched on in chapter 2 will also be considered to some degree in chapter 3 in relation to the scholars discussed there.

Chapter 4 first gives a general outline of Quechua grammar with emphasis given to those aspects that are of major significance to the present study. The latter part provides a few insights into Quechua culture, particularly related to cultural patterns as perceived in social structures as well as in various forms of verbal art. The information is mainly based on various Quechua scholars' works.

The insights presented in these first chapters provide the framework for the analysis to follow in the remaining chapters. Their order and organization within each chapter follow the analysis step by step.

Chapter 5 presents a detailed analysis of the lengthy Ayacucho Coracora *Juan del Oso* text which provides a point of departure for the analysis of the texts to follow.

Chapter 6 presents a rather detailed analysis of four smaller Ayacucho Coracora texts. It also provides a comparison between the analysis of these and that of the *Juan del Oso* text and concludes with observations on general patterns of the texts.

Chapter 7 presents the analysis of various Shausha texts, for which the analysis done in the previous chapters creates a natural basis. The final part of the chapter provides a comparison of patterns as perceived in the two varieties being scrutinized.

Chapter 8 presents further discussion of some questions raised in the course of the analysis and tentative conclusions.

All the texts treated in the present work are presented in the appendices, if not included earlier, as in the case of two of the shorter texts. The texts are all displayed to show the structural organization as I perceive it. All textual examples given in the main text have an English translation; so do all the Shausha texts in the appendices as well as the Ayacucho Coracora *Juan del Oso* text. In the case of the other texts from the latter variety, they only have a semiliteral translation in Spanish as given by the Quechua-speaking authors. In a few places I have made some changes, e.g. I reordered the phrasing and corrected the Spanish spelling to aid the reader. However, for the understanding of the discussion related to these texts, I trust that the overall structures as they are displayed in the presentations of the texts will provide the necessary background.

2
Assumptions about Texts

2.1 Preliminaries

It is assumed that certain cognitive domains are common to mankind and this is reflected in language. Without some shared cognitive domains, e.g. concepts related to the reality of the world around us, there would be no basis for developing an understanding between different ethnic groups. Talmy (1987), in comparing various languages, suggests that there is a general, universal set of notions to make up a "basic schematic framework for conceptual organization within the cognitive domain of language" (in Slobin 1991). The question is, how general and how universal? The study of many hitherto unknown languages has brought to our attention the vast differences that exist; this has been especially revealing in the different ways languages denote time, use color terms, use metaphors, etc. Language in this respect reflects cognitive processes and domains for categorization that differ between cultures (G. Lakoff 1987, Berlin and Kay 1969, Givón 1984).

From what has been said above, one can assume that the study of language can be an important tool in gaining insight into culture and cognitive processes and domains; on the other hand, studying other cultural aspects within a society might help shed light on specific language structures. It is a fairly common view that language should be studied in its cultural context (e.g. Givón 1984, Hymes 1981, Longacre 1983, Palmer 1996, Pike 1967, 1990). Not only should language be studied in its cultural context but one also has to consider how language is used in situational contexts within a specific culture. In both these respects anthropology has had a major influence on various linguistic approaches:

> Anthropology...anchors the study of language and cognition within the matrix of social structure/function and cultural world view. The role of language and communication within this matrix, and the way different language communities solve the task of coding and communicating knowledge, shed light on the balance between cultural and cognitive universals, on one hand, and culture-specific codes of behavior, cognition and communication on the other hand. (Givón 1984:2)

Although most theorists, whether linguists, anthropologists, psychologists, or others, agree that "context" is of vital importance for the understanding of, and for the very existence of, human communication, there are different orientations as to the concepts used to treat of context. Some trends are cognitively oriented; other trends are socioculturally oriented. The concept of context, as expressed above by Givón, stresses the importance of sociocultural factors, as well as cognitive factors. In my approach to the analysis of the texts, ideas from scholars within different traditions have been helpful.

2.2 Text, communication, and context

2.2.1 Different orientations

For the socioculturally oriented scholars the study of the social and cultural environment has been imperative in regards to the study of human communication; they study how speakers form their utterances within a pre-existing extra-linguistic context. Dell Hymes, who developed the "Ethnography of Communication," is a good representative of such scholars (Gumperz and Hymes 1986). For others, the study of mental processes involved in the conceptualization of what is being communicated has been of major interest. Within both major trends there are different focuses. Wallace Chafe, for example, approaches text analysis mainly from a cognitive point of view; he uses concepts related to perception as a basis for explaining narrative processing. He states that the way people use language has to do with "what they are conscious of from one moment to the next—on the focus of their internal attention, coupled with a concern for what is going on in the consciousness of the listener" (1980b:9). The cognitive aspects of communication do not seem to play any overt role in Hymes's writings but according to Palmer, he rather took them for granted. Palmer (1996:23) says that Hymes "never denied the importance of cognition, or 'knowledge', in language...because such an interest is implicit in the notion of communicative competence." However, the sociocultural context and the cultural conceptions of discourse or narrative (the ethnopoetics) are what one perceives as being of greatest importance to Hymes. The theoretical contributions of the Ethnography of Communication "are centered around the study of *situated discourse*, that is, linguistic performance as the locus of the relationship between language and the socio-cultural order" (Duranti 1988:210 in Palmer 1996:26). Chafe's views and those of Hymes, are both of major importance to the present study and will be discussed in more detail in chapter 3. Another cognitively based theory that has gained much influence lately and has been of some interest for the present study, is Relevance Theory. In the following I will give a few details in regards to the concept of context as it is perceived within Relevance Theory.

2.2.2 Relevance Theory

The founders of Relevance Theory, Wilson and Sperber (e.g. Sperber and Wilson 1995), base their theory on the claim that relevance is fundamental to communication because it is also fundamental to cognition. They also claim that the principle of relevance "is an exceptionless generalization about what happens when someone is addressed" (Wilson 1994:56). When a speaker addresses a hearer with an utterance, she does so with a presumption of its relevance (that it is worth while for the hearer to process it); this is what is called ostensive communication. The hearer on his part has an expectation of relevance in regards to the utterance. Ostensive communication need not be a verbal message; various acts or gestures may also be communicative.[1]

---

[1] The term "relevance" was already introduced by Grice as one of his maxims: "Be relevant." According to Fretheim (2000:123), "Grice (1975, 1989) developed an alternative to the traditional code model of communication, an inferential model that accounts for human communication in terms of the speaker's communicative intentions and the hearer's recognizing those intentions." Grice views human communication as a co-operative effort which, moreover, is governed by certain norms (maxims) which "would be necessary for the participants in *any* conversation to assume to be true" (Palmer 1996:191), that is, norms based in the human rationale. According to Blakemore (1992:26–27), Grice recognized the social aspect of the maxims but his concern was to "find a basis for the maxims," that is, a basis for a theory of utterance interpretation grounded on underlying universal principles. Grice also stressed that "the key to such an explanation lies in the notion of relevance," a notion which was also expressed as one of his maxims but which "his account leaves undefined." This is the principle that Sperber and Wilson build their Relevance Theory on, although not in terms of a rule-based maxim but rather as a principle that is fundamental to cognition. This

However, what is said is not always what is meant. The first step in interpreting utterances is making a hypothesis about what the speaker intended to say, by recovering the explicitly communicated propositional content. Our knowledge of the language used will severely constrain our assumptions about what was overtly said. The next question would be, what did the speaker intend to imply in saying what was said?

So relevance theorists are occupied with how an addressee selects, by inferential processing, a very restricted set of assumptions, called his context, which it is hoped resembles as closely as possible the communicator's intended context, thus making communication possible. According to the relevance theorist, mutual knowledge is unattainable because we all as human beings have different experiences and perceptions of the world surrounding us.

Although the concept of context to the relevance theoreticians has first of all a psychological basis, "context" includes mental representations triggered by external factors such as the information derived from the immediate surroundings of the communicative situation as well as information obtained in a preceding text or discourse. Context is defined "as a subset of the hearer's beliefs and assumptions about the world" (Blakemore 1992:18). These beliefs and assumptions play a crucial role in arriving at the speaker's intended interpretation. Although the state of the surrounding world is the same for both speaker and listener, they may perceive it differently, based on prior knowledge and experience.

The selection of the appropriate contextual assumptions then becomes crucial to the interpretation or understanding of an utterance. Wilson says that, "once we know what contextual assumptions we [are] intended to use, the intended implications follow by straightforward logical deduction" (1994:41).

Our knowledge of the language helps us in our inferencing process, otherwise we would have no need of a language. Accordingly, relevance theorists make a distinction between lexical expressions that encode CONCEPTS versus those that encode relevance PROCEDURES. Procedural indicators encode information about the CONTEXT, which the hearer must bring to bear in order to arrive at an interpretation that makes the utterance relevant to him/her. In other words, the principle of relevance and the procedural indicators operate together in the inferencing process in order for the hearer to derive the intended meaning of the utterance(s). So the so-called procedural indicators are a means to constraining contextual choices in the inferencing process; those indicators may be intonation

---

principle is expressed in the following terms: "Every act of ostensive communication communicates a presumption of its own optimal relevance" (Sperber and Wilson 1995:158).

patterns, specific syntactic constructions, the use of various connectives, reference markers or pronouns, and also certain particles.

In terms of Relevance Theory, it is some of these procedural markers (connectives and reference markers) that are of importance to the present study. I have found it helpful to also view these from the perspective of constraints on context for processing concepts like plot and event line, although these are not treated in literature on Relevance Theory that I am aware of.

Languages differ as to the kinds of procedural indicators they possess. In my opinion, they may also differ as to the degree of constraining that seemingly similar procedural indicators (e.g. discourse connectives or pronouns) may exert on context selection across languages. While certain markers in a given language may heavily constrain the contextual choice for utterance interpretation and reduce the processing effort on the hearer's behalf, in another language they may provide for a greater choice of contextual frames and hence cause greater effort on the hearer's part in selecting the correct frame for a given utterance.

In the Quechua varieties, for example, there is only one pronoun to refer to third person; there is no distinction as to gender. The use of the third-person pronoun *pay* provides for a greater choice of contextual frames. Often there is no need to specify the gender because the context makes it obvious; however, in a specific context it may not be clear as to whether a person referred to is a male or a female and additional information is needed. This applies to other languages as well, e.g. Finnish. In both Quechua and Finnish, one can say, that the third-person pronouns do not constrain context as to gender.

However, in the Quechua varieties there is a neat system for constraining context through the use of the adverbial clause markers that indicate whether the subject of the dependent adverbial clause is the same as or different from the subject of the independent clause; these are referred to as switch-reference markers. This mechanism immediately constrains contextual choice, which bears directly on reference assignment. In the discussion of the texts at hand other functions will be accounted for in regards to the switch-reference markers. It will also be noted that their reference function is different on text/discourse level.

2.2.3 In conclusion

Most scholars, whether they tend toward one philosophical trend or another, do not completely disregard the other trends; it is all a matter of emphasis.

Although the question of context is at all times and in all situations of vital importance to utterance understanding, it is obvious that it becomes even more crucial in meeting with foreign languages and cultures. This is clearly expressed in the writings of Hymes and many other scholars following the same trend of thinking. For a foreigner who tries to learn and understand the Quechua language, for example, it is of the utmost importance to be able to grasp the various subtle functions that linguistic items may have. This is a process that takes time and compels the language learner/researcher to study language in all its aspects in various social and cultural contexts, including narrative texts of various kinds. This is where ethnographic or sociolinguistic methods of research become crucial. Foreigners cannot expect native speakers to be able to tell them about subtle functions of various linguistic items, hence the necessity for detailed studies in various settings. Only when a foreigner knows how to use language in specific contexts is he/she able to aid the hearer in creating the necessary contextual assumptions in the processing effort of utterances. If not, the processing effort and the search for contextual relevance may put the hearer in too difficult a position trying to derive the intended information, and in the worst case can make communication break down altogether.

It is the view of the present research that a sociolinguistic perspective is indeed necessary in order to arrive at how some of the procedural markers (as viewed by Relevance Theory) function to help constrain contextual choice in the Quechua languages, at least in the varieties considered.

On the other hand, I think it is also important to keep in mind that (according to Relevance Theory) there is no mutual context between interactors in a communication situation, even within the same social and cultural context, but that personal experiences play an important role in our perception of the world around us. Different perceptions, I believe, would also be based on different human gifts and what is important to us at the time. For example, entering a friend's new house, an artistically minded friend would first of all look at interior design and color schemes; while a more practically minded friend might first of all notice the practicality of the house's layout.

These truths should help all scholars approach their analysis of any text with insights and interpretations based on both linguistic items and structures used in a body of texts, as well as extralinguistic, that is, historic and sociocultural knowledge.

2.3 Culture and orality

Another aspect to consider in regards to what has been discussed above has to do with orality versus literateness. Some cultures have not been introduced to literacy and only operate in an oral mode, as opposed to others that for centuries have been accustomed to express themselves both orally and in writing.

Goody (1977) analyzes "the relation between means of communication and modes of 'thought'." Although he recognizes that "The thought ways of human societies resemble each other in many respects," he still asserts that "cognitive activities of individuals differ from society to society in many ways" (p. 16). He attributes some of the differences to different means of communication, that is, some cultures being oral, others literate. His claim is that with writing man develops new ways of thinking, which also changes the nature of language itself. There is no need to memorize cultural knowledge in specific patterns in order to transmit it from generation to generation; you can develop a thought process on paper and pass on information that is not apt to vanish so easily through space and time.

Arnold and Yapita (1999:253) criticize Goody (as well as Ong) for his view which they perceive as a prejudice against oral societies because it implies a lack of abstract thinking by such societies. They assert that Goody's view is a view inherited from as far back as Plato and is a view that is being more and more rejected these days. In regards to American ethnic groups they say that it is a view that cannot be accepted when taking into account *"la compleja multitextualidad de las tradiciones nativas americanas"* (the complex multitextuality in the American native traditions). They also state that abstract thought in the Andean communities can be related to their textiles and the relation between parts and wholes in the textile patterns (p. 245). In the case of Keith Basso's idea of developing an "ethnography for writing" in the occidental world, Arnold and Yapita (1999:253) say that for comparison it would also be necessary to develop an "ethnography for weaving" which is the means of communication *par excelance* in the Andean world. In the conclusion of their interesting article they claim that weaving and singing are systems of complex knowledge and "incarnations of science, logic and philosophy in the Andes" (1999:264, translation is mine). In my opinion Goody's view (as well as Ong's and others' cited) need not necessarily be considered as signs of prejudice against oral societies. Although many oral societies can show forth complex oral textual patterns which reflect complex thought patterns, these patterns may still change when people are introduced to writing and often to the society at large. Several studies show that rhetorical patterns will change (e.g. Wise 1990), while others claim that they may persist (Beyersdorf 1986). The differences in these studies may be due to various other social and cultural factors related to the introduction of literacy. At any rate, the need for memorization tools certainly will be less necessary with the introduction to writing and this may in turn change "modes of thought." Arnold and Yapita (1999:264, 251) say themselves that the songs in the Aymara culture serve like mnemonic tools and function like *"enciclopedias aurales."* But they also say, in another connection, that many of the songs are disappearing or are not as common in many Aymaran communities. I assume it means that the introduction to or knowledge of writing is one of the change factors in these communities, although the authors don't say so.

Forstorp (1992) also criticizes Ong and Goody for making a polarized opposition between orality and literateness in regards to cognition. He refers to Scollon and Scollon (1981) who consider orality and literateness from the perspective of worldview. Their idea is that changes in discourse patterns also mean changes in people's worldview, which consequently change their identity. They base this view on results of their research among the Athabaskan people in northern Canada. In the Athabaskan worldview the social relationships between participants interacting in face-to-face communication is very important. With the introduction to literacy this aspect is being lost. They are not only introduced to a new technology of communication but also to a new way of "knowing" in regards to their values and social customs, which often are in conflict with their worldview. Forstorp concludes that literateness versus orality cannot be considered in terms of changes of cognitive patterns but rather in terms of changes in social relations and/or customs. If the social customs are related to worldview, I cannot see why this wouldn't also be related to cognitive patterns and "modes of thinking," which, according to Ong and Goody, are bound to change with the introduction of literacy (cf. quote from Givón in section 2.1).

Goody obviously has been confronted with various criticisms, because in some more recent publications (1995) and (2000) he attempts to meet such criticisms, either supporting previous claims or clarifying what he considers to be misunderstandings of previous claims. In the latter publication he is amplifying on previous themes and "stressing the transforming effects of literate activity on human life," and at the same time claiming that this does not mean that he intends to say that "logic" or "abstract" thinking do not exist in oral societies. His point is that, e.g. "the rules of 'logic,' (in the formal sense...) are not found everywhere...[and]

2.3 Culture and orality

that the formal logical operations involved in the development of the Aristotelian notion of contradiction, of arguments such as the *modus tollens* or of the explicit notion of the syllogism, were critically dependent on the introduction of writing" (2000:6). In regards to the development of graphic modes throughout history, he says that

> Many anthropologists are reluctant to see these techniques as facilitating cognitive advances, as instruments of intellectual operation. Their immersion in "other cultures" has led them to be suspicious of many of the lines drawn between these cultures and our own. This is rightly so from some standpoints, but wrongly so from others. One cannot overlook the advances in knowledge that have been made by mankind; that would be to engage in a sentimental relativism that neglects the welcome given to most of these techniques, or their products, by the vast majority of people when offered the opportunity. That includes the book as well as the sword or the loom. (2000:137–138)

Whether Goody, Ong, or others cited above are wrong in some of their perceptions is not a major concern for my research. In the following sections I will discuss different aspects related to text and orality and will also draw on insights from the writings of both Ong and Goody, as well as other authors. My research is, however, based on the assumption that oral communication patterns are to certain degrees different from the written ones and that in oral societies these are also related to certain cultural patterns as well as the need of memorizing knowledge, in addition to having an aesthetic function. My interest is to uncover "hidden" oral communication patterns which I assume exist in the text—patterns created through the use or extended functions of certain linguistic categories, as well as underlying semantic structures. I also assume that these patterns not only have helped but may still help in the task of memorizing knowledge, at least in some Quechua communities. Although some of the texts (especially from the Ayacucho area) were in fact written down by literate Quechua speakers, I believe they still reflect oral Quechua patterns. The not-so-fluent translations into Spanish of some of the texts, also written by the same people, indicate that at least Spanish language style has had little influence. It is most likely that several of the Quechua speakers concerned were newly literate—and barely so—in Spanish rather than Quechua, and that their newly acquired skill of writing was then applied to the transcribing of the Quechua texts. Several of the sections to follow in this chapter will focus on various aspects related to text and orality in cultures that are predominantly oral.

Ong defines a "primary" oral culture as "a culture totally untouched by any knowledge of writing or print." He proceeds to say that, "Today primary oral culture in the strict sense hardly exists, since every culture knows of writing and has some experience of its effects" (Ong 1997:11). Ong might be overstating the case as even quite recently cultures have been discovered that can be claimed to be "primary" oral cultures. However, there are probably very few cultures left that have not had any experience with writing or print.

In all societies that today are considered literate there has been a long period of transition from one mode of communication to another. For centuries literacy was a mark of the elite; the majority of members in the society operated in the oral "mode." People knew about reading and writing but had not been affected by the art. And even after a general introduction to literacy, people may continue in an oral mode. Goody says (2000:110) that "Oral communication obviously continues to play a fundamental role after the advent of writing, just as writing continues to be fundamental with the advent of the electronic media." Also, in the more modern societies where most of us know reading and writing, there also exists an oral mode or register, not only in our everyday conversations but also in regards to more formal functions, as well as artistic ones.

During the past centuries, the Quechua people have been exposed to the art of writing to various degrees. Some Quechuas were exposed to writing following the Spanish conquest in the sixteenth century (as in the case of Guaman Poma, section 2.4.). But both Guaman Poma and other Quechuas who have learned to read and write over the years have for the most part become literate in Spanish, and many Quechuas are still pre-literate. Although coexisting with the Spanish-speaking population that for hundreds of years has been in political power, Quechua is still being spoken by millions of people in several countries in South America. Many Quechua speakers are monolingual; this applies especially to the older generation and to women. Monolingualism is partly due to geography because most Quechua-speaking people have lived in the Andean mountain regions, many of them in quite isolated areas, distant from western civilization and school systems where Spanish has been the language of instruction. As a consequence, many Quechuas even until this day are pre-literate. Though there are also other historic, social, and cultural factors that play a role in this respect, I am not going into those here. What is of interest is that an oral mode has long existed in the Andes mountains, in some places with hardly any interference from a written mode; in other places the oral and written modes coexist in the sense of some people being literate, others not.

One problem in regards to the introduction to literacy is that in many societies around the world this has meant literacy in the language of a

2.3 Culture and orality

powerful elite rather than the mother tongue of the individual. In such cases, when later the art of writing is transferred to the mother tongue, there are bound to be some stylistic influences in the transition. This holds true for the Quechua languages (as well as with many other language families in South America); they have coexisted to various degrees with the Spanish language. This makes it difficult to know to what degree even oral texts reflect true Quechua oral patterns. In the case of Quechua speakers who have become literate in Spanish, one would expect a change or a synchronizing of textual language patterns after a while, when stories are told or written in their mother tongue; but maybe mother-tongue patterns persist longer than one would think. The urban areas of Peru have in more recent years received a major influx of people from the Andean areas, and according to Beyersdorf (1986:45) "forms of expression in the verbal arts...are beginning either to transform literary genres constituting the Hispanic tradition or to take their place among them as unique innovations."[2] This would suggest that in the more rural Quechua-speaking areas where people are exposed to Spanish and may even speak it, when telling stories in their mother tongue they will still hold onto patterns typical of storytelling in Quechua.

Scholars who have done research on oral "literatures" of mestizo societies in other parts of Latin America where the language is Spanish have also noticed Amerindian structural elements in the texts (e.g. Vázquez 1977).

Someone who intentionally tried to transpose Quechua language characteristics into Spanish narrative prose was the well-known Peruvian author, José María Arguedas, whose mother tongue was Quechua. According to Beyersdorf (1986) this was a major endeavor for him in order to develop his own unique identity as an author. However, with the majority of Quechuas speaking at least some Spanish, features from the Quechua language probably become a natural and integral part of their new, adopted language, just as Quechua has adopted Spanish vocabulary over the years. In many areas they have exploited this language mix for artistic purposes, as claimed by the authors referred to in footnote 2.

---

[2]Some of the studies referred to in *Quechua Verbal Artistry: The Inscription of Andean Voices* (Schechter and Delgado 2004), show how the two languages (Spanish and Quechua) often mix in the creating of Quechua verbal arts; for example to create interesting puns in riddles (Gnerre 2004) and *waynos* (Muysken 2004) and Adelaar (2004). This mixture is also used in order to create certain rhyming or alliterative effects; e.g. Gnerre (2004:378–379). However, what these studies also show, is that the underlying structures typical of Quechua verbal art very much remain the same.

2.4 Linearity, structures and recall

2.4.1 The problem of linearity

One of the first Quechua speakers to be exposed to western culture (after the Spanish conquest) and the art of writing was Guaman Poma (1980). He was first of all a historian but he was also a poet.[3] What he wrote down was not organized in any particular way; it was simply written out in the linear order of any prose text. The reason might be that this was the only way he had been exposed to the art of writing; also, he had learned to write in Spanish first, then adapted his new skill to Quechua. His poetry was not like the poetry of the Spanish speakers, and he might not have known how to set his own poems in poetic lines. But what was his mental organization of the poems like before the time he was exposed to writing, patterns that were probably still coexisting in his mind along with the written, linear rendition? The poems, later organized by western literary scholars according to traditional western models, might not reflect true Quechua patterns.

The conception of linearity in the western world and many other societies may be a result of our conception of time as progressing in a certain linear order along the scale past-present-future. A story always has a beginning and progresses toward an end, which is manifest in writing as mentioned above. Some cultures do not seem to have this strong linear perception of time, in the sense of past-present-future, since the temporal-aspectual systems in their languages do not have any means for expressing it—though most probably have some other means of expressing it. Some languages have a system where one thinks of actions in terms of realis or irrealis. Other languages have a system where one thinks of every action in terms of going back to its cause. A story may somehow be perceived as cyclic, with every action being caused by some previous action(s). However, in the case of Quechua the temporal-aspectual system shows a clear perception of time in terms of past-present-future (seen in Quechua grammars, e.g. Weber 1989, chapters 8 and 9).

2.4.2 Structures and recall

My memory is to a certain degree photographic for I often recall things read as to where on the page something was written; it is attached to the written exposition of the material that is to be recalled or remembered.

---

[3]It is questioned whether Guaman Poma was a poet himself or only wrote down collected traditional poetry.

2.4 Linearity, structures and recall

In my project description, when referring to a section in an oral Quechua narrative which had been transcribed to writing, I at one point said "what comes below," my mind clearly being bound to the written exposition. My advisor's comment was: "Wouldn't it be better to say "after" since these are oral texts?" He was right. But even then, is "after" the right concept? In progression of time, yes, but in structural organization maybe not. What kind of mental framework (cf. D. Payne 1992a, Goody 1987) does a pre-literate Quechua have for creating and/or storing a text in his memory, e.g. a legendary narrative; and when passed on, how is the progression and organization perceived by the receiver? Is the patterning something we, as literate people and outsiders, cannot get hold of, and something that Quechua speakers are unable to explain? And as soon as they become literate, do their patterns of organization—and thinking—change according to the written tradition they are being submerged into? Goody (1977), as noted, asserts that writing changes thought patterns as well as the nature of language.

That language use changes with the arrival of literacy is, as already noted, testified to by many linguists who have worked or are working in oral societies which are becoming literate. Even in the case of no interference from another elite language, the literate person writing down a story does not write it down in the way he would have told it orally. Wise in her article "Lo tradicional y lo moderno en la literatura indígena" (1990:142) says that oral literature changes into new literary genres as various rhetorical devices change. She gives examples from three different ethnic groups in the Amazonian rain forest of Peru. A new way of thinking seems to be developing along with writing. As Goody says (1977:109–110):

> "[Writing] encourages reflection upon and the organization of information, quite apart from its mnemotechnic functions. It not only permits the reclassification of information by those who can write, and legitimises such reformulations for those who can read, but it also changes the nature of the representations of the world (cognitive processes)...."

Obviously, thought processes (also literary genres) do not change over night, especially in a society where few people are literate and the majority still operate in the oral mode—and where in addition you might be literate in a language that is not your mother tongue.

2.4.3 In conclusion

Is it possible for me or other outsiders to find out about any other frameworks for storing knowledge, like a story, without being bound to the written tradition in our minds? How can we possibly detach ourselves from it? And where can we look for other possible frameworks? Maybe some specific cultural pattern could give us a clue, like those of the weavings, as mentioned in section 2.3, or some other pattern?[4]

For many of the thoughts and questions posed in the sections above we will probably never find an answer, nor is it my purpose to account for the many issues raised.[5] Still, it is important for the present research and the study of orally delivered texts in general to keep in mind that differences exist between a written and an oral mode. However, in newly literate cultures it can be assumed that rather than writing influencing the native patterns, native patterns influence the written form. This is particularly true when it is the goal of the writer to lead the reader to understand and appreciate the indigenous language/culture, as was noted above in the case of Arguedas's work; he consciously transported Quechua patterns of expression into his Spanish publications. Any conscious attempt on the authors' or storytellers' part of making a reader or listener appreciate Quechua patterns of expression in the texts to be studied, cannot be proved, but it is assumed that they nevertheless reflect genuine Quechua patterns. On the other hand, some of them may reflect Spanish influences. There are indigenous authors who obsequiously seek to gain acceptance in the majority language and try to conform to majority patterns; others, through constant use of Spanish over time, may unconsciously be influenced by some patterns of expression in the majority language.

2.5 "Text" versus "oral literature"

I am using the term "text" well aware of the different notions that the term carries. For a literate person, the word "text" immediately brings to mind one or several printed pages of text, and in the case of our western world, printed from top to bottom in a linear order, going from left to right. This is because we perceive the sentence as a linear constellation of the various grammatical parts going from left to right. In a strict sense, the word text is therefore not a good term in reference to oral renditions,

---

[4]Arnold and Yapita (1999:243) say that in the Andean cultures causal relations are different from those of the western world and that "similarities" between things play an important role in their discourse. This, they claim, is encouraged by the act of weaving. Their research has been done on Aymara language and culture. See their article for more details; see also section 2.5.

[5]The authors referred to in footnote 4 have more detailed discussions related to these aspects.

2.5 "Text" versus "oral literature"

because the organizational patterns in a pre-literate speaker's mind might be nothing like the way we conceive it.

The term "oral literature" which is widespread in reference to verbal folk art also has its problems. According to Bright (1984:80–81) there are several questions related to the term "oral literature": (a) how do we define literary language in the first place, whether written or oral?, and (b) how can something oral be connected with writing?

In relation to the first question Bright (1984:80) suggests that "'literature' refers, roughly, to that body of discourses or texts which, within any society, is considered worthy of dissemination, transmission, and preservation in essentially constant form."

In relation to the second question, Bright (1984:80) says that "the term [oral literature] has been widely used for literature which is composed, transmitted, and performed orally..." (e.g. the Homeric poems). It has also been used in relation to myths and legends from oral societies which have been "transcribed and transmitted into the written medium." He concludes that if such printed materials are read aloud to an audience, "the text passes back into the oral medium. It must be recognized, then, that the difference between speech and writing is not necessarily basic to a definition of literature" (p. 81).

On the other hand, Ong (1997:10–15), in discussing the use of various terms, strongly rejects the term "oral literature," which he claims is losing ground, and he says "...it reveals our inability to represent to our own minds a heritage of verbally organized materials except as some variant of writing, even when they have nothing to do with writing at all" (p. 11).

The term "text" is in Ong's opinion a better solution, if not optimal:

> 'Text', from a root meaning 'to weave', is, in absolute terms, more compatible etymologically with oral utterance than is 'literature' which refers to letters etymologically/(literae) of the alphabet. Oral discourse has commonly been thought of even in oral milieus as weaving or stitching—*rhapsòidein,* to 'rhapsodize', basically means in Greek 'to stitch songs together'. But in fact, when literates today use the term 'text' to refer to oral performance, they are thinking of it by analogy with writing. (p. 13)

Ong mentions various other terms but does not come to any conclusion as to what is to be preferred, except for saying that he will resort to "self-explanatory circumlocutions" like "purely oral art forms," "verbal art forms" and the like.

In this present study I will use the term "text" for the sake of convenience and because some of the stories were actually written down by Quechua speakers though they still show oral patterns. Thinking of text in terms of "weaving" does not necessarily give the notion of strict linearity. Weaving is also a very important aspect of Quechua culture. However, in dealing with oral traditions, one may ask whether we as literate people will ever be able to completely detach ourselves from the image of a written text in our minds?

2.6 Poetic versus formula

2.6.1 Constancy of form

In the discussion above on text and orality, Bright's definition of "literature" was also introduced as "that body of discourses or texts...worthy of dissemination, transmission, and preservation in essentially constant form." Regarding the "essentially constant form," there is obviously a difference between texts that have been handed down through the ages in oral form versus those that have been written down. According to various studies (Goody 1977, 1987, Havelock 1963, Ong 1997, Bright 1984) most oral texts have not been transmitted in verbatim form; even such famous poems as the Homeric *Iliad* and *Odyssey* have not been memorized and handed down in a constant form. This seems to apply to other famous oral literature of the past as well. The constancy seems to be expressed in the general structure of the texts as wholes, as well as through formulaic expressions. In the passing on of texts there seems to be room for both creativity as well as constancy. There is a question of genre related to this; some genres seem to be more liable to change than others. Goody (1977) says that folktales change more rapidly than metrical texts, like songs. The many versions of European folktales testify to the likelihood of their liability to changing rapidly.

The notion of formula was, according to Goody (1977:113), developed by Milman Parry through his work on the Homeric poems as well as the Yugoslav epics (Lord 1965). The formulas of the texts from these languages are fixed metrical patterns with a variety of epithets to go into these patterns, from among which the oral poets could choose the ones of preference for each telling. Ong (1997:35) says that "the more sophisticated orally patterned thought is, the more it is likely to be marked by set expressions skillfully used." There are, however, some reported cases of texts that seem to have been transmitted through verbatim memorization;

2.6.2 Is formula art?

One question that arises in respect to the above, is, if texts are formulaic according to a standard pattern, can they be considered art? Jakobson (1959:13–16) claims that metrical texts, like verse, make use of the "poetic function" without necessarily being poetry. I understand Jakobson to say that metrical templates are in a sense formulaic and need not contain poetry. But these templates have also been used by famous poets over the centuries because within these templates there is room for much creativity and you have to be skilled in order to work within already created formulas. In every culture, in every kind of artistic expression, some people are more skilled than others. This is a well-known fact for both literate and oral societies. There are people who have special gifts in expressing themselves verbally. I would think that the most artistic and beautiful expressions and/or structures are those that would tend to survive—in line with Bright's definition of literature.

Bright also raises the question whether oral literature is qualitatively the same as written literature. He refers to Finnegan (1973) who, for African oral art, seems to think that there is no difference as far as quality is concerned. She claims that various kinds of genres show "the same types of content as written literatures, including intellectual perception and aesthetic expression" (in Bright 1984:81). Goody (2000:13) says that there is no "hard-and-fast line" between the oral art forms of oral and literate societies but that certain genres are products of the latter, like the novel. He also says that an oral composition may be added to at any time, while in the case of a written work there is always "a beginning, a middle, and an end."

Ong, on the other hand, seems to think of verbal art from oral cultures as art of "high artistic and human worth, which are no longer even possible once writing has taken possession of the psyche" (1997:14).

Whether art or not, it is a fact that many of the orally delivered texts that we have been aware of in the western world are poetic in the sense of being metrical and/or rhythmic. Havelock (1976:34) claims that "orally preserved statement has to be 'poetized statement'" according to specific

---

[6]Goody (2000:26) does not agree with Parry and Lord about the Homeric poems and the Yugoslav epics being created in an oral culture, but that they rather "like most epics, are products of early literate cultures even if they are performed orally." In the case of the Vedic hymns, Goody (2000) questions the verbatim memorization of these, as described with more details in his chapter 1.

rhythmic laws that "would tend to preserve the statement in its oral form." Ong (1997:34) also makes similar claims. He says that in order to retain and retrieve "carefully articulated thought," that is, in a primary oral culture, "you have to do your thinking in mnemonic patterns," like rhythm, repetitions, antithesis, alliterations, assonances "in epithetic and other formulary expressions, in standard thematic settings...Mnemonic needs determine even syntax." Rhythm, Ong (1997:35) claims, helps recall, and formulas not only "help implement rhythmic discourse" but "they form the substance of thought itself. Thought in any extended form is impossible without them, for it consists in them." The latter statement can, of course, be questioned. However, in regards to the memorization of knowledge there are many examples of how knowledge in now literate societies was earlier memorized and transferred through the means of rhythmical texts and/or songs. One example from my own country is from the time around 1670 to 1707 when Petter Dass, one of our old north-Norwegian poets, also a priest and businessman, used songs to teach people both the basics of theology as well as more mundane knowledge on how to handle their own resources, whether they be from agriculture or from fishing (cf. the Aymara songs, referred to in section 2.3).[7]

Hymes in his writings does not necessarily exclude any of these more traditionally recognized patterns as presented above, but in his opinion they are not the only poetic markers that exist in languages. According to his analysis of orally delivered American Indian texts it is the recurrent sentence-initial particles that define the verse (which can of course create a rhythmic effect), in addition to co-occurring abstract features. To him there exists a strong relationship "between form and meaning" and "a recurrent pattern of narrative organization." I take this to mean a specific pattern seen in relation to the rhetorical structuring of the texts as well as underlying cultural patterns, like certain cultural "pattern numbers" (which will be dealt with in chapter 3).

Recurrent sentence-initial particles in oral texts have been noted by others as well. Ong (1997:37–38) makes note of the additive, rather than subordinative, nature of oral texts, which often results in some recurrent initial particle or connective. He makes reference to the Biblical creation story and the repeated "and" for each recounted act of creation in the Hebrew original. Ong does not, however, suggest that these are markers of verse, occurring in some specific recurrent pattern.

The expression "recurrent pattern" brings to mind Jakobson's important principle of PARALLELISM in verbal art (to be treated in section 3.3.4).

---

[7]Delgado-P. (2004:190) says: "Naturally, memory songs form part of the expressive art for Quechua and Aymara and their function is to reproduce the social memory in the absence of writing…" (translation is mine).

The principle of parallelism is seen at work on various linguistic levels in more traditionally recognized verbal art but may play a role also in the kind of verbal art not traditionally recognized as such. I believe parallelism is also some kind of a fixed formula or template on whichever level it operates. The principle of parallelism has also proved to play a significant role in the formation of the texts analyzed in the present study.

In sum, I believe it is difficult to draw any hard and fast line between poetic forms as art as opposed to being plain formulaic; formula and creativity seem to interplay and intertwine in the creation of new artistic expressions. The question of what is art or not is also a matter of individual taste and opinion and may also differ greatly between cultures. The temporal aspect is important as well because tastes and opinions in regards to forms of expression change over time.

2.6.3 Prose, poetry, and genre

A question that arises in respect to the discussion above is "how do we distinguish between prose and poetry?" Bright (1982, 1984) is concerned with this question and wonders whether "free verse" as used in more modern poetry is to be found in oral cultures as well. He mentions the Biblical Psalms that are not defined by metre but by syntactic parallelism—according to Jakobson's definition. Bright (1982:172) defines a poem as

> a text in which linguistic form—phonological, syntactic, and lexical—is organized in such a way as to carry an aesthetic content which is at least as important, as regards the response of the receiver, as is the cognitive content carried by the same text.

I will adopt this definition as mine but with the possibility of expanding the "linguistic form" so as to also include higher levels of text.

From what has been said above, it is to be expected that orally delivered texts, that have survived through the centuries, must be marked by poetic features of some kind.

The question of genre also arises, because orally delivered texts within one and the same culture may show different kinds of organizational patterns as well as poetic devices depending on genre; this was already alluded to in relation to the constancy of form through the process of transmitting texts. Texts that are sung and chanted are usually metrical and rhythmic, while most epic texts, folktales, legends, and myths of various kinds are typically neither metrical nor rhythmic, in the sense of syllabic patterns or repetition. However, there are also metrical texts of epic nature, e.g. the Homeric poems and the Yugoslav epics (Lord 1965).

Concerning genres like folktales, legends, and myths, it is not unlikely that even these might originally have contained more formulaic patterns and poetological devices than what we find in printed versions in current literate cultures. Through the various processes of writing down and editing the texts, many formulaic features were probably weeded out and the texts little by little moved away from oral patterns to the more accepted prose-style of the literate society (e.g. Sparing 1984).

2.7 Linguistics and text analysis

2.7.1 General assumptions

Already being concerned with oral textual patterns, I had a feeling that at least some of the Quechua legendary narrative texts were of a poetic nature, and I approached this study with that in mind. I have paid attention to how specific linguistic features as well as certain semantic features possibly play a role in the creation of the artistic features. Early in this chapter, I made it clear that context is of vital importance to the study of linguistic patterns. I will now discuss some assumptions underlying the present study with regards to text and context from the perspective of linguistic and literary discourse studies in relation to linguistic categories and their extended functions.

First, it is assumed that a text embodies a certain situational context in which language functions in specific ways to meet with certain perceived standards and expectations for the type of text it represents within a specific culture (cf. Givon's statement in 2.1).

Second, it is assumed that the speaker producing an oral monologic narrative text and the hearer processing it both have a certain "mental representation of a narrative as a coherent cognitive structure" (D. Payne 1992a:376). This includes "representations of participants or referents, events and event-sequence units, certain nonevents, and relations between the units." This mental representation is not necessarily the same in every culture and the linguistic means used to express these representations may also differ. Oral cultures, as noted, might also operate with completely different frameworks from those of literate cultures, e.g. by the use of formulaic and artistic patterns, probably both as mnemonic devices and for the pure joy of the art (Havelock 1963, Ong 1997, and Goody 1987).

Third, the speaker is free to make certain choices about relations between different events or event units. Some events the speaker might want to convey to the hearer as main events and others of less importance as background events. Some languages operate with several levels, with events ranging from most important to least important, providing specific linguistic means for marking these (cf. Longacre's salience scheme, section 3.4). To a certain degree these are stylistic choices, but having a pragmatic function; that is, one has to see the speaker's choices in relation to his goals vis-à-vis the hearer (cf. Relevance Theory, section 2.2). The different ways this is expressed vary from language to language. Different points of view found in various studies related to this aspect will mainly be discussed in chapter 3 (focusing on different scholars) and chapter 4 with focus on a particular Quechua study.

Fourth, the speaker is also free to vary the forms or linguistic means of the text within the limits of what would be considered grammatical, e.g. certain formulations might seem more effective or artistic. I think that these choices are usually considered to be of a stylistic nature. Occasionally in poetic texts the artistic sense is so strongly bent toward regularity that certain patterns pursued can violate what is strictly grammatical. Aviram (1994) quotes Jakobson to say that poetry is "organized violence exercised by poetic form upon language." Kruckenberg, who discusses Jakobson's theories about the poetic language, talks about his claim that although the poet all the time is always aware of the grammar, he may consciously make ungrammatical choices in order to submit to another superior pattern, the artistic one, and which in such cases he refers to as *un beau désordre* 'a beautiful disorder' (1979:57–58). The term "disorder" is of course used in reference to the deviances that are due to ungrammatical structures.

2.7.2 Linguistic categories and extended functions

Although there are many factors that play a role in the analysis of poetic texts, e.g. various kinds of figurative language, I believe the analysis of linguistic CATEGORIES is crucial. The present work pays specific attention to certain grammatical categories, because I believe their function may be of crucial importance to the understanding of textual patterns on various levels, indeed also in the discovering of figurative meanings of metaphor or other kinds of images. The analysis of grammatical categories is the more important when one is dealing with texts of possibly poetic nature from cultures and languages that are not of an Indo-European background and which have not as yet been thoroughly scrutinized. On the other hand, to repeat from the quote of Wallace (1982:201), "one does not truly understand the meaning of a linguistic category until one comprehends its function in a text..." Let me add that this includes the need to study a linguistic category by also taking into account its possible usage within formulaic and poetic structures within a text. Only then can a proper understanding be gained. This applies specifically to the analyses of texts from various oral cultures.

According to Givón (1984:33–34), the correlation between structure and function in language is not absolute, but rather an approximation. He further states that "In particular the diachronic change in syntax often removes a particular structure from its original functional domain—while at least initially leaving the structure itself relatively intact. Going by structure alone may lead the linguist, on such occasions, to the wrong definition of a functional domain."

Inherent in Givón's view is the notion of prototypes or prototypical meanings of categories that may adopt extended senses or meanings over time. This does not apply only to the meanings of lexical words but also to grammatical categories. This is a position taken by Prototype Theory developed by linguists like Ronald Langacker (1987) and George Lakoff (1987) and whose ideas go back to the philosopher Ludvig Wittgenstein.

We can extend this vision into the realm of language use in poetic texts, which often have adopted extended meanings and/or senses. Young, Becker and Pike (1970:363) stress the importance of studying poetry and the characteristics of verse, because: "the expressive capacities of language are most fully exploited in verse." This is a view they share with Roman Jakobson.

Jakobson was a forerunner in the linguistic analysis of poetry; he adopted and propagated some of the ideas presented above, although he uses a different terminology. He says (1959:4–5) that

> the insistence on keeping poetics apart from linguistics is warranted only in such cases when the field of linguistics appears to be illicitly restricted, for example, when the sentence is viewed by some linguists as the highest analyzable construction or when the scope of linguistics is confined to grammar alone or uniquely to non-semantic questions of external form or to the inventory of denotative devices with no reference to free variation...No doubt, for any speech community, for any speaker there exists a unity of language, but this overall code represents a system of inter-connected sub-codes; each language encompasses several concurrent patterns which are each characterized by a different function.

It needs to be stressed then, that in poetic texts the meanings of certain linguistic devices may not be isomorphic with the meanings assigned to them by the lexicon of the language or its rules of grammar but may diverge from those meanings in ways that mark the discourse as a poetic text. In some cases the extended meaning of one particular linguistic entity from its everyday prosaic meaning may even be constitutive of the poetic text, a necessary (if not sufficient) element that makes the text poetic. The grammatical categories may adopt additional or complementary meanings as part of an overall artistic pattern. In other words, an artistic pattern may be superordinate to the grammatical patterns or meanings as normally understood. Leech (1969:5), in regards to poetic texts, talks about extended meanings in terms of "deviations" from normal language use. He also says about the linguist that "His approach to literature may be in many ways a crude one, but it results in generalizations and particular observations which could not easily be made from the [literary] critic's point of view."

Wendland (2004:124 fn135), on the other hand, says that

> A literary approach to discourse analysis...is rather different from a strict linguistic methodology, but I would expect the respective results to correspond and converge in a number of important areas. The occurrence of clashes and contrasts may mark points that require further study from one perspective or the other. No single method is sufficient to analyze a literary text completely, accurately, and relevantly; the most credible and helpful study normally involves a combined approach that selects and applies the principles and techniques of several different modes of analysis.

Particularly in view of the latter statements, it is indeed necessary and important for textual analysis to make use of a combined method with an eye to both linguistic and possibly artistic features, taking into account extralinguistic aspects, like specific historical and cultural features. According to Jakobson (1959:32), "Folklore offers the most clear-cut and stereotyped forms of poetry, particularly suitable for structural scrutiny."

2.7.3 An example of extended functions

To aid our discussion later let us look at some simple examples of extended or complementary functions of a couple of Norwegian connectives as perceived in two different poetic pieces, the first one a little rhyme and the other a stanza taken out of a longer poem.

The little rhyme is called "Killingdans" (The dance of the kids) and is from Garborg's *Haugtussa*. Garborg is one of the old Norwegian poets and *Haugtussa* is the name of a volume of his poems. The poem is presented as in Åsfrid Svensen's book (1991) *Tekstens Mønstre* (Textual patterns); a literal translation into English is provided to aid the reader.

Og det er rull-i-sving,	And there is "rolling-around"
og det er sull-i-sving,	and there is "rocking-around"
og det er lett-på-tå,	and there is "easy-on-toe"
og det er sprett-på-tå,	and there is "jump-on-toe"
og det er hei-san,	and there is "*hei-san*"
og det er hopp-san	and there is "*hopp-san*"
og tra-la-la.	and "*tra-la-la*"

In this little rhyme the phrase *og det er* 'and there is' is repeated at the beginning of every little line, which also corresponds to a sentence, with the exception of the last one, *og tra-la-la*. The prototypical function of *og* 'and' is that of conjoining on different syntactic levels, although it also has some extended functions or meanings in our everyday language use. In this little poem, according to Svensen, the whole phrase *og det er* 'and there is' is devoid of meaning. Surely the copula *er* does not contribute much by itself, and the reference of the subject pronoun *det* must at best be called loose, or vague, but I do not think the phrase is completely devoid of meaning. *Og* together with *det er* still has a conjoining function and the whole phrase functions as an attention-drawing device for the descriptive predicates which are not onomatopoetic but still have an onomatopoetic tinge and therefore are difficult to translate. In addition, the phrase has a formulaic meaning as a verse-line introducer at the same time as it provides for a rhythmic effect. These are all extended, complementary uses of *og det er* 'and there is'.

Let's look at a different poem with a literal translation provided below:

Da drypped der frugtstøv fra blodsdråbeklyngen,
da blomstred det frem fra blomstermunde,
da mumled det kjælent fra skjulte kilder,
da risled det og skummed det i bække og elve,
da dryssed det og kyssed det og fossed det og blussed det:

"Indtil nu, indtil nu, indtil nu."

Then there dripped flowerdust (pollen) from *blodsdråbeklyngen*[8]
then it bloomed forth from the mouths of flowers
then it murmured lovingly from hidden springs
then it trickled and foamed in brooks and rivers
then it sprinkled and kissed and streamed and flared:

"Until now, until now, until now"

The stanza above is by Sigbjørn Obstfelder and is from a poem called "Al skabningen sukker" (All creation is sighing), a theme taken from the New Testament of the Bible. It starts out with a rather negative outlook on life but in this stanza deep despair is converted into an ecstatic feeling of

---
[8] A kind of flower; the literal translation of its name is 'the cluster of blood-drops'.

joy with life, according to Kittang and Aarseth (1993) who have included this stanza in their book *Lyriske strukturer* (Lyric structures). Kittang and Aarseth, however, do not say much more concerning this stanza, and how it is that both grammatical categories and the syntactic structure of the stanza play an important role in demonstrating this exuberant joy. For the moment I just want to point to the fact that even the initial *da* plays a crucial role in this respect. The meaning of *da* here has to be translated by 'then' in English, in the sense that when the poet made a specific discovery, *then* all these joyous feelings emerged from within, all introduced by *da*, all pointing to a specific moment of time when all these feelings seemed to emerge more or less at once. In each line, the complement of the initial *da* is a conclusion based on a premise which *da* represents anaphorically, and the premise is the same throughout the verse. The meaning of *da* as a marker of a specific point in time has not been lost in this poem, but the constant repetition of *da* would be considered abnormal language use in prose; here, however, in the same initial position, it gives a specific force to the feelings described, and as such has adopted an extended function in this poem. It has adopted the same function as *og det er* in the previous poem, by marking or introducing the poetic lines, as well as providing a specific rhythm to the poem.[9]

We will return to these examples in the next chapter when discussing other aspects of extended functions and poetic analysis.

2.7.4 In conclusion

Questions to be raised in relation to the above and in regards to the present study are whether certain grammatical features have extended functions on text level. If there are any forms of verbal art or other regular patternings in a text, is it an expected conventional feature for a certain type of text, applicable to varieties of Quechua in general? Are there different conventions for different varieties? Is it narrator dependent and a consequence of individual stylistic choice? If specific patterns are found, what function could such features have on the text level, e.g. with respect to rhetorical patterns? Although the study is basically focused on texts from only two varieties of Quechua, the analysis should be able to give us a tentative answer to these questions, specifically since the two varieties concerned belong to the two major branches of Quechua, those of Quechua A and Quechua B, respectively. (Chapter 4 will give more details on

---

[9]In the case of the Norwegian poems, the repetition of the initial connectives is not what would be considered the main poetic feature of the poems; these might even have a tendency to be overlooked, since poetic features like rhyme, meter, and figurative meanings play more overt roles.

this.) Whatever might be the case, possible patterns can at least tell us something about what forms are acceptable within the framework of text in the different varieties of Quechua considered.

As mentioned in chapter 1, there is a risk that we miss out on important aspects in our linguistic analyses of languages not previously analyzed if we do not keep in mind the possible existence of artistic patterns, maybe unusual in our own cultural background. Dell Hymes in his research on native American oral texts says that it took him twenty years to discover the artistic patterns in the texts that he had analyzed. It was his rather non-traditional approach that led him to find these patterns.

Among transmitted Quechua texts, there are many that have a typically lyrical nature; many of these have been sung or chanted throughout the years. It is reasonable to expect that even in the orally transmitted narrative texts there would be artistic features of some kind. But what are they? And what differences exist between different dialects or varieties of Quechua? The various degrees of exposure to literacy also plays a role in this respect because, according to Goody (1987:99), the more formulaic a text is, the closer it is to the oral mode. Patterns typical of the oral mode tend to get lost with the introduction of literacy.

As already stated, various scholars have made important contributions to the analysis of text in Quechua. I will seek to show how the analysis of the texts at hand, which are close to the oral mode, will add other insights and reveal still living artistic patterns not yet discerned, as far as I know. Legends and tales do serendipitously communicate something to the hearer. Most often the stories having an entertaining aspect also communicate a particular worldview and have some ethical or moral message to teach. There are studies that mainly focus on these aspects or at least include some analysis of the message of texts. Some scholars have analyzed folktales from the perspective of worldview; for example, Sparing (1984) has analyzed folktale texts circulating in Germany, showing how they demonstrate a particular worldview (most probably a worldview that has undergone changes throughout the centuries). In the case of Andean studies, the works by Arnold and Yapita (1992, 1999) can be mentioned. It is not the intention of the present study to dwell on such analyses. Based on the study of linguistic structures, however, I will show how these play a role in communicating certain aspects related to plot and eventline of the texts at hand, and at times allude to possible other aspects of communication.

3

Theory and Methodology

3.1 Preliminaries

As stated earlier, I want to adopt as a general basis for the study of artistic patterns Dell Hymes's theoretical/methodological approach to his studies of North American Indian legendary or mythical narratives. Hymes has a global perspective: both the cultural and social aspects of language behavior are very prominent in his research at the same time as he stresses the importance of a thorough linguistic analysis. In section 3.2 Hymes's approach will be looked at in some detail. I will also present insights from other works, e.g. by Roman Jakobson and Geoffrey Leech, that are of a more traditional nature (section 3.3).

Sections 3.4 and 3.5 will be dedicated to the second aspect: theoretical and/or methodological approaches related to the analysis of rhetorical plot and event line (storyline) structure; Robert Longacre's model for textual analysis plays an important part in this regard. Longacre, like Hymes, has a global perspective. Apart from the insights gained from Longacre and linguists with similar views, Wallace Chafe's perception of textual structuring has proved to be very significant for understanding the structuring of the Quechua texts. While Longacre and Hymes mainly approach text studies from a structural-functional point of view but with different focuses, Chafe approaches the study of text from a cognitive point of view. I believe insights from both perspectives have proved to be important for the analyses I present. However, I want to add that a functional perspective (as presented by Hymes and Longacre) necessarily also takes into account cognition though not explicitly stated (see the discussion on context in chapter 2.)

In section 3.3, I will present some ideas from Axel Olrik's article on the "epic laws"—laws that could pertain to both of the main aspects of the study as outlined above. Insights gained from Olrik's findings on general laws in folkloric genres will tie the present study to certain universal principles/patterns related to folklore, in addition to revealing culture specific ones.

3.2 Hymes's approach

3.2.1 Theoretical

Hymes developed the Ethnography of Speaking during the 1960s and 1970s. According to Palmer (1996:26), the Ethnography of Speaking "is not yet a tightly articulated theory of language. It is better described as a comprehensive and eclectic approach, borrowing its methods from structural linguistics and ethnography and its theory somewhat diffusely from linguistics, cultural anthropology, philosophy, and sociology."

It was mentioned in the previous section that Hymes has a global perspective in his research and scholarship, something the above quote also underlines. Some of Hymes's theoretical ideas, as presented in the paragraphs to follow, are taken from his article "Models of the Interaction of Language and Social Life" (1986). Although Hymes's theory may be eclectic, the title of this article reflects his basic view of language, namely that language can only be properly understood in its social (and cultural) context, a view which Hymes (1986:39) expresses in this way: "A general theory of the interaction of language and social life must encompass the multiple relations between linguistic means and social meaning." Toward this end he sees the need of a descriptive analysis that is "jointly ethnographic and linguistic." A main concern is to ensure the soundness of descriptive analyses from different communities, for which he suggests an "initial heuristic scheme" under the heading "Toward a Descriptive Theory." The goal is to be able to "conduct arguments analogous to those now possible in the study of grammar as to the adequacy, necessity, generality, etc., of concepts and terms" (1986:52).

The SPEECH COMMUNITY is a core term for Hymes, which he defines as "a community sharing rules for the conduct and interpretation of speech, and rules for the interpretation of at least one linguistic variety. Both conditions are necessary" (1986:54).

3.2 Hymes's approach

In addition to the speech community, Hymes makes use of various other terms (1986:56–57), a few of which I will mention. Within the speech community you can identify the SPEECH SITUATION, e.g. a ceremony or meal; within the speech situation you can identify the SPEECH EVENT, e.g. some monologue or conversation taking place. A SPEECH ACT is seen as operating as a mediary level between "the usual levels of grammar and the rest of a speech event or situation in that it implicates both linguistic form and social norms." Hymes sees the analysis of speech into acts as an analysis into genres (1986:65) and states: "The notion of genre implies the possibility of identifying formal characteristics traditionally recognized." This is what he has sought to do through much of his work on legendary narrative texts in several North American Indian languages. This is what I also attempt to do through my research. The analysis admittedly represents just one aspect of language use, and more specifically, the way it is used within a specific genre.

I do, however, have one serious disadvantage in this study, at least according to Hymes, because I have not been able to watch and study the speech event in its speech situation. I also do not know the situation around every recording or writing down of the various versions of the texts. However, by working through a rather big body of Quechua legendary narrative texts, I should be able to identify how certain linguistic markers function in legendary narrative texts and whether certain patterns are "formal characteristics traditionally recognized."

Whether Hymes presents a tightly articulated theory is not a major concern; it is his methodological approach to the study of North American Indian texts that is of specific interest for the present study.

In this respect, Hymes's approach in his own words is "stucturalist in a fundamental sense, the sense of the Prague School of Trubetzkoy and Jakobson and of the American tradition of Sapir, that of seeking form-meaning covariation and patterning based upon it. It is also structuralist in its insistence on language, a requirement that anthropologists so often forget. Interpretation of myth must be grounded in philology" (Hymes 1981:333). In this statement lies a critique against Lévi-Strauss, who, based on the works of Propp (*Morphology of the Folktale*, 1958/1968/1977), sought to create a universal model of structuring for folktales, not so much based on linguistic structures, but on binary "motifs" within the tales.

Hymes's words above reflect his emphasis on the functional perspective needed in every aspect of language study. In this respect the sociocultural context is viewed as crucial for the proper understanding and/or interpretation of language use.

Although Hymes stresses the importance of linguistics in the analysis of legendary narrative texts, the socio-cultural aspect seems to be even more prominent. My desire for the present research is to focus on linguistic aspects, but when possible I also want to seek an explanation for patterns in the texts drawing on knowledge of nonlinguistic cultural patterns.

3.2.2 Methodological

As mentioned previously, Hymes assumes that texts from oral cultures in North America are organized according to certain principles formulaic in nature and of artistic value. That texts from oral cultures may be formulaic and artistic is not a new idea, for others have claimed the same for other languages. The most famous oral poetry of the past in the western world are the Homeric poems. They have been considered art of high value, and it has been believed that they were created by *one* man with specific artistic gifts. More recently this long standing tradition has had to give way to a different view.

Ong (1997) and Goody (1987) both refer to the studies done by Milman Parry (found in Adam Parry 1971) on the Greek epics as well as the studies done by Albert Lord (1965) on Yugoslav epics. Significant for both the Greek and Yugoslav epics, according to the mentioned authors, are that they are strictly metrical because their languages lend themselves to metrics, but both Parry and Lord assert that they were stitched together differently at each telling, making use of different epithets to fit into the metrical system, the metrical systems being different, though, for the two languages.

Hymes also makes reference to Milman Parry and Albert Lord, but what is new with Hymes's approach is that the principles of organization he is basing his studies on are so completely different from what had previously been considered the marks of art:

> The principle of organization has to do with the initial elements of sentences. Certain initial elements frequently recur in structurally significant roles...the recurrent initial particles that have annoyed so many linguists, ethnographers, and readers by their monotony...turn out to be far from the tedious trivia of primitive minds. They are markers of "measure." (1981:318)

Hymes uses the term MEASURE as a substitute for meter because the text material does not exhibit phonological or grammatical regulation of lines. Although he recognizes a completely different, non-traditional kind of organization in the texts, he nevertheless uses traditional terms like verse, stanza, and so on for the groupings of patterns.

3.2 Hymes's approach

In Hymes's analysis the sentence-initial particles define the verse; within verses, lines are typically based on predications. The verses are grouped in stanzas which are again grouped in scenes, and then acts for the longer narratives; these are defined in terms of active participants to a unit and change of scenes.

Although the sentence-initial particles typically define the verse, Hymes notes "Once such [verse] patterning has been discovered in cases with such markers [e.g. sentence-initial particles], it can be discerned in cases without them...To determine the organization of...narratives, one has to recognize and abstract features that co-occur with the use of initial particle[s]" (1981:319).

And for the Chinookan language Hymes states the following for the units called verses:

> "verses", however, appear to be the pivotal unit. And verses are recognized, not by counting parts, but by recognizing repetition within a frame, the relation of putative units to each other within a whole. Covariation between form and meaning, between units and a recurrent Chinookan pattern of narrative organization, is the key. (1981:318)

Three aspects of textual structures are included in what Hymes calls the "presentational form": POETIC form, RHETORICAL form and VOCAL REALIZATION. The poetic form constitutes the organization into lines, verses, stanzas, and acts. The rhetorical form has to do with the organization of a text "in terms of sequences of onset, ongoing action, and outcome." Vocal realization has to do with the use of "direct quotation, rather than reported speech; the taking of the voices of those who speak, differentiating them; onomatopoetic precision, giving the words that define characteristic sounds..." (Hymes 1981:321). These three aspects of performance are, according to Hymes, interwoven.

For the present research I will be looking only at the first two aspects from the point of view of Hymes and adding insights from others. I am aware of the fact that I am working on a language family very different from those of Hymes' research,[1] and I cannot take for granted that I will find the same kinds of organization.[2] For analysis of the function that certain patterns might have in the rhetorical structuring of the texts, I consider Longacre's

---

[1] According to Greenberg (1956, 1987) the Amerindian languages constitute eight major branches. Three of these are represented in South America, namely the Andean branch, the Ge-Pano-Caribe branch, and the Ecuatorial-Tucano branch. Quechua belongs to the Andean branch. (Wise 1993:76–77 notes problems with his classification, which is not widely accepted).

[2] There are, however, other studies done that suggest that similar patternings to those of Hymes's findings in the North American Indian texts also exist for texts in varieties of Quechua, as well as in Aymara. These will be referred to in relation to my own analysis.

model as adding important insights, for his model in some areas is more differentiated and takes into account aspects of rhetorical structuring not mentioned by Hymes. Chafe's insights have also proved to be significant. As far as vocal realization is concerned, I am quite limited. The onomatopoetic expressions are not abundant in the texts and will not be of much importance to the present study, but when significant they will be mentioned. However, various studies show that they may function on different levels of the text and that they also have grammatical functions in some varieties of Quechua, shown by the studies made by de Reuse (1986) and Nuckolls (1992, 1996).

Another factor that Hymes considers in his analysis is what he calls "cultural pattern numbers"; these are prevalent in other areas of the culture and are also reflected in the texts in the way of grouping different units; e.g. "verses are grouped in sets of three and five (stanzas)" in one of the languages he is working on, and three and five are typical pattern numbers even in other areas of the culture. The pattern number may also be reflected in other ways, such as number of participants. The well-known American folklorist Alan Dundes also points to the fact that certain numbers are significant in cultures; he specifically deals with the number three in American and also European culture. He states that "The nature of culture is such that if one finds a pattern in social organization and religion, one is likely to find that pattern manifested in time and language (or vice versa, of course)" (1980:150).

In the present analysis I will attempt to explore possible pattern numbers and their significance in the structuring of the texts.

3.2.3 Other approaches similar to Hymes's

Not many scholars within linguistic circles seem to have undertaken studies similar to those of Hymes although there are a few studies done by anthropological/ethnographic scholars. One reason is the limited view many linguists have had about what constitutes linguistic analysis, for they have focused on the sentence as the major and ultimate unit for linguistic analysis. And when discourse/text level has been focused on by some linguists, formulaic patterns and poetological devices have often been overlooked. Bright (1982, 1984), already referred to in chapter 2, is one linguist who has approached linguistic studies taking into account Hymes's perspectives, but in his analysis on narratives among the Karok he has used Tedlock's criteria in addition to Hymes. Tedlock (in Bright 1984), in his work among the Zuni, based his analysis on features like pause, pitch, loudness, and rhythm; of these features the pause was said to be of major importance. Hymes (1996), although he applauds Tedlock for his work, rejects his criteria, especially the pause, as a feature defining verse. He reanalyzes one of Tedlock's texts showing how he misses the beauty of organization of the text because of his failure to base his analysis on linguistic structures. In this respect it should be noted that Hymes mainly worked on texts in written form, many of them from extinct languages.

Bright (1984:84), however, used both methods and found that "the two approaches coincide 90 percent of the time in their identification of basic units."

For the present study I will not be able to check on the degree that my analysis, which is based on linguistic structures, coincides with intonational features. (I do recognize that there might also be linguistic structure in intonation.)

3.2.4 In conclusion

The studies mentioned in Bright (1984) have been on North American Indian texts, written or oral. According to Hymes himself (1996), very little work exists in this area. However, according to a more recent article by Hymes (*Anthropology News,* May 2002), specific implicit textual patterns have been found in more than seventy languages. He also says, "In classes taught by Virginia Hymes or myself, students have found it again and again in English (and sometimes other languages)."

At the time of my research there were to my knowledge few similar studies for South American languages, including the Quechua varieties (Carpenter 1985, Sherzer 1990, Schottelndreyer and Levinsohn 1976). Various other studies and publications related to Andean texts, some of them referred to in chapter I, have later been brought to my attention, many of these done by anthropological scholars. One of these publications, *Tradición oral andina y amazónica* (Godenzzi 1999), is a collection of text studies made by various scholars on languages of the Andes, that is, Quechua varieties and Aymara, as well as including a study of Ese Ejja, an Amazonian language. Some of these make use of at least parts of Hymes's methodology (e.g. Hornberger, Mannheim, Dedenbach-Salazar). The various articles refer to many other publications also dealing with verbal art in Andean cultures.[3]

---

[3]See, for example, Schechter and Delgado-P., eds., 2004 *Quechua Verbal Artistry: The Inscription of Andean Voices.* As mentioned in chapter 1, this volume also includes articles written by Quechua linguists.

Within SIL circles many linguistic text studies have been done.[4] The study of text in regards to the function of linguistic markers has always been stressed as important within SIL. However, as already stated, not many linguists seem to have taken into account verbal artistic features in their approaches. And in general, although Hymes has been quoted and referred to in various studies, not many linguists seem to have taken seriously this particular aspect of his scholarship. Some of Hymes's ideas might seem too farfetched, like his suggestion that all oral narratives "even personal accounts" within speech communities are structured into units which can be divided into (verse) lines. Hymes (in earlier versions) does admit that much more work is needed in this area, as he builds his idea on just a few studies in the English-speaking world of America and Britain, in addition to his American Indian studies. To sum up, I use Hymes's own words:

> First, all oral narrative discourse may be organized in terms of lines. Second, each change of predicate is likely to coincide with a change of line...Third, lines are grouped into what can best be called verses. Fourth, the relationships between verses...are grouped in an implicit cultural patterning of the form of action, a logic or rhetoric of experience...Fifth, such patterning frequently, but not necessarily, is marked by devices at the beginning of lines.
>
> These patterns may be universally present but made use of in different degrees and ways. (1996:139)

A question that arises in this respect is whether Hymes sees any difference at all between prose and poetry (depending on one's definition of poetry).

3.3 Literary/folkloric studies

3.3.1 Generalities

In the course of the last century, impressionism within literary studies had to give way to more objective approaches (Hallberg 1992, van Dijk 1985e). Influences from other fields within the social sciences—above all structural linguistics—have forced literary scholars to look for more generally applicable laws in literary creation rather than focusing on individual works. Pavel (in van Dijk 1985:85e) states the following:

---

[4] I have myself edited one publication including text studies from several Amazonian languages; namely *Estudios lingüísticos de textos de la Amazonia peruana* (1996).

It was gradually understood that not only many properties which were previously attributed to individual works or to the genius of individual authors can be explained by structural or poetological principles, but also that features, which for a long time were thought of as purely literary are, in fact of a more general nature and their study goes beyond science of literature proper.

The new approaches devoted to seeking general laws in narrative creation were directed toward oral literature first of all. It has already been noted that the works of Lord and Parry on Yugoslav and Greek epics showed that what had been considered the hallmarks of art of high quality could in fact be explained more adequately in terms of "structural and poetological principles," typical of each culture concerned. Similar studies have been done on African and Asian oral literature (Goody 1977, 1987, 2000, Havelock 1963, and Ong 1982/1997).

Two Russian scholars deserve some attention in this regard: the folklorist, Vladímir Propp, who sought to find general structural features in Russian folktales and the linguist and literary scholar Roman Jakobson, who looked at poetological principles from the perspective of linguistic studies.

Another scholar that deserves some attention is the Danish folklorist Axel Olrik. He may not be so well-known in the American world but he is highly esteemed by folklorists in Europe (Dundes 1965).

Some ideas from these scholars, as well as Leech, will be presented below.

3.3.2 Propp's approach

Propp was a forerunner in regards to structural analysis of folktales through his well-known work *Morphology of the Folktale*. Although his book was completed already in 1928 it took nearly 30 years before it caught interest in Europe and the United States (Propp 1958/1968/1977: Introduction). His research focused first of all on Russian folktales. According to Propp, the structure of folktales is seen in terms of various motifs expressed in a common chronological ordering of elements in the story. These elements are called functions in Propp's analysis and constitute a "block of actions...Any specific action may be a part of a variety of functions since 'function must be taken as an act of dramatis personae, which is defined from the point of view of its significance for the course of action of a tale as a whole' (Propp 1958:20)" (in Wise 1971). Hymes criticizes Propp for not paying enough attention to language structures in his analysis. Another critique against Propp has been his lack of contextual/cultural considerations (seen in the introductory remarks by Dundes to Propp 1977).

Propp's work was expanded by Lévi-Strauss who sought to create a universal model of folktale structures, not so much based on chronological ordering of elements, as in Propp's work, but rather on underlying motifs taken out of the sequential order of the story. The main critique against his analysis is that the way one arrangement is chosen at the expense of another is rather arbitrary (Pavel 1985, Propp 1977).

Although Propp's work has given us new insights into the structure of folktales, these structures were not based on linguistic features. The terms "patterns" or "structures" as used in the present study, should be understood neither in the sense of Propp nor in the sense of Lévi-Strauss, but in terms of linguistic and poetological structures. When, in turn, certain structures are studied with respect to their function in the text as a whole, it is not in terms of Propp's functions (Propp 1977 and Pavel 1985) but in terms of more general rhetorical structures as outlined above and in section 3.4 and 3.5.

3.3.3 Olrik's approach

According to Dundes (1965:129), Olrik presented his paper "Epic Laws of Folk Narratives"[5] as early as 1908 at an interdisciplinary congress in Berlin. The concept *Sage* as defined by Olrik includes both folktale, myth, legend, and folksong and the "epic laws," he felt, were applicable to all these genres. Olrik conceives of these laws as superorganic, in the sense that they exert control of the narrator as laws that must be blindly obeyed. According to Dundes, Olrik's findings "need to be tested in areas other than Europe to see which principles apply elsewhere and which do not" (p.130).

It is not my intent to test these laws; still, it may be of interest to bear them in mind when analyzing the texts. The *Sage*, according to Olrik (in Dundes 1965) includes the following "laws":

- The *Law of Opening* and the *Law of Closing*: "The *Sage* does not begin with sudden action and does not end abruptly" (Dundes 1965:131). The *Sage* moves from calm to excitement to calm (some final loosely attached episode). "A longer narrative needs many such rest-points" (1965:132).
- The *Law of Repetition:* Because few descriptions are presented, repetition is the solution, often seen in connection with the number three. "There is intensifying repetition and simple repetition, but the

---

[5]The article was originally published as "Epische Gesetze der Volksdichtung," *Zeitschrift für Deutsches Altertum* 1909(51):1–12 (in Dundes 1965).

3.3 Literary/folkloric studies

important point is that without repetition, the *Sage* cannot attain its fullest form" (1965:133).
- The *Law of Three:* The number is predominant in oral versions: "...in hundreds of thousands of folk traditions, three is the highest number with which one deals" (1965:133). However, there exist other "numeric" laws in folklore around the world, e.g. in Indic traditions (1965:133-134).
- The *Law of Two to a Scene:* "Two is the maximum number of characters who appear at one time" (1965:134-135).
- The *Law of Contrast:* A correlative to the Law of Two; e.g. polarized characters: "...works from the protagonist of the *Sage* out to the other individuals, whose characteristics and actions are determined by the requirement that they be antithetical to those of the protagonist" (1965:135).
- The *Importance of Initial and Final Position*: When persons or things occur, the principal character will always occur first, the last one is always the one who arouses sympathy.
- "Folk narrative is *single-stranded."* To fill in details, it uses dialogues; attributes of a person or thing are expressed in actions. "With its single thread, folk narrative does not know the perspective of painting; it knows only the progressive series of basreliefs. Its composition is like that of sculpture and architecture; hence the strict subordination to number and other requirements of symmetry" (1965:137).
- "The *Sage* invariably rises to peaks in the form of one or more major *tableaux scenes (Hauptsituationen plastischer Art).* In these scenes, the actors draw near to each other..." (1965:138).
- "The *Sage* has its *logic (Logik).* The themes which are presented must exert an influence upon the plot...an influence in proportion to their extent and weight in the narrative...not always commensurable with that of the natural world" (1965:138).
- *"Unity of plot (die Einheit der Handlung)* is standard in the *Sage*...loose organization and uncertain action in the plot structure is the surest mark of cultivation."
- *Concentration on a Leading Character:* "the greatest law of folk tradition" (1965:139).

There are also other "laws" included as subpoints under the major ones listed above. Some of Olrik's laws will be discussed in relation to the Quechua texts in section 8.3.3. In conclusion I again quote Olrik (in Dundes 1965:139, 141):

...we find that folk narrative is formally regulated to a far greater degree than one would think. Its formal rules we may call the epic laws...From these stable features, we can determine the characteristics of particular peoples, their special types of composition and cultural themes. Our work on individual traditions can properly begin only when we can measure them along these sharp lines. And this is perhaps the best thing about our theories: they compel us to make empirical observations of things.

3.3.4 Jakobson's approach

Above (3.2) Hymes was quoted as saying that his approach was structuralist "in the sense of the Prague School of Trubetzkoy and Jakobson and of the American tradition of Sapir, that of seeking form-meaning covariation and patterning based upon it" (Hymes 1981:333). Jakobson saw the verbal art forms as an integral part of linguistic analysis and, on the other hand, linguistics as the basis for a literary analysis. According to Hallberg (1996), Jakobson was probably the most influential advocate for a literary study based on linguistics.

The term POETIC FUNCTION is a primary term in Jakobson's article "Linguistics and Poetics" (1959), also in Sebeok (1960). According to Jakobson, the poetic function has to do with the "focus on the message for its own sake." I understand this to mean the verbal form of the message. It is primarily an object of study within literary circles.

However, poetic function is found outside of the poetic realm proper and Jakobson states

> the linguistic study of the poetic function must overstep the limits of poetry, and, on the other hand, the linguistic scrutiny of poetry cannot limit itself to the poetic function. The particularities of diverse poetic genres [e.g. epic poetry versus lyrics] imply a differently ranked participation of the other verbal functions along with the dominant poetic function (1959:13-14).

About verse he says the following:

> ...verse actually exceeds the limits of poetry but at the same time verse always implies poetic function. And apparently no human culture ignores versemaking, whereas there are many cultural patterns without "applied" verse...[Many] metrical texts make use of poetic function without, however, assigning to this function the coercing, determining role which it carries in poetry. (1959:16)

The above quote seems to imply that texts may or may not be made in verse forms; and those that are, are not necessarily poetry. Hymes's claim is that all oral narratives are organized in lines and verses; however,

3.3 Literary/folkloric studies

Hymes does not claim that these texts would in all cases be considered art, but rather that units are grouped according to implicit cultural patternings. Jakobson does not speak about oral texts in particular, and his criteria for defining verse is from a more traditional point of view than those of Hymes.

According to Jakobson (1966:399), verse is defined by recurrent patterns on various linguistic levels, "occurring in metrically or strophically corresponding positions." These recurrent—or PARALLELISTIC—patterns are typical within languages around the world, although manifest in different ways. Another important principle that operates along with the principle of parallelism is the principle of EQUIVALENCE—an important concept with Jakobson—and which signals which linguistic categories may "function as equivalent" in a given parallel pattern within a specific language.

The principle of parallelism is well recognized within literary circles; it is not a concept created by Jakobson. Hopkins (in Jakobson 1966:399) more than a century ago said, "The structure of poetry is that of continuous parallelism." According to Hallberg (1992:122) this "stylistic figure" had its own name already in the poetry of ancient India. In the western world, the term has probably had greatest significance in relation to the semantic parallel structures of Biblical Hebrew poetry. Robert Lowth in his studies on Hebrew poetry, (first published in 1778, referred to in Jakobson 1966:399–400), used the term and lined out three different kinds of parallelism: PARALLELS SYNONYMOUS, PARALLELS ANTITHETIC, PARALLELS SYNTHETIC. According to Lowth, "Synonymous lines 'correspond one to another by expressing the same sense in different, but equivalent terms...' Two antithetic lines 'correspond with one another by an Opposition...sometimes in expression, sometimes in sense only...Synthetic or Constructive [correspond]...only in the similar form of Construction'" (p. 400). This last kind of parallelism is what Jakobson calls "grammatical parallelism" and which "belongs to the poetic canon of numerous folk patterns" (Jakobson 1966:403). Jakobson refers to works on various languages, from peoples of Asia, Eurasia, and the Semitic world. For several Turkic languages he reports: "The older the features we observe in the cultural pattern of a Turkic people, the more sustained is the parallelistic groundwork of the native oral poetry, especially the epic" (1966:405).

When Jakobson refers to the "poetic canon" he means poetic patterns that are typical within specific cultures. For example, in regards to the Indo-European world, Jakobson says that it is only in Russian that you still find a living oral tradition for the use of grammatical parallelism "as its basic mode" in the creation of poetry, "both songs and recitatives." (Section 3.3.5 and chapter 8 contain a more detailed discussion on the "poetic canon.")

According to Jakobson (1968), all the linguistic elements may have an aesthetic function, not only the word-classes but also inflectional and derivational morphemes of various kinds. He says that through analyzing all kinds of grammatical structures, one may come up with interesting and surprising patterns of artistic nature, something I think my research will underscore.

To give an example of grammatical parallelism I return to the Obstfelder poem which I introduced in chapter 2. The verbs in the poetic stanza are all different but they occur in the same syntactic position, the second position in the sentence. They also have the same past tense marker and are followed by the impersonal (formal) subject *det* corresponding to the English expletive "it" or, in the first line, the older Dano-Norwegian *der* corresponding to the English impersonal "there" in existential constructions. This is a pattern of grammatical parallelism. However, the grammatical parallelism is not there to fit into some poetic canon for Norwegian/Scandinavian poetry, but is rather a creative act by the poet. As noted, in numerous patterns for folklore around the world, grammatical parallelism may be part of the poetic canon, often within the constraints of a specific meter as well. In the case of North American Indian literature, only the initial connective played such a role, apart from an underlying semantic pattern, corresponding to a scenic stanza.

According to previous studies on Quechua languages (Mannheim 1986, Harrison 1989) verbal art forms are not so much based on metrical patterns, although they do exist. Mannheim particularly mentions grammatical and semantic parallelism. Carpenter (1985) found parallel structures in a text from an Ecuadorian variety of Quechua and if grammatical and/or semantic parallelism has been noted in other oral epic traditions of the past, it is not unlikely that it also exists in Quechua narratives/epics.[6]

---

[6]Dedenbach-Salazar Sáenz (1999), for example, analyzes two Aymara (also an Andean language) texts and shows various kinds of parallelism found in the texts. However, the texts do not seem to demonstrate any parallelism typical for the structure of the epics as wholes. Nevertheless, she makes reference to both Huanca and Briggs who both have noticed parallel structures in the way scenes are formed throughout the texts they have analyzed in the Aymara language. Hornberger (1999) has analyzed two Quechua texts showing parallel structures (cf. Hymes and my own analysis of the Quechua texts in chapters ahead).

3.3.5 Leech's approach

3.3.5.1 Deviations

Geoffrey Leech, in regards to poetry, talks about complementary meanings in terms of deviations from the normal language use. According to him there are three kinds of deviations that he refers to as primary, secondary, and tertiary deviations. In the case of primary deviations, it has two main forms:

> (a) Where the language allows a choice, the poet goes outside the normally occurring range of choice; and
>
> (b) Where the language allows a choice, the poet denies himself the freedom to choose, using the same item in successive positions. (Leech 1985:45)

The latter kind of deviation is what we see in the use of the repeated initial connectives in the two Norwegian poems/stanzas introduced in chapter 2. The stanza by Obstfelder is repeated here:

> Da drypped der frugtstøv fra blodsdråbeklyngen,
> da blomstred det frem fra blomstermunde,
> da mumled det kjælent fra skjulte kilder,
> da risled det og skummed det i bække og elve,
> da dryssed det og kyssed det og fossed det og blussed det:
>
> "Indtil nu, indtil nu, indtil nu."

> Then there dripped flowerdust (pollen) from *blodsdråbeklyngen*[7]
> then it bloomed forth from the mouths of flowers
> then it murmured lovingly from hidden springs
> then it trickled and foamed in brooks and rivers
> then it sprinkled and kissed and streamed and flared:
>
> "Until now, until now, until now"

In the case of the stanza above, the poet could easily have started the poem with the use of *da* and used the connective *og* (and) for the rest of the lines, or he could have used it in every other line and still have a neat initial pattern. However, he would have had to change the syntactic positions of the following verbs and another parallel structure very important to the initial rhythm would have gotten lost. *Da* is an adverb and as such it triggers subject-verb inversion in the sentence, *og* on the other hand, or the absence of any initial connective, would demand straight word order and the consistent, syntactically defined parallelism would be lost. In terms of Leech this kind of deviation creates a pattern of "abnormal

---
[7] A kind of flower; the literal translation of its name is 'the cluster of blood-drops'.

regularity," a concept which would include both grammatical and syntactical parallelism as well as verse forms, like meter, rhyme scheme, and stanza form. The latter would not in itself be a "form of stylistic variation," the way Leech puts it, but would rather be "a set of schematic structures which allow their own stylistic variation" (Leech 1985:47).

The poems referred to above do of course also have specific metrical structures that the poet follows. A deviation from this pattern would be what Leech calls secondary deviation. Secondary deviation is a deviation from the poetic canon, "including norms of author or genre," according to Leech. Jakobson talks about the poetic canon in terms of culture-specific patterns; he does not mention norms of the author.

Returning to the stanza above, the initial repetition of both the connective and the following impersonal syntactic construction with various intransitive verbs, all denoting a kind of sensory experience, also create a structural expectancy chain internal to the stanza. This might be peculiar to this stanza, and not dictated by artistic (and possibly culture-dependent) conventions; if broken, it would cause a deviation from the internal language use of the stanza. This is what Leech refers to as tertiary deviations. In the case of the Obstfelder stanza, its construction is different from the rest of the poem, and as such the stanza in itself causes a deviation from the pattern of the poem as a whole, so one could talk about not only one tertiary deviation, but two.

Deviations usually serve the purpose of foregrounding and must "be seen as forming a meaningful pattern in themselves," according to Leech, who also makes reference to Mukarovský (1958:44). To return to Obstfelder's poem, I earlier said that the repeated initial connective gave force to the following descriptions, indicative of the poet's feelings. And it has to be remembered that this stanza is only a part of the poem, which when viewed in its totality, displays various other poetically determined linguistic structures. The use of the initial *da* is one means of foregrounding this specific stanza by giving force to the following events/feelings, directing the reader's attention to that specific moment in time that the author is alluding to. The two last *da*-lines of the poem show a break in the internal expectancy chain, because the penultimate line of those initiated by *da* 'then' adds another verbal phrase following the first and conjoined with this through the use of *og* 'and'. The final *da*-line includes no less than four such verbal phrases conjoined by *og*. This is a tertiary deviation and marks a mounting tension in the poetic stanza itself, both through vertical and horizontal parallelism. The tension is calmed by the final line with the triplet elliptic complement *indtil nu* 'until now', indicating that the ecstatic joy has persisted until the moment of the author's writing the poem. This is again a grammatical/syntactical parallel pattern, an exact repetition of the elliptic complement. The stanza with its specific use of *da* and the other final grammatical parallelisms would correspond to what is often referred to as climax with some culminating point and/or final resolution in linguistic text/discourse studies.

In sum, the Obstfelder stanza demonstrates primary deviation through the abnormal repetition of the initial connective *da* with the following "forced" syntactical constructions. It shows tertiary deviation in the latter part, through the deviation from the poetic pattern as established in the first part of the stanza; and also in that the whole stanza deviates from the poem as a whole. The poem does not demonstrate secondary deviation as it cannot be said to deviate from either a Norwegian or other Scandinavian poetic canon, nor a canon typical of the author.

3.3.5.2 Different perspectives on foregrounding

The concept of foregrounding can be perceived from two different perspectives; on the one hand, the author's choice of language use, and on the other hand, the readers' or audience's response to the linguistic signals (cf. D. Payne (1992a) and Relevance Theory, sections 2.7 and 2.2, respectively). Concerning the grammatical and the syntactical parallelisms just discussed, we can be quite certain that they are deliberate choices by the author in order to create both an expectation chain and a mental halt by the reader or audience when the expectation chain is broken.

According to Leech, FOREGROUNDING is a term for an effect brought about in the reader by linguistic or other forms of deviation...the normal linguistic features of a poem become the background against which the deviant features are FOREGROUNDED. The degree of deviation varies, and so does the strength of foregrounding" (Leech 1985:47).

Some of the same ideas are inherent in Pilkington's view. From a relevance theoretic viewpoint, he approaches the issue of poetry from the perspective of the reader/listener and his/her response. He says that, "verse features, exploited poetically, might be said to encourage the accessing of a wide range of assumptions in the same way as poetic metaphor..." (Pilkington 2000:131).

He takes an example from metrical variation and unexpected stress, and says that "the extra time this enhanced stress gives to the lexical access process...causes the encyclopaedic entry to be more thoroughly explored and assumptions within it to be made more highly salient" (Pilkington 2000:134). This, of course, does not pertain to metrical variation alone, but also to other unexpected changes relating to, for example, grammatical parallelism.

An important point to stress here is that by analyzing grammatical categories in a poetic context, a wide range of new assumptions (in the hearer's world) may be activated. Or, in terms of our previous perspective, new and extended functions may be discovered regarding the grammatical categories in question, as I have tried to demonstrate through some of my previous examples. Jakobson (1968) says that in studying the grammatical categories one will discover unexpected patterns of both symmetry and asymmetry, creating meaningful balanced forms as well as contrasts and equivalent forms. He says that the reader/listener senses the poetic effect but unconsciously. I think it is worth stressing that the grammatical parallelisms, or even the metric ones, are not just ordered adornments pleasing to the ear, but that their functions carry over into the semantics and pragmatics of the poetry, something I hope has been recognized in my discussion so far.

As far as the concept of foregrounding is concerned it does not belong to the study of poetry alone, but to discourse studies in general. However, the terms foregrounding and backgrounding as used by Leech should not be confused with the way they are used by some linguistic scholars, for example, Hopper and Thompson, Longacre, D. Payne, and others in the following sections. The latter group does not talk about foregrounding in relation to poetic texts; rather, they contrast main event line features as opposed to background information features in discourse/text in general. The terminology used by the scholars mentioned above also differs. The term foregrounding as used by Leech corresponds better to the notion of "climax" as perceived by the mentioned authors.

3.3.6 In conclusion

So far, I have looked at general studies relevant primarily to the first aspect of the present research, that of discerning specific artistic patternings, although many insights also bear significance for the second part of the study, that of exploring functions of specific patterns in the texts. In the following sections I will present aspects of various works that will be taken into consideration in my analysis of the Quechua texts. These do not pay specific attention to poetic texts but to text (discourse) in general. Other authors, as well as other aspects of the studies now mentioned or mentioned below, will be discussed, when appropriate, as I proceed in my analysis.

3.4 Longacre's approach to text analysis

3.4.1 Preliminaries

Seen from a literary point of view, most narratives have a "story" and a "plot." The story has to do with the chronological ordering of events (often called the event line, at least in linguistic circles (Longacre 1996:23ff.); the plot has to do with some kind of causal relationship between the events, seen as building tension toward a climax (Svensen 1991:170; Ong 1982/1997:142, etc.).

Since for years the focus of study in linguistic circles was limited to the sentence, few linguists took notice of such concepts as story and plot; these were concepts that belonged to literary scholarship. However, as linguists have increasingly become aware of the importance of context in their analysis of sentence structures, the concepts of story and plot have gained interest in linguistic circles as well, in particular where the study of narrative text is in focus. These concepts are also of major importance in exploring the functions of specific patterns in the text in the present study. Some literature of relevance in this regard is presented in the following sections.

3.4.2 The profile and salience scheme of a text

An inherent assumption in Longacre's approach is that "language is language only in context" (1996:1). This is an assumption he shares with Hymes as well as with many other linguists of the last decades. Longacre's insistence on the necessity of discourse (text) studies has sprung from his research on many languages from around the world, as well as his studies of narrative structure in Biblical Hebrew. Whether one agrees or not with Longacre, the theoretical basis found in his methodology for textual analysis has been and still is a very useful tool in the study of lesser-known languages.

Longacre (1996), in line with many literary scholars, looks at the study of text from two perspectives, in terms of a PROFILE and of a SALIENCE SCHEME of the text.

The profile of the text has to do with its rhetorical structure. Longacre makes a distinction here between (1) the underlying notional structure (the rhetorician's schema or plot) and (2) the surface structure which displays how the underlying notional structure is encoded. Parts of the notional structure, like exposition, inciting moment, developing argument or conflict, climax, denouement, final suspense, and conclusion, may be coded in specific ways in the surface structure. For example, the climactic episodes are often set apart from other episodes in the surface structure through shift in language use in various ways, like change of tense, heightened vividness through a shift along the narrative-drama parameter, and change of pace through variation of length of units, to mention but a few. Longacre calls this part of the surface structure the "peak" of the narrative. As for the term plot, Longacre chooses to use it for the notional structure of narratives in general, "even for those of episodic nature where the plot is in low relief due to absence of any perceptible climax" (Longacre (1996:34).[8]

It may be necessary to give a definition to some of the concepts mentioned above, since Longacre's definitions (1996:34–35) may not exactly correspond to those of literary scholars. "Inciting moment" is the name for the episode that starts off the episodic development through an event or events that trigger the subsequent events in the developing conflict. "Climax, 'Knot it all up proper,' is where everything comes to a head" and where the author "adds all sorts of tangles until a confrontation is inevitable" [a culminating point]. "With...denouement 'Loosen it,' a crucial event happens which makes resolution possible. Things begin to loosen up. We see a way out—even if not to a happy ending...Final suspense, 'Keep untangling,' works out details of the resolution." The final suspense may encode as one or more episodes following the denouement. In the case of the latter this may encode in the surface structure through the same features as climax, but it may also encode with other features that set it apart from the climax as seen in my analysis of the text in chapter 5; this may differ between languages as well as between narrators. It should be noted, however, that the different parts of the plot structure may not all occur in the same story and sometimes they may overlap; much depends on the length of the story, which the analysis of the texts included in this research also shows.

I have found it helpful to look at the texts from the perspective of both notional and surface levels, although it seems to me that this division is

---

[8]Ong asserts that in narratives from oral cultures there is a lack of a clear perceptible climax; he mentions the Greek epics as examples of this and makes the following claim: "In fact, an oral culture has no experience of a lengthy, epic-size or novel-size climactic linear plot. It cannot organize even shorter narrative in the studious, relentless climactic way that readers of literature for the past 200 years have learned more and more to expect..." (Ong 1997:143). Ong also assumes no clear beginning, middle, or end to the narratives of the oral poet. The oral poet, according to Ong himself and others he quotes, usually plunges the hearer into the middle of actions. However, his views do not seem to go along with Olrik's findings (section 3.4.3). Powlison (1969, 1985, 1993), who worked more than 40 years among the Yagua of the Peruvian Amazon, says that their mythic narratives show clear epic tendencies. D. Payne (1992a) and T. Payne (1996) both point to the fact that Yagua narratives have clearly marked climactic parts.

3.4 Longacre's approach to text analysis

too simple because the texts display other aspects of information also. However, my findings do support the idea that different underlying semantic patterns on a higher level are marked in specific ways in the surface structure.

The salience scheme of the text has to do with the difference between main event line information versus that of "all other material," referred to as "supportive" material. Longacre, however, along with literary scholars, uses the term "storyline" rather than "eventline" (p.21). As far as "supportive" material is concerned, Longacre assumes that it is "encoding progressive degrees of departure" from the main event line development (1996:23).

Languages around the world have different ways of "encoding progressive departure" from the main event line, or in other words, different ways of marking the importance of the information conveyed. Longacre refers to languages in Africa that have a SECONDARY STORYLINE and even a TERTIARY STORYLINE:

> The secondary storyline may encode happenings of lesser importance (often preparatory to or resultant from happenings reported on the primary storyline). Sometimes the secondary storyline encodes actions which are performed by a secondary or minor participant, since there is a correlation of action prominence with participant prominence...The tertiary storyline reports a series of actions that are habitual or script-predictable. (1996:27)

Based on information from around twenty-five different languages, Longacre proposes an ETIC SALIENCE SCHEME (1996:28) as a frame of reference for analyzing verb or clause functions in narrative. The salience scheme lists nine different levels of information, numbered from 1 to 9:

$1'$ Pivotal storyline (augmentation of 1)
  1. Primary storyline (S/Agent > S/Experiencer > S/Patient)
    2. Secondary storyline
      3. Routine (script-predictable action sequence)
        4. Backgrounded actions/events
          5. Backgrounded activity (durative)
            6. Setting (exposition)
              7. Irrealis (negatives and modals)
                8. Evaluations (author intrusions)
                  9. Cohesive and thematic

However, above the primary storyline, Longacre posits a $1'$ as a pivotal storyline. In regards to the latter, he says that

> Here two functionally different constructions are marked by very similar devices: (i) happenings which are marked as pivotal constitute a rough abstract of the story, and (ii) happenings which are marked as pivotal, although they are for some reason weighted, when taken together do not constitute such an abstract. In situation (i), the pivotal elements rank hierarchically above the primary storyline in a salience scheme. In situation (ii), however, the pivotal elements are simply weighted happenings which are tagged for prominence but still simply on the primary storyline. (1996:28–29)

According to Longacre (1996:3) the main event line of a given type of discourse may be marked

> by a characteristic tense, aspect, or mood (or some combination of the three), by word order in the clause, or by a mystery particle. Various further features can also mark the more pivotal parts of the mainline from the more routine parts and can classify background, supportive, and depictive material so that the more crucial bits of such information stand out.

From this quote one can see that the profile and the information salience of a text will intertwine and overlap. For example, Longacre asserts that at discourse "peak" the markers of the main event line in a given language "may be phased out, be used less frequently, or be used much more frequently than in other parts of the discourse" (1996:3).

3.5 Other approaches in line with Longacre's salience scheme

Few linguists seem to acknowledge the profile-salience scheme distinction, at least not in an explicit way. However, in line with Longacre, but approaching the matter from different perspectives, various linguists recognize the difference between main event line information versus background information. Some of these linguists are also referred to by Longacre in his 1996 publication.

Hopper (1979) claims that it is a universal feature of narrative text to make a distinction between main line events (which he refers to as foregrounded events) and supportive material. Grimes (1975) makes similar distinctions, but talks about them in terms of events versus non-events; Wallace (1982) talks about them in terms of figure and ground. Jones and Jones (1979), referred to by Longacre, have also pointed to the fact that languages may display several levels of information, ranging from the most important to the least important.

3.5 Other approaches in line with Longacre's salience scheme

Aspects of these different perspectives will be looked at a bit more in detail below, as well as some insights from D. Payne (1982a) and Kalmár (1982), related to specific text analyses. Chafe's somewhat different way of looking at narrative processing, in terms of principles of cognition, will be outlined in more detail.

3.5.1 Hopper and Thompson

According to Hopper and Thompson, foreground information constitutes "the chief, event-centered, sequential actions of a discourse" (Hopper and Thompson 1982:4).[9] In a study carried out in the 1970s, Hopper and Thompson (1980) proposed a TRANSITIVITY HYPOTHESIS and listed ten parameters or characteristics of a clause important to the notion of transitivity. They claimed that high transitivity correlates with foregrounding, as the degree of transitivity is related to the agent-patient relationship and the salience of the agent or patient in the type of action involved.

Kalmár (1982:241), however, who did an analysis on a Czech folk tale based on the hypothesis referred to above, claims that transitivity did not correlate with foregrounding proper, but rather with the sequentiality of events. Kalmár stresses that temporal sequence is only one mode of foregrounding and that different languages also use other means for "communicating essential information." For the Czech folktale that he analyzed, the quotation is one such means. Of particular interest for the present study is the idea of "communicating essential information" rather than focusing on the most important events as they are conceived of in temporal sequence in a narration.

3.5.2 D. Payne

D. Payne (1992a:375), in line with Hopper (1979), states that it seems to be a universal feature in languages to distinguish between main event line information and background information. She is explicit about the underlying reason for this distinction: the speaker-hearer relationship, particularly the speaker's need to inform the hearer about which events belong to the main event line or not. She states that "such instructions are necessary because, depending on the speaker's goals, semantic events are not always to be integrated as part of the main event line; thus the speaker cannot rely on sheer communication of eventive versus noneventive information to be a sufficient clue of how to integrate incoming information" (D. Payne 1992a:375). Her statement here seems to be in line with Longacre and Jones and Jones, who distinguish between levels of event

---
[9]Cf. section 3.3.5 on Geoffrey Leech; specifically subsection 3.3.5.2.

information. Grimes, as noted above, makes a distinction between events versus non-events.

D. Payne, based on Labov and Waletzky (1967) and Hopper (1979), identifies "a clause as part of the 'semantic main event line (MEL)' if it has two properties: (a) It must report an event as actually occurring. The event cannot be a hypothetical one that is presented as possibly occurring in the future or one that might have occurred in the past. States, which are nonevents by definition, are also excluded. (b) The actual reporting of the event must advance the action of the narrative along a chronological time line" (D. Payne 1992a:379). Simultaneous and partly overlapping events, as well as repetition, are also excluded from what D. Payne considers to be the main event line.

In a study of the use of a particular particle in Yagua (an Amazonian language) texts, based on the criteria above, Payne found her analysis to support "Hopper's claim that languages do overtly mark MEL [main event line] in narratives..."; however, she also found that "simple MEL" is not always the category overtly signalled; in Yagua we need to acknowledge two kinds of MEL: ordinary and peak. She found the ordinary MEL to be marked by the particle in question, while the "latter [was] not in any simple formal way distinguished from non-MEL material." This finding is a point that refines Hopper's claim, according to Payne. Her findings also confirm Longacre's claim as well as the findings of Jones and Jones that events at peak often have a different significance and are marked differently than other events on the main event line.

3.5.3 Jones and Jones

Jones and Jones did their research on several languages in Meso-America; they list the following "levels of significant information that may be grammatically marked in narratives in different languages": peak, pivotal events, backbone events, ordinary events, significant background, ordinary background (1979:7). Not all these levels are expected to occur in any given language. In their study, Jones and Jones also found that some languages show a preference for one specific way of marking peak grammatically, while other languages showed more variety. They say that "this suggests an important question with respect to levels other than peak: Are there levels other than peak in languages that are marked *not* by a preferred device, but by one or other device selected from a bag of tricks available to the speaker?" Jones and Jones are here using the term level for grading the importance of information in discourse, not for rhetorical structuring like plot development (e.g. the profile of Longacre).

3.5.4 Wallace

Wallace (1982), in line with Hopper and Thompson, also looks at the interrelationship of various linguistic categories, although from a somewhat different perspective. His main focus is on verbal categories (e.g. tense, aspect, voice, and mood) and how they "fit into extended discourse" for, as he says, "a fundamental task of linguistics must be to understand and organize the facts of the totality of linguistic behavior: not just isolated sentences, but whole discourses" (Wallace 1982:207). The notion of voice also brings in a discussion on "the categories of nominal expressions associated with verbs," e.g. "person, number, animacy, humanness, definiteness, and the like" whose degree of salience is not just a matter in syntax but in discourse as well. (In my opinion any salience in syntax is related to its salience in a wider discourse context.) In a table he lists linguistic categories according to their degree of salience: more salient versus less salient; e.g. among the nominal features are: human versus nonhuman, animate versus inanimate, proper versus common; among the verbal features are: perfective versus nonperfective, present-immediate versus nonpresent-remote, eventive versus noneventive, transitive versus intransitive, action verbs versus stative verbs, deliberate versus accidental action. The more salient features (the first in each contrastive pair) have a tendency to occur in foregrounded units in discourse.

Wallace then turns to the question of why some categories are more salient than others and suggests that the answer might be found in an "innate, universal perceptual distinction between figure and ground." The concept of figure and ground is taken from the Gestalt psychologists (from early in the twentieth century) and is related to our visual perception. According to the Gestalt theorists, human beings are naturally equipped with an ability to organize details on the cognitive level according to specific laws grounded in perception; e.g. small fragments will be organized according to principles like "likeness" and "distance"; in the case of figure and ground, human beings tend to perceive certain figures or objects against a more diffuse background (Harald Rørvik 1968). Wallace's hypothesis is that "linguistic categories of the sort mentioned above function to differentiate linguistic figure from linguistic ground: the speaker uses such categories to structure an utterance (of one or more sentences) into more or less salient portions, and the listener uses such categories as clues to interpreting the speaker's verbal picture" (Wallace 1982:214).

Wallace objects, however, to the Gestalt theory's "strong claims about universal innate perceptual mechanisms" and states that individual, social, and cultural factors "play a role in determining, among other things, perceived figures and grounds" (Wallace 1982:217). This would apply to language as well.

Wallace concludes his paper stating that his goal is "not to promote the figure-ground distinction as *the* principle of grammatical organization, but to call attention to it as *a* principle" along with others "in determining why human languages are as they are" (Wallace 1982:218).

3.5.5 Chafe

Chafe (1980b) approaches text studies mainly from a cognitive point of view. Wallace, as noted above, sought an explanation to the distinction in language between salient and less salient categories, in the "perceptual distinction between figure and ground." Chafe also uses concepts related to perception as a basis for explaining narrative processing, albeit from a somehow different perspective than Wallace. The concepts "focus" and "consciousness" are very important in his approach.

Introductorily Chafe states that the way people use language has to do with "what they are conscious of from one moment to the next—on the focus of their internal attention, coupled with a concern for what is going on in the consciousness of the listener" (Chafe 1980b:9).

The basic unit in a narrative in Chafe's view is the "idea unit," marked by intonation, pause, and/or syntactic features and which often corresponds to a clause, which might also contain embedded clauses, such as relative clauses. These idea units are linguistic expressions of "focus of consciousness." He defines consciousness as a mechanism through which one uses old information, whether from memory or from our immediate sociocultural or situational context. Another factor is what he calls "self"; this self chooses and decides what is important to share from the old information; in this respect, sociocultural factors also play a role, e.g. in respect to how much attention one would give this or that piece of information.

In a narration the major focus is on people, their characteristics and their actions. The backbone of a narration consists of the introduction of people, their description, and especially their states and activities that are considered important enough to share with others. The focus of interest can again be organized into centers of interest; this could be a series of punctual actions that terminates in some type of conclusion and which would correspond to a single "mental image." A center of interest might correspond to one syntactic sentence or more, what Chafe calls an "extended sentence." According to Chafe (Chafe 1980b:38), "Centers of interest, as expressed in extended sentences, show significantly greater variation in the amount of information they contain than do focuses of consciousness, as expressed in idea units." Chafe found that the number of words in an extended sentence ranged from 1 to 153, and says, "I take this as evidence for an important hypothesis: *that centers of interest are not governed by capacity and duration limitations of the sort that restrict the content and duration of focuses of consciousness*" (Chafe 1980b:38). "Sentences per se, whether intonationally or syntactically defined, are less expressive of cognitive interests than are extended sentences" (p. 36).

In regards to background orientation and the transition from one center of interest to the next, Chafe (1980b:40) states:

> The division into focal and peripheral processing may well have evolved in eye and brain together as a way of dealing with both perceived and remembered information. The well-known properties of the eye are thus likely to be a manifestation of a more general division of information-processing functions into a focal component with high acuity and a peripheral component with lesser acuity [cf. Wallace's figure and ground above] which serves to provide a context for the focus, and to guide the focus to possible next resting places.

It seems as if Chafe departs from other views as presented above, in that he considers states and descriptions, too, to form part of the "backbone," and not just main events. Of special interest is the concept of center of interest, which, according to Chafe, could be a series of punctual actions terminating in some kind of conclusion. I take it, from what he says about the backbone of a narrative, that states and descriptions may also be part of a center of interest and that a center of interest can be characterized as "a focal component [or unit] with high acuity," while transitions (some kind of background orientation) between these centers of interest are characterized as peripheral components with lesser acuity, serving as resting places.

Chafe's approach differs from those of the others, as described above, in that focal components or centers of interest, etc. are not in any way defined in terms of linguistic structures but in terms of intonation and pause. Although he does mention linguistic units like clause and sentence in relation to focus of consciousness and centers of interest, they do not seem to be interesting as specific syntactic units, but rather in some extended sense. If one talks in terms of foregrounding versus backgrounding in relation to Chafe's view, his focal components or units, rather than particular events, would correspond to foregrounding, while the peripheral component would correspond to background.

In dealing with written texts, not marked by intonational features, it may be difficult to see the usefulness of Chafe's approach in respect to the present study. However, there are factors from his insights that help shed light on the organization of the Quechua texts studied. Also, as far as intonation is concerned, other Quechua studies give helpful insights to be examined in the following chapter.

3.5.6 In conclusion

Longacre makes a distinction in an explicit way between two different aspects of information in a text, which he calls the salience scheme and the profile of the text (described in 3.4.2). Although others emphasize different parts of the rhetorical or plot structure of texts, especially the peak (e.g. D. Payne, also Jones and Jones), these are mentioned in relation to the main event line information (Longacre's salience scheme). I have found Longacre's approach to be very helpful in my analysis; the distinction made between salience scheme and profile has made it easier to handle all the textual information, and it has given me interesting insights that probably would have escaped me without this particular perspective on the texts. This applies in particular to the profile or the plot structure of the text.

In regards to the salience scheme or the main event line versus background information in the texts, Chafe's views have been of great importance. However, the various works presented above have provided useful insights. Those insights will be discussed when appropriate in relation to the analysis presented in chapters 5, 6, and 7, as well as discussed in some detail in chapter 8.

The question of context, as already discussed, is very important to this study, as well as to the study of discourse/text in general. Throughout the account and discussion of the various scholars above, although having different perspectives, it is clear that they all view context in one way or another as crucial to the study of narrative texts. In chapter 2, I discussed the concept of context as perceived by cognitive scholars, specifically that of Relevance Theory, as well as the view taken by sociolinguistic scholars, and have pointed to the importance of both perspectives.

Several of the theories presented above are explicitly said to be cognitively based, like those of Chafe and Wallace. Their focus is, however, different from that of Relevance Theory although including parallel thoughts. Chafe, for example, states that the way people use language has

3.5 Other approaches in line with Longacre's salience scheme

to do with "what they are conscious of from one moment to the next—on the focus of their internal attention, coupled with a concern for what is going on in the consciousness of the listener" (Chafe 1980b:9). He defines consciousness as a mechanism through which we use old information, whether from memory or from our immediate sociocultural or situational context. Another factor is what he calls self which chooses and decides what is important to share from the old information; in this respect sociocultural factors also play a role, but in a mental sense, e.g. in respect to how much attention one would give this or that piece of information. D. Payne talks about "mental representations" of narratives, events and event-sequence units, etc. She also expresses the importance of the speaker-hearer relationship in the choice of linguistic clues, e.g. the speaker's need to inform the hearer about which events belong to the main event line or not, as already discussed—thoughts clearly in line with Relevance Theory and the concept of construing as well as constraining context, although none of the theoretical accounts of Relevance Theory that I am aware of mention such notions as event lines and narrative processing.

Hymes was presented as an example of the sociolinguistic approach to the concept of context. However, as already noted, it would not be fair to say that mental representations or cognition did not play a role in Hymes's theories and writings; he rather took them for granted (Palmer 1996). Hymes in his own words, has a structural-functional approach to language studies and talks about both the intention behind and the consequence of the act of communication, which would be related to both social and cognitive aspects. I have already stated that a functional approach to language studies necessarily implies cognition and this applies to Hymes, Jakobson, and Longacre. Longacre, for example, is explicit about the underlying notional or semantic structures in text processing, structures that are perceived as being universal, but manifested in different ways in the surface structure, depending on the language.

To return to Givón, he says that "the study of texts, and the study of the functional distribution of various morphosyntactic structures within the text…is the *sine qua non* for discovering the communicative conditions under which various syntactic structures—or rules—apply," and continues to say that "language and its notional/functional and structural organization is intimately bound up with and motivated by the structure of human cognition, perception and neuro-psychology" (Givón 1984:10–11).

4

Quechua Language and Culture

4.1 Facts about the Quechua languages

4.1.1 Geographical situation

Quechua has the most speakers of any indigenous language family[1] in South America. According to Cerrón-Palomino (1987) Quechua is spoken in as many as seven different countries: Peru, Ecuador, Bolivia, Colombia, Argentina, Chile, and Brazil, with the majority of speakers found in Peru, Ecuador, and Bolivia. In the other countries, especially Argentina, Chile, and Brazil, there are only minor "pockets" of Quechua speakers. In Colombia, Quechua is referred to as "Inga," in Ecuador as "Quichua." In the jungle area of Peru, close to the border between Ecuador and Peru, one variety is referred to as "Inga" (South Pastaza).

Peru is the country with the widest geographical distribution of Quechua; it is spoken in almost all of the Andes regions as well as in a few areas in the Amazon rain forest. (See Cerrón-Palomino (1987) and Landerman (1991) for more details.)

Quechua is spoken by several million people in Peru. Both Torero (1964) and Parker (1963) classify the many varieties into two major

---

[1] It is not only a linguistic question but also a political one whether to consider Quechua one language or a family of languages. This is not a question I want to get into here. However, most linguists recognize various separate languages which are not mutually understandable (see, e.g. Cerrón-Palomino (1987) and Landerman (1991)). The degree of mutual understanding varies. Within SIL Peru, we have opted for the term "variety" in reference to the "languages/dialects" of the major groups referred to as Quechua A and Quechua B.

language groups, where the varieties in the north and in the south constitute Quechua A according to Parker (Quechua II according to Torero), and the varieties in the central part of Peru constitute Quechua B (or I). The varieties spoken in the other countries mentioned above all belong to Quechua A/II in terms of Parker and Torero. Landerman (1991) classifies the varieties of Quechua into the Southern, Central (Peruvian), North Peruvian, and Northern language groups (see Landerman for more details). The classifications are based on phonological, morphological, and lexical differences. In the present study I will be focusing on varieties from the southern and central part of Peru, and in reference to the major language groups, I will be using the terms Quechua A (QA) and Quechua B (QB).

In Peru, SIL has been or is engaged in work on between fifteen and twenty different varieties; extensive research has been and is still being done in order to distinguish the different varieties of Quechua.

4.1.2 Grammatical features of Quechua

Quechua is agglutinative with SOV word order; the word order is, however, rather free in main clauses, less so in subordinate clauses. All affixation is by suffixing and, according to Weber (1989), in Huallaga Quechua more than half of the morphemes in any kind of text are suffixes. This would probably be true of most of the other varieties as well.[2] The suffixes thus carry a heavy information load and play a very important role in word formation.

The two major lexical classes are verbs and nouns. Within the noun class there are subclasses like noun-adjectives, pronouns, quantifiers, etc. Nouns and adjectives are considered to constitute one subclass, based on their morphosyntactic similarities. Some of the minor classes are adverbs, negation words, interjections, and connectives.

4.1.2.1 Word classes

Some characteristics of the word classes are given below. (All examples except the sixth one in this section are taken from the *Juan del Oso* text, North Junin Quechua (Weber 1987:141–157). The sixth example is from the Ayacucho Quechua text, pp. 169–180 in the same volume. The examples are labeled "(a), (b),...")

---

[2]According to David Weber (pers. comm.) the Ecuadorian varieties ("Northern" according to Landerman 1991) "depend less on morphology" than the Quechua varieties farther south.

4.1 Facts about the Quechua languages

Verbs have the following characteristics:

- They are obligatorily marked for tense[3] and subject (and object on transitive verbs), often called the transition suffixes.
- They may take pre-transitional suffixes which include aspectual suffixes, reflexives, passives, causatives, and others.
- They may take both derivational and subordinating suffixes and consequently take on nominal and adverbial functions.

(a) witrqa-ra-ya:-chi-n[4]
     lock-OUT-IMPRF-CAUS-3
     'he locks (them) up (in a cave)'

(b) witrqa-ra-ya-pti-la-n-shi
     lock-OUT-IMPRF-ADVDS-ONLY-3P-RPT
     'locking (them) up (in the cave)...'

Nouns have the following characteristics:

- They are marked for case.
- They may take possessive and plural suffixes and at times "shading suffixes."[5]

(c) matray-la-n-tru
     cave-LIM-3P-LOC
     '(only)in the cave'

(d) aycha-la-ta-sh
     meat-LIM-OBJ-RPT
     'only meat'

CONNECTIVES (links) usually occur sentence-initially in narratives. According to Weber (1989:355) they "function as boundary markers between sentences, and indicate—to a very limited degree—the relation of the second sentence to the first."

---

[3] Zero tense marker is considered present tense.
[4] In the examples, colons indicate length of the preceding vowel. The digraph *tr* represents a retroflex affricate; *ll* represents a palatalized lateral.
[5] The suffix *-la* in (c) is one of the so-called "shading suffixes," so called "because they add fine shades of meaning." The gloss is only suggestive (see Weber 1989:357).

Exploring the use and function of connectives and their import in legendary narratives is an important part of my research. Weber (1989:75) lists the following as the most common connectives in Huallaga Quechua:

> *chawra(s)* 'so, then' is derived from *chay oora(s)* 'that time'
> *chaypita* 'thereafter, then' is *chay* 'that' and *-pita* 'ABL'
> *nirkur/nikur/niykur* 'thereupon, then' is derived from *ni-* 'say',
> a pre-transition suffix, and then *-r* 'adverbial clause, same subject'"

Although these items are listed as the connectives in Huallaga Quechua, they are also quite typical of most of the other QB varieties, with some minor variations. As for the QA varieties, the most usual sentence-initial connective seems to be the pro-verb *(h)ina-* 'do like this', often with various suffixes attached, as in (f). *Chay* also occurs with the QA ablative *-manta*.

(e) (Q North Junin)
Chay-pita-sh chay matray-la-n-tru
this-ABL-RPT this cave-ONLY-3-LOC

    witrqa-ra-ya:-chi-n.
    lock-OUT-IMPRF-CAUS-3
    'Then he (the bear) locked them up in his cave.'

(f) (Q Ayacucho)
Ina-pti-n-ña-taq-si padreno-n-qa
do.like.this-ADVDS-3P-NOW-EMPH-RPT godfather-3P-TOP

    lliw-ña piña-ru-ku-n.
    all-NOW annoy-ASP-REF-3
    'Now when he did that, his godfather got very angry.'

4.1.2.2 Suffixes

Some of the suffixes that are of special importance for this study are found in (g) below, which is a small excerpt from the text *Juan del Oso* in North Junin Quechua. That example also includes some of the expressions cited above.

Switch-reference-adverbial suffixes:

One very interesting feature of Quechua—though by no means restricted to Quechua—is that of switch reference. The switch-reference markers have traditionally been analyzed from a strictly syntactical point of view as marking the verb for adverbial subordination to an independent or matrix verb, and at the same time indicating whether the referent of the adverbial clause is the same or different from that of the independent clause. Weber (1989:301–302) says that switch reference "is based on the relation of subordination, i.e. same/different subject is always with reference to the immediately superordinate clause," not necessarily to an immediately preceding or following clause, nor the last clause of the sentence.

However, there are many instances that do not comply with the rules and make it difficult to come up with an explanation based on an analysis with the sentence only as its scope.

Anne Stewart, in a study done on Conchucos Quechua (a QB variety), claims that switch-reference marking can only be understood in a discourse context and that "instances which 'break' syntactic rules, however they are defined, are seen to be consistent at the discourse level, if, that is, the notion of central, or focal participant is taken into account" (Stewart 1987:285). What this implies is that "Same-Subject switch reference in narrative…is reserved for central participants" (p. 289). Different-subject switch-reference marking, on the other hand, "is reserved for clauses which refer to discontinuous or not-yet-continuous participants and events…[that is] for less central, adverbial kinds of reference ('background' in the sense of Hopper 1979)" (Stewart 1987:301–302). This is also in line with what Conrad Phelps (pers. comm.) claims for Ayacucho Quechua. Stewart also claims that the "asymmetry" between the two switch-reference markers "is indicative of a discourse-driven system" where same-subject switch reference marks the "expected" and different-subject switch reference marks the "unexpected" (Stewart 1987:302).

The most usual switch-reference suffixes are the following:

QB	QA	
-pti	*-pti*	'different subject'
-r/l	*-s(h)pa*	'same subject'

More details in regards to the claims made above will be discussed in view of my findings in the Ayacucho Coracora texts, which will be dealt with in chapters 5 and 6.

Evidential suffixes

Evidential suffixes were mentioned in chapter 1. Quechua operates with three main evidential suffixes: *-mi, -shi, -chi;* the phonological manifestation of these may differ somewhat between varieties. What follows is a general characterization of each of them (based on Weber 1989):

-mi 'direct information/convinced'
-shi 'indirect information/unconvinced'
-chi 'conjecture'

The function of these on discourse/text level is, according to previous studies, somehow uncertain, and may differ from variety to variety. Weber sees their location as giving the sentence an information-structural profile, in the sense of a theme/rheme relation (according to the view of the Prague school), where the "topic" marker "tends to occur on old information (with 'old information' suitably defined to include things alluded to, generics, etc.)" (Weber 1989:401), while the evidentials tend to occur on the new information but are not restricted to such markings. But Weber admits that these distinctions are somewhat fuzzy. (See Weber 1989 sections 20.1, 20.2, 21.2, and 21.3 for more details.)

The evidential of interest for this project is the suffix *-shi/-si* 'indirect information', also named 'reportative' or 'hearsay', and which is a typical marker of folktales, myths, and legends although the consistency of its usage varies a lot between different varieties.

Usually, but not always, the evidentials occur sentence-initially together with the connectives. Floyd suggests at least for Wanka Quechua (a QB variety) that their function in the kinds of text mentioned is not that of "hearsay" but "that what we have here is a sort of discourse level grammaticalization. Reportative marking here is principally a characteristic feature of the genre…" (Floyd 1999:135). Floyd also recognizes the formulaic use of the evidential *-shi* in the genre of riddles. He further states the following (p. 141):

> The hearsay prototype is characterized by short turns and irregular evidential marking and the subject matter is mundane. The prior information source is a specific, cognitively-salient nonspeech-event participant, and the speaker is the possessor of privileged information. On the other hand, a folktale is characterized as an extended monologic turn with very regular evidential marking with content that is typically alien to normal everyday experience.

All of the texts being analyzed in the present study have a very regular repeated use of the evidential *-shi/-si*. I trust my study will shed light on some areas of function that have not previously been considered.

The "topic" suffix

The suffix *-qa* is generally called the "topic marker," though its function as a topic marker has been questioned. Weber (1989:418) points to various uses of *-qa* and suggests that "some very general pragmatic function underlies the various uses of *-qa* and that this function is roughly that *-qa* marks those constituents of a sentence which—in the speaker's eye—are most responsible for that sentence's relevance to its context."

The use of the so-called "topic marker" is seen to vary considerably between varieties and also from narrator to narrator. It seems to be used very infrequently in the texts at hand and will not be particularly focused on in the present study.

The following excerpt from a text from North Junin Quechua gives an example of the use of some of the suffixes mentioned above:

(g) Chay-pita-sh chay matray-la-n-tru
 this-ABL-RPT this cave-ONLY-3P-LOC

 witrqa-ra-ya:-chi-n. Oso-qa
 lock-OUT-IMPRF-CAUS-3 bear-TOP

 witrqa-ra-ya-pti-la-n-sh kasa-ku-q
 lock-DUR-IMPRF-ADVDS-ONLY-3P-RPT hunt-REF-PRMC

 aywa-r, aycha-la-ta-sh mas apa-q.
 ir-ADVSS meat-ONLY-OBJ-RPT more bring-HAB

 mantini-na-n-paq
 keep-NOM-3P-PUR

 'Then he (the bear) locked them up in the cave. The bear, having locked them up, going hunting, just brought them meat, to keep (feed) them.'

Tense and aspectual suffixes

The tense-marker -*naq* 'narrative past' for QB is very frequent in legendary narratives. Its equivalent in QA is -*sqa*. Its discourse functions will be discussed later on.

Some other tense markers will be discussed in connection with the analysis of the texts.

As for aspectual suffixes, there is a host of them, and those that are important for this study will be discussed as part of the textual analyses.

As can be gathered from the information on the connectives and the suffixes above, a proper understanding of these is only gained through their study in a wider discourse context.

4.1.2.3 Sentence, clause, and predicate

In the introduction to the connectives (4.1.2.1), it was noted that Weber sees them as functioning as "boundary markers between sentences." Weber defines the sentence "in terms of clause, and clause in terms of predicate" and says that a "sentence must contain a main clause, and may contain other elements such as adverbial clauses, interjections, and links...A clause must contain a predicate, and may contain other elements such as adverbs, adverbial clauses, and substantive phrases...A predicate is usually a verb (finite or non-finite) with its "closest" argument (e.g. an object). However, it may also be a substantive (either simple or derived)." (For more details see Weber 1989:13.)

Larsen (1974:420–421) in a study of a text from the Huaraz variety of Ancash Quechua says that "the basic grammatical unit of the narrative" is the "narrative sentence" which "consists of one or more clauses and a sentence marking construction. In its fullest variation the sentence marking construction has three parts, two of which are connective":

The two connectives are (1) the "antecedent connective" *tsay* (demonstrative); or a dependent clause: a repetition of the preceding verb root with switch-reference markers; and (2) the "sequence connective" -*na*.

The third part of the "sentence marking construction" is, according to Larsen, the reportative -*sh(i)*.

The notion of grammatical sentence has validity in all traditional grammars. However, many Quechua linguists (in conversation with Weber) seem to recognize the fact that often natural pauses or falling intonation are lacking at the end of the units referred to as sentences, as Quechua texts are often written with two to four grammatical sentences punctuated as one sentence;

the grammatical sentences are sometimes separated by commas, sometimes by nothing.

Stewart (1987) in her study on clause-combining in Conchucos Quechua, claims that the clause tends to coincide with pauses, which gives evidence for the clause as the basic intonational unit in Conchucos Quechua. She bases her claim on Chafe's study of English where the clause likewise is the 'prototypical intonation unit.' The intonation unit, according to Chafe (1980b), expresses a basic cognitive unit or single "focus of consciousness." Stewart (1987:31–32) further claims the following:

> Conchucos Quechua clauses cluster together into intonational paragraphs. Much as Chafe noted for English, these paragraphs manifest 'the major schematic structure of the story' ([Chafe] 1984:58) in narratives. Evidence for these paragraphs in Chafe's analysis of English is exclusively pausal, whereas in Quechua, there is also pronounced falling intonation. In Quechua monologic discourse, there are clear breaks between paragraphs, signalled clearly by the intonational patterns of speech, and reflecting major shifts in orientation of the discourse, regardless of genre. The situation is thus similar in this regard to what Chafe reports for English spoken paragraphs, which, he says, 'result from major shifts in a speaker's peripheral consciousness' ([Chafe] 1984:48).

Chafe recognizes the sentence as some kind of intonational entity indicated by falling intonation in English but sentences "do not seem to have the same cognitive correlates as clauses, extended clauses, or paragraphs, that they 'appear to be determined by a speaker's decisions based on rhetorical effect'" (Stewart 1987:32).

Stewart says that there are factors (some of those mentioned above, e.g. the connectives) that appeal to the notion of grammatical sentence, but she claims that the lack of pauses does not "support the notion of 'sentence' as an intonational entity" (Stewart 1987:32). She discards the sentence as useful for her discourse study on clause-combining strategies and resorts to an analysis in terms of independent and dependent clauses.

Also Burns and Alcócer Hinostrosa (1975:44) analyze a text from the Ayacucho area in terms of independent and dependent clauses, and their conclusion is that (translation is mine) "the paragraph is a legitimate element of the grammatical structure of Quechua" and the connectives "give the sensation that there is no corresponding final stop to the anterior clause." They further state that "the role of the dependent clause and the clausal connective is crucial to the Quechua style." The *sentence* is never mentioned.

While Stewart finds the notion of sentence to be of little value to her study, the structural unit defined as the sentence by other linguists seems to be very relevant to the present study, particularly the *narrative sentence*, as defined by Larsen. Larsen also asserts that the nature of the sentence differs according to its place in the narrative; e.g. the sentences in what is considered the background (or stage) of the story often lack the narrative "sentence marking construction." (1974:422).

The nature of these "units" will be dealt with in more detail in relation to the analyses in the following chapters.

4.2 Some aspects of Quechua culture

A few cultural aspects relevant to the present study will be considered in this section.

According to Quechua worldview and culture, notably their art and old social structures, there are strong organizational principles where symmetry and "pattern numbers" play an important role (personal observations, David Coombs (pers. comm.), Harrison 1989, Howard-Malverde 1989, López-Baralt 1979, Rostworowski 1999). The term "pattern number" is taken from Dell Hymes (1981:319) who has pointed to the significance of certain pattern numbers within different North American Indian cultures. The pattern number seems to be reflected in various ways in stories or acts in a rite: the number of repetitions of an incident, the number of participants in a story, or the number of verses in a stanza. For most North American Indian cultures the number is four, but for some the number is five.

In Quechua culture one cannot point to a single number as *the* specific cultural pattern number, as various numbers seem to play that kind of role. However, some seem to be more prominent than others. According to both López-Baralt and Rostworowski there seems to be a basic structure in the Andean culture based on an old principle of organization in the Inca empire. This principle of organization is well demonstrated in the organization of the city of Cusco which was the religious and cultural center of the Inca empire. According to López-Baralt (1979:88–89):

First, duality: the city is divided into two big halves, the upper and the lower, and four regions or "barrios". (I assume she means that there are two "barrios" in each of the halves as four names for the "barrios" are mentioned.)

Second, triology: each region or "barrio" is divided into three sections. Triology is also seen in the cosmic ordering: Viracocha (the creator god), the sun, and the moon.

4.2 Some aspects of Quechua culture

The sun and the moon again represent two elements each, so the maximum cosmic pattern number according to López-Baralt is $4+1=5$, where 1 stands for Viracocha. I believe I have seen the cosmos represented with other numbers but the maximum pattern number is apparently 5.

López-Baralt's conclusion is that duality is the most prominent of the numeric principles, and it still plays a major role in the social, ritual, and spatial organization of the Andean communities.

Rostworowski in her ethnohistoric description often refers to numbers (structural quotients) in relation to the Andean political and social structures; however, the number three is never mentioned. All the numbers represent "multiples of the dual and quadripartite divisions." The number eight, according to her, is of "great significance in the Inca social structure" (1999:18, 26). The duality is seen in both opposition and complementarity of halves, e.g. in the sense of upper *(hanan)* and lower *(hurin)*, left *(ichoc)* and right *(allauca)* (1999:7).

In the case of duality, Rostworowski claims that the opposition of halves "formed a dual division throughout the Andean world" during the Inca rule. This was expressed through dual partitioning of valleys, towns, and *ayllus*. Gender also played an important role in these physical divisions of space. This was particularly demonstrated through the moieties in the city of Cusco, where "the upper moiety relates to the masculine gender and the lower to the feminine" (p. 7).

These divisions were not only important as far as physical space was concerned but the concepts of opposition and complementarity was fundamental to Andean thought and worldview (see Rostworowski 1999 for more details).

Rostworowski pays attention also to the extensive practice of dual rulership, a practice that seems to have been normal, not only among the Inca rulers, but also among other ethnic groups later included in the Inca "empire" (pp. 144–148).

Although the number three is never mentioned as significant by Rostworowski, certain cultural combinations reflect three different units. For example, prior to the Inca ruler, Pachacutec, the Sun was the most important deity. However, Pachacutec introduced two other deities. The image of the Sun still occupied the most important position in the "Temple of Gold," but next to it, on either side, were images of Viracocha (the creator god) and Chuquiylla (the deity of lightning). Also, Rostworowski (p. 4) mentions that the armies of the Andean world typically were "divided into *three* parts" (italics are mine), but each army was "commanded by two chiefs."

In regards to the lack of a writing system in the Inca realm, Rostworowski says that the various chroniclers agree "that the natives possessed special songs in which each *ayllu* (a lineage group or kinship-based community) or *panaca* (a royal *ayllu*) narrated the principal events of its past during certain ceremonies..." (Rostworowski 1999:vii). Other ways of preserving memories of the past were through paintings and the *quipu*, a special mnemonic tool which nobody today knows how to use. According to Rostworowski (p. viii). "...the absence of writing was not an insurmountable obstacle to the Inca people's keeping and commemorating their past."

Mannheim (1986) presents us with some different forms of parallelisms seen in Southern Peruvian Quechua verbal art, patterns which he claims to be usually binary but which can also be ternary. However, he does not draw any comparison with these and any cultural "pattern number." At the writing of an earlier draft of this study, no one, to my knowledge, had ever suggested that these numeric principles serving as culturally defined pattern numbers might be found in any form in stories from the Andean culture. Although I initially did not think this aspect would be of major interest in my study, my project work led me to believe the opposite.[6]

4.3 Verbal art forms

Apart from what is already mentioned above in relation to the pattern numbers, I will in this section present some insights from studies related to different aspects of verbal art. The studies represent work on different varieties of Quechua, although most of them belong to Quechua A.

4.3.1 Mannheim

Mannheim (1986) discusses how verbal art functions as a tool for learning grammar, especially the semantics of grammatical categories, in Southern Peruvian Quechua. The two genres he considers are riddles and popular songs, the so-called *waynus*. Mannheim presents us with some of the

---

[6]More recently I have also become aware of several authors who have found Aymara texts to be organized according to certain numeric principles, e.g. in triplets, couplets, or quadruplets (Huanca (1989) and Briggs (1994)) in Dedenbach-Salazar's article (1999:189), published in *Tradición oral andina y amazónica* (Godenzzi 1999), although Dedenbach-Salazar does not talk in terms of cultural pattern numbers in regards to these structures. Arnold and Yapita (1999:243), in the same publication, mention the "paratactic" or binary constructions in songs and narratives in Aymara, where textual elements (I believe verses or stanzas) are seen to be placed "uno al lado de otro" (one at the side of the other), reflecting textile patterns. See also Mannheim in the next section.

4.3 Verbal art forms

most typical features of these two genres and mentions typical features of Southern Peruvian Quechua verbal art in general, some of which will be mentioned here.

"Apart from children's riddles, Southern Peruvian Quechua verbal art—poetry, song, and formal rhetoric—is primarily non-prosodic in organization" (Mannheim 1986:55). This statement is puzzling because the *waynus* seem to also be composed in meter, according to what Mannheim himself says: "*Waynus* are a dance form, rhythmically regular and strophically organized" (Mannheim 1986:60).

Mannheim also claims that rhyme is not "aesthetically valued"; the nature of the language is such that suffixing and clause chaining easily create rhyming words in everyday discourse. In personal conversation with a literate Ayacucho Quechua speaker a few years back, he claimed that in Quechua poetry lines could be rhyming both at the beginning, within, and at the end. This claim, I think, could indicate that rhyme must also have some aesthetic value, even when it is only based on rhyming suffixes. In some of the *waynu* examples Mannheim gives, *all* couplets have lines ending with the same grammatical suffix(es) as well as initial words ending with the same grammatical suffix(es). Although there are other features in these songs that are of higher value aesthetically (see the discussion on "semantic coupling"), the fact that all lines are rhyming, seems to indicate that rhyme in itself also is of some importance. However, it might be the grammatical parallel structuring of the clausal units as wholes that is of real artistic value. The following excerpt from a *waynu* taken from Mannheim (1986:61) provides an example of what might be considered initial, internal, and final rhyme, but, I have to admit that what might be considered initial rhyme in this example is pure repetition (for the parts in bold, see the discussion on semantic coupling below):

*Noqachu **muna**kurayki*	Was it me you desired?
*Noqachu **wayllu**kurayki*	Was it me you loved?
Sonqocha munarasunki	A heart desired you
Ñawicha qhawarasunki	Eyes watched you

According to Mannheim, metaphoric iconicity and semantic and syntactic parallelism seem to be the most valued features in Southern Peruvian Quechua verbal art. As far as semantic and syntactic parallelism is concerned "they apply over a limited range of textual material and do not exhaustively versify entire texts" (Mannheim 1986:55). One problem with this statement is that there are no examples given, and I do not know what kind of texts Mannheim is referring to. Of all the material I checked into at the time of writing my dissertation, I was not able to find Peruvian Quechua narrative texts of any kind displayed in such a way as to show features of verse of the sort mentioned above. However, Mannheim mentions "formal rhetoric" and could be alluding to such kinds of texts. In another publication (1991:125) he mentions "versified secular and religious dramas," but here, too, without any examples. The dramas he mentions belong to the written body of literature and some of them date back to as early as the beginning of the seventeenth century. One question in regards to these is whether they rather reflect Spanish style. The Spaniards were well established in the country by then, and literacy was introduced by them. But Mannheim seems to think that they are composed according to Quechua rhetorical patterns.

However, in a more recent publication, Mannheim presents an analysis of two texts which are divided into lines; these are, according to him, based on

> grammatical parallelism and pauses in the discourse of the narrator. These lines are grouped in bigger units (sometimes called verses), taking into account grammatical parallelism, the structure of the sentence, and, when there is direct speech, taking into account the changes of interactants. These are again grouped into bigger blocks which are separated through some change in the narrative line (normally marked through a change in the location of the narrated events) or a change in the rhetorical posture of the speaker (Mannheim 1999:63, translation is mine).

As far as grammatical parallelism is concerned, this is not explained or defined in the article; readers are left to make their own observations. (See the texts as they are lined out in the same publication.)[7]

Mannheim (1986:56) lists three kinds of parallelism typical of Southern Peruvian Quechua verbal art. These kinds of parallelism are typically binary but sometimes ternary:

---

[7]Mannheim, in his article (1999:52ff.) tries to combine three different perspectives to textual analysis; that of Hymes, dividing the texts into lines, etc.; that of Lévi-Strauss, amplifying his views on intertextuality, saying that, once organized, intertextual networks serve to establish "normative social frames" (translation is mine); and that of "*La etnografía de la actuación,*" which claims that "the importance of the narrative is a property emerging from the interaction" between various participants in a social event. Mannheim (1999:61) claims that in his research he was not able to find "oral narratives that were like the concise expositions" that he had read in his studies over "'temas actuales' and in the chronicles from the colonial era." Instead, he says, "I found actions (actuaciones) that questioned the stereotypes that I had in regards to the texts and the textuality." He (1999:62) further claims that the Southern Peruvian Quechua texts seem to be "fragmented and highly dependent on context" because the texts are adapted (acted out) according to some situation within the sociocultural framework.

4.3 Verbal art forms

- *Referential parallelism*—typical of formal rhetoric: "Formal rhetoric often involves referential parallelism with superimposed parallelism of grammatical categories."
- *Morphological parallelism*—"in derivational and inflectional suffixes but not enclitics."
- *Semantic coupling*—the most typical kind of parallelism. According to Mannheim this is

> a peculiarly Quechua poetic device in which two otherwise morphologically and syntactically identical lines are bound together by the alternation of two semantically related word stems...The stems are a semantic *minimal pair*; they differ by a single semantic property, and there is no word stem with a value for that property mid-way between them. Semantic coupling is found extensively in Quechua popular song (p. 56).

The excerpt of the *waynu* cited above, in relation to the discussion on rhyming, includes an example of paired lexical stems, shown in bold, namely *muna* and *wayllu*, where *waylluy* (the infinitive form) 'to love with tender displays of affection' is "a hyponym of the unmarked" *munay* 'to want, to desire, to need, to love' (the translations are Mannheim's). Mannheim says that "...any utterance with *waylluy* entails an utterance with *munay* replacing it. (The reverse is not the case.)" (p. 61). The marked (and also more complex) stem occurs in the second line and the unmarked stem occurs in the first line (p. 60).[8]

From Mannheim's study it can be concluded that although metrical verbal art exists in Southern Peruvian Quechua, non-metrical verbal art is most typical.

Harrison (1989), who worked with Ecuadorian Quechua (*Quichua* in Ecuadorian terms) speakers, states that the poetry of the song is often marked by an internal rhythm (referring to the more modern Quechua songs) but she does not say or show how in her analysis of several Quechua poems. She further states that "Although many scholars over the centuries have attempted to distinguish genres and formal versification of Quechua poetry, much of the analysis stems from a European tradition, with expectations of what poetry should be" (1989:22).

---

[8]See also Adelaar (2004) and Muysken (2004) and their analyses of *waynus*. Muysken says (p.47) that "It is not always clear whether to count Quechua verbs as a doublet; often there was [in the data] no direct correspondence, not even in the sense that the first item was less specific in meaning than the second item, as Mannheim assumed to be the case." Adelaar (p.63) says that the semantic pairs may be "synonyms, near-synonyms, antonyms, or just members of a same semantic class."

I do, however, believe that some of Mannheim's and other scholars' discoveries show some genuine Quechua verbal art features; it is left to see whether there is more to be discovered in regards to different genres.

4.3.2 Szemiński

Szemiński (1997), through his research on Andean (Peruvian Quechua) theology, based his studies first of all on prayers (adorations and supplications) to the various deities. Important to the research has also been the study of the vocabulary and structure of the prayers. Although these prayers belong to the written material (from the time between 1550 and 1662) and some of them are obviously influenced by a Christian way of thinking, Szemiński claims that it is possible to recognize the more ancient prayers of Andean origin through their organization into complementary semantic pairs. Sometimes these patterns have other subordinated patterns of such complexity that they suggest a system of writing or some other method of "codifying and representing the prayer in such a way that the author could verify mistakes in the internal structure of his composition" (1997:327, translation mine).

Szemiński further claims (1997:327, translation mine):

> I do not doubt that a major part of the prayers were memorized and repeated. Some of them, specifically the more simple ones, seem to be based on common memorized schemas which served as a basis for the composition of an adequate prayer for a particular situation.

The idea of *schemas* as a memorization tool is interesting but, although Szemiński presents us with structures of the different prayers considered, he does not propose any specific patterns for possible schemas used for memorization. As stated, Szemiński claims that complementarity of semantic pairs is fundamental to the prayers of Andean origin, but he also shows that the prayers may have very different structures and consist of a number of different lines, no prayers being completely identical in this aspect. However, if schemas were used in the memorization of prayers it is not unlikely that these—or other kinds of schemas—were used in memorization of other kinds of texts, e.g. folktales, legends, and mythical texts. In the studies referred to in chapter 2, rhythm and other poetic devices, often in the form of verse, have been regarded as tools for memorization but no one has proposed that these form specific patterns on higher levels of text.[9]

---

[9]Thematic modules, serving in the reconstruction of stories by individual authors, as well as serving as memorization tools, have been mentioned by various authors (see Godenzzi 1999).

4.3.3 Carpenter

Carpenter (1985) has done a study of Ecuadorian lowland Quechua (Quichua) mythical narrative texts. During his stay with this particular Quechua-speaking group he was repeatedly told that his way of telling their stories was not quite right. This prompted him to try and find what underlying patterns existed in their mythical texts.

In his article he presents the analysis of one particular myth whose patterns he claims to be representative of the rest. He says,

> the myth is composed of a series of couplets. In the majority of these couplets the first line contains a subordinated verb and the second line contains an independent verb....This verbal construction is usually followed by the reportative *nin* 'they say/one says'....In many cases the couplets are tied together in that the independent verb of one couplet becomes the subordinated verb in the next couplet....Throughout the myth there are quotations and these generally occur as the first line of the couplet....The final couplet type consists of a question and answer scheme with the first line being the question and the second line the answer. (1985:57–58)

Although Carpenter's study was done on Ecuadorian Quechua,[10] the Peruvian Quechua texts might display patterns similar to those he discovered.

4.3.4 In conclusion

From the literature that has been looked into so far, all the authors seem to believe that Quechua verbal art is typically non-prosodic in nature. Their claim is that there is a basic binary pattern of parallel organization in Quechua verbal art. According to Mannheim, ternary structures are also found. If binary semantic/syntactic patterning is a typical feature of so many genres looked into so far, it is reasonable to expect similar patterns in legendary narratives as well.[11] What other patterns may exist? Mannheim says that only parts of texts may be versified. If that is the case, one also has to ask "why is it so?" Most of these studies (the exception is

---

[10] As stated introductorily, Quechua scholars consider the Ecuadorian Quechua to belong to the Quechua A branch.

[11] As noted earlier, Arnold and Yapita have found both songs and narratives to have binary patterns in Aymara (an Andean language coexisting with Quechua in the southern part of Peru). Mannheim (1999:51–54) uses the term *cultura del lenguaje* 'the culture of language' which may pertain to certain areas. In relation to Quechua he says that the culture of language in the southern part of Peru is very distinct from that of lowland Ecuadorian Quechua. On the other hand, he reminds the reader that languages that are not genetically related, but which exist in the same or neighboring areas, may belong to the same culture of language.

Szemiński) concern varieties of Quechua A. It will be of interest to see whether the same features exist in the varieties of Quechua B.

5

Textual Patterns (I)—Ayacucho Coracora Quechua

5.1 The textual data

In the first chapter I said that my analysis would be based on texts from two different varieties of Quechua: Shausha, belonging to Quechua B and Ayacucho Coracora, belonging to Quechua A. I also said that I would first focus on texts from the Ayacucho Coracora area, first of all *Juan del Oso* (Weber 1987). A rather detailed analysis and discussion of this text will be given below. In the following chapter, the analysis will be compared with the analyses of other Ayacucho Coracora Quechua texts, (called simply Coracora).

The theoretical and the methodological bases for the study—specifically those of Hymes, Longacre, and Chafe—have been outlined, and various other works and theories have been looked into in the previous chapters. Of these Jakobson and Leech have been of specific interest, but all the works, approaching textual analysis from different perspectives, have provided insights useful for the present study. Insights from other authors still not mentioned, will be referred to in my discussions and analyses of the various texts.

The title of this work indicates that I will be looking at structures in *legendary* narrative texts. The Peruvian folklorist Morote Best (1987) ascribes to *Juan del Oso* several factors of legendary nature (in Weber 1987: Introduction). However, whether this story should be considered a legend or a fairytale is not a major question for this research. As pointed out in chapter 4, Floyd (1999:141) suggests that the evidential *-shi* is a marker of genre which includes legends, fairytales, and myths. Still, it could be that other structural features set these apart as different genres. Since I will be comparing structures in the *Juan del Oso* story with structures in stories that are more typically fairytales, the comparison may also give an indication in this respect. One factor of significance is that *Juan del Oso* is much lengthier than any of the other stories, at least as far as the Ayacucho Coracora texts are concerned. The main character is heroic, a feature that is typical of old epics of European origin, and found in African folklore as well (see Goody 1987). This does not necessarily set the story apart as structurally different from the others. In chapter 3 insights from the works of the folklorist Axel Olrik were presented. His *Sage* included both folktale, myth, legend, and folksong; and the "epic laws," he felt, were applicable to all these genres. However, whether this holds true for Quechua folklore from the areas studied cannot be answered based on a study of folktales alone.

5.2 The basic organization of the *Juan del Oso* text

I believe the Coracora version is quite representative of most of the others; in very general terms one can say that the story comprises three major parts and basically unfolds in three major locational settings: the cave-site (for most versions), the village, and the woods (or, in some versions, a different village and/or hacienda). Within these major locational settings there is a lot of moving back and forth to different sites/locations within the major specified area. This is particularly obvious in the second setting, the village. In fact, the moving from one location to another seems to be a very important part of the basic underlying structure of the text, at least the Coracora version.

The main character, whom I will call by the name "Osito" 'little bear', is depicted as struggling against various (three) forces: human (children, men, priest); natural (lions); spiritual (a condemned spirit or a little devil, as in the case of the Coracora version).

The first part of the story often depicts life in the cave. It sets the stage for the episodic development to come, and is the part that has been best preserved in the different varieties. According to Morote Best (1987:7) this is the basic form of the story. In fact, in some areas this is the only part of the story that exists. In other areas this first part and the subsequent parts exist as separate stories.

In the Coracora version as well as in most other versions, the first part relates the story of Osito's father who is a strong and dangerous animal; he has taken prisoner a young woman who becomes the mother of Osito. They live in a cave and the father sustains his wife and son by raiding and killing people; the Coracora version also expresses the assumption that his wife suffers from this kind of behavior. When Osito gets older he kills his father and he and his mother escape. (See appendix 1 for the glossed text with a semiliteral translation.)

The second part relates his introduction to life in the village, living in the priest's home, and the many difficulties he encounters due to his strength and eating habits. Osito's struggles in the village are against both human and natural forces. (Morote Best 1987:13 terms the human forces "social institutions.")

The third part mainly relates Osito's final struggles with spiritual forces of some kind in the woods (in some versions related to some hacienda) and his victory—death in the case of the Coracora version.

Osito, through his strength inherited from his father, is able to overcome most of these forces. But one underlying problem, and also a major reason for the many different struggles, is Osito's incredible demand for food. Though the need for food to survive is basic both to human beings and animals, in Osito's case the need for food grows out of proportion due to his animalistic heritage, and it becomes a major struggle for him to survive in a more civilized setting. The unfulfilled craving for food is what in the end causes Osito's death, in some versions. The Coracora version and the Ambo-Pasco version end on a sad note, while most other versions have a happy ending. Whether this fact sets the Coracora version and the Ambo-Pasco version apart as closer to the original, cannot be determined. But probably this is one of the older versions in *Juan del Oso*.[1]

According to various Quechua scholars, many of the Quechua tales contain elements typical of European folklore. This is not surprising considering the Spanish influence in the country for centuries. It is quite typical for European tales to end on a happy note, and this feature might have become a part of some of the stories already centuries ago. On the other hand, stories of European origin may have become so Andeanized that they have lost many of the original features typical of the European origin, and possibly as such also have exchanged the happy ending for a sad

---

[1]According to the note in the introduction to Lauriault (1958), the Ayacucho Coracora story might have been told as early as 1951. The author tells that he met the narrator of the story already in December of 1951 and that the text was dictated to him during about a month of working together with the narrator (the time of this is not specified, however, but it may be assumed that it happened around the time of their first getting to know each other). The Cusco story was written in 1952 (but not published until 1975) and has a happy ending (Loriot 1975).

one, reflecting metaphorically a negative outlook on life and the hopelessness of the Quechua within the powerful Spanish society.

However, many scholars seem to assume that *Juan del Oso* is of Spanish origin. Morote Best (1987:9, 11, 12), refers to José María Arguedas (1964) and Aurelio M. Espinosa (see Morote Best 1987:9 for more details) and says that the story "without doubt" is of Spanish origin, and that "it is in no way strange that what is now considered the Peruvian folktale originates from two sources, both of them powerful" (1987:11, translation mine). Although the basic form may be of foreign origin, it still has been "Americanized" to such a degree that it has adopted "local colors with individual narrative elements loaded with significance" (Morote Best 1987:12).

5.3 The presentational form of the story

The term "presentational form" was introduced in chapter 3 with the introduction to Hymes's methodological approach to text analysis. It was stated there that I would be using the term in a slightly different sense than Hymes (see 3.2.2), who uses the term to cover *poetic* form, *rhetorical* form, and *vocal* realization. The poetic form is, as discussed above, the organization of the text in terms of verses, lines, stanzas, scenes, and acts. The rhetorical form has to do with the organization of the text as a story, like "onset, ongoing action, and outcome" (Hymes 1981:321). My focus will be on these first two forms for obvious reasons. Concerning the poetic form I will be drawing on the works of Hymes, as well as Jakobson and others. For a discussion of the rhetorical form, and in relation to the study of various interacting aspects of the text, I will mainly be drawing on works by other linguists, particularly ideas from Longacre and Chafe.

I could have started the study of the text by trying to identify underlying semantic units and see how these are marked in the surface structure, but I wanted to use Hymes's approach where the identification of sentence-initial connectives plays a major role in discovering other patterns. This methodology turned out to be of great help, because certain patterns that stood out as salient to me in the surface structure helped to identify underlying semantic patterns that I might have missed if I had started the analysis the other way round. In fact, keeping an eye on several aspects of information at the same time helped me to discover the presentational form of the story. Hymes also claims that the different aspects of text (in his analysis three, as mentioned already) are interwoven. I by no means claim to have discovered all that is involved in the often intricate interplay between different aspects or types of information within the text; there are many unanswered questions yet. Still, some patterns have become clear. These patterns will also serve as a point of departure for the analysis and discussion of the other texts.

Although I will try to discuss the different aspects of information one at a time, it will be necessary at times to discuss some of these at the same time to show how they interact.

5.3.1 Surface features—artistic patterns?

5.3.1.1 Discovering specific features in the text

Ternary structures

By and large, the story is composed of a series of triplets, interspersed with units—bridges—of one or two sentences (called sentences for the time being).

The key to the structure—in line with Hymes's analysis—is found in the recurrent connective clause, which is also the equivalent to what Larsen (1974) called the narrative sentence-marking construction in her analysis of Huaraz Quechua (see 4.1.2.3).

When I first started to study the text I was not able to recognize any specific patterns of the particular surface features in the introductory part. A few instances of *chay* 'this' were occurring in sentence-initial position but at the time I was not able to see them as part of any pattern. When I got to the second section—the village setting—the pattern started to fall into place, at which point I realized that I could also apply it to the introductory part, albeit my criteria for doing so were based more on semantic unity than surface characteristics. I should admit that I am unsure about some of my groupings in this part.

For the village setting it is the regular occurrence, in sentence-initial position, of *ina-pti-n-si* 'do.like.this-ADVDS-3P-RPT' that plays the major role in the pattern formation. The sentences initiated by these can easily be grouped in units of three based on semantic unity and can be seen as small episodic units or—in terms of Hymes (and that of dramatic performance)—a little scene with three takings of turn.

In the final section of the story it is the regular occurrence of *ina-spa-(n)-si* 'do.like.this-ADVSS-(3P)-RPT' in sentence-initial position, as well as the grouping of sentences in units of three, that provides for a regular pattern.

Because all the units show such a consistent patterning of three I choose to call them by the poetic term *triplet*, the nature of which will be discussed in more detail below.

The ina-pti- *triplets*

The conformity of the triplets lies partly in the presence of a recurrent sentence-initial connective clause whose initial pro-verb *ina*- 'do like this' signals a tie to the previous sentence. In addition, part of the connective clause, the suffix *-pti*, also signals a change of subject or referent for the independent (or immediate superordinate) clause of the new sentence.[2] Description of other events or background information is usually found in a subordinated form (also using *-spa* and at times *-pti* but without the *ina-*). At times an independent clause serves the same function. In a sense the conformity lies in both "likeness" and "unlikeness," to borrow terms from Hopkins, quoted in Jakobson (1959). "Unlikeness" is produced by the suffix *-pti* through the constant change of referent, but together with the rest of the connective clause it also accounts for a regular repetition of surface structure.

There is another kind of conformity seen between the triplets because most triplets have the same kind of internal structure—in terms of a little story—where the first sentence creates a circumstance or situation for the second sentence of the episode, while the last expresses a result or conclusion.

To facilitate the reading of the discussion below, consider the following excerpt from the text in appendix 1. The numbers in parentheses are the numbers of the triplets and the "bridges" (to be discussed below). The other numbers are the numbers of the sentences as they occur in the published text. The arrangement of the text is my responsibility. It is intended to show the triplets and to indicate possible lines if one were to consider the *ina-pti-n-si* connectives to be markers of verse (see 5.3.1.3). (The free translation does not reflect the layout of patterns.

---

[2]Weber (1989:301–302), says the following: "Switch reference is not defined in terms of the order of clauses (as, say, by reference to the immediately following clause, or to the preceding clause, or to the last clause of the sentence). Rather, it is based on the relation of subordination, i.e. same/different subject is always with reference to the immediately superordinate clause. [In a footnote (p. 302) he says: "This is true across Quechua dialects."] Subordinate relationships (i.e. what is subordinate to what) are not always obvious; in fact, they are sometimes quite subtle…extra-syntactic considerations sometimes enter into determining the chain of subordination."

5.3 The presentational form of the story

(7) 16 Chay-ta-ña-taq-si   mana muna-sqa-chu   warmi-n.
     this-OBJ-NOW-EMPH-RPT   no   want-PRT-NEG   woman-3P

     17 Ina-spa-s   wawa-n-ta   ni-n:
     do.like.this-ADV-RPT   son-3P-OBJ   say-3

                "Imayna-raq   iskapa-ru-ku-chwan?"   ni-spa.
                how-YET   escape-ASP-REF-12CND   say-ADV

16 His wife didn't like (want) this [that her "husband" raided and killed people]. 17 Then she said to her son: "How do we escape?"

(8) 18 Ina-pti-n-ña-taq-s   chay   wawa-n   ni-n:
     do.like.this-ADVDS-3P-NOW-EMPH-RPT   this   baby-3P   say-3

            "Suya-yku-y   mama-y.
            wait-IN-2IMP   mother-VOC

            19 Ñoqa-m   tayta-y-ta   orma-yka-chi-saq
            I-DIR   father-1P-OBJ   fall-IN-CAUS-1FUT

            kay   qero-nta-kama   amu-chka-pti-n."
            this   trunk-ALONG-LIM   come-IMPRF-ADVDS-3P

     20 Ina-pti-n-si   ok   vez   chay-na
     do.like.this-ADVDS-3P-RPT   one time   this-SIM

            torillo   tonto-ri-sqa
            bull   carry-ASP-PRT

            qero-ta   pasa-mu-chka-pti-n
            trunk-OBJ   pass-AFAR-IMPRF-ADVDS-3P

            qero-ta   moyo-rpari-chi-sqa.
            trunk-OBJ   move-MOMENT-CAUS-PRT

     21 Ina-pti-n-si   mayo-man   pasa-yku-n.
     do.like.this-ADVDS-3P-RPT   river-GOAL   pass-IN-3

18 And her son said: "Wait, mother! 19 I will make my father fall when he comes (walking) along the trunk." 20 And once when he was passing along the trunk, carrying the bull, he (the son) made the trunk move. 21 And he fell into the river.

(9) 22 Ina-spa-n remolino-man pasa-yku-n
       do.like.this-ADV-3P whirlpool-GOAL pass-IN-3

   23 Ina-spa-n-si wañu-n.
       do.like.this-ADV-3P-RPT die-3

22 And he went into the whirlpool. 23 And he died.

(10) 24 Ina-pti-n-si chay wawa-n
        do.like.this-ADVDS-3P-RPT this baby-3P

        mama-n-ta apa-ri-ku-spa-n
        mother-3P-OBJ take-ASP-REF-ADV-3P

        ri-pu-n llaqta-man.
        ir-BENEF-3 village-GOAL

    25 Ina-pti-n-si llaqta-pi
        do.like.this-ADVDS-3P-RPT village-LOC

        mana bautiza-sqa ka-pti-n
        not baptize-PRT be-ADVDS-3P

        ok kura-man qo-yku-n
        one priest-GOAL give-IN-3

        bautiza-chi-na-n-paq.
        baptize-CAUS-NOM-3P-PUR

    26 Ina-pti-n-si bautiza-ra-chi-spa
        do.like.this-ADVDS-3P-RPT baptize-ASP-CAUS-ADV

        yacha-y + wasi-man chura-n.
        learn-INF + house-GOAL put-3

24 And his/her son, taking his mother along, went to the village. 25 And in the village, since he wasn't baptized, she gave him to the priest for him to baptize him (her son). 26 And after having baptized him, he/they put him in the school.

5.3 The presentational form of the story

(11) 27 Ina-pti-n-si   pichqa wata-yoq-ña.
       do.like.this-ADVDS-3P-RPT   five   year-HAVE-NOW

   28 Ina-pti-n-si   barba-n wiña-ra-mu-n.
       do.like.this-ADVDS-3P-RPT   beard-3P grow-ASP-AFAR-3

   29 Ina-pti-n-si   chay-manta chuta-n
       do.like.this-ADVDS-3P-RPT   this-ABL   pull-3

        chay-pi   waron-kuna.
        this-LOC young.man-PLUR

27 And now he was five years old. 28 And his beard was growing. 29 And because of this the children pulled it (the beard).

(12) 30 Ina-spa-s
       do.like.this-ADV-RPT

          "Padreno-y,
           godfather-VOC

           kay warma-kuna-m   bastidia-wa-n."
           this child-PLUR-DIR   bother-1O-3

30 Then (he said): "Godfather, these children are bothering me."

(13) 31 Ina-pti-n-si
       do.like.this-ADVDS-3P-RPT

          "ok   taka-ta   qo-y,
           one fist.knock-OBJ   give-2IMP

           macho zonzo" ni-pti-n-si
           big   fool   say-ADVDS-3P-RPT

           taka-ta   qo-n.
           fist.knock-OBJ give-3

   32 Ina-pti-n-si   wañu-rari-n.
       do.like.this-ADVDS-3P-RPT   die-REPET-3

   33 Ina-pti-n-si   padreno-n-qa
       do.like.this-ADVDS-3P-RPT   godfather-3P-TOP

sipi-na-n-paq   ni-sqa.
kill-NOM-3P-PUR   say-PRT

31 And as he said "give them a punch, you big fool," he gave them a punch. 32 And so many died. 33 And it was his godfather who had told him to kill.

(14)   34 Ina-pti-n-si
          do.like.this-ADVDS-3P-RPT

    chay   sacristan-nin-wan
    this   catechist-3P-ACCOMP

    atun   ochko-ta   ochku-ra-chi-n
    big   hole-OBJ   make.hole-ASP-CAUS-3

    pichqa   negro-wan.
    five   negro-ACCOMP

  35 Ina-pti-n-si   chay   okumarí
    do.like.this-ADVDS-3P-RPT   this   bear

    chay   ochku-pa   pata-n-ta   pasa-chka-pti-n
    this   hole-GEN   edge-3P-OBJ   pass-IMPRF-ADVDS-3P

    tanqa-yku-rpari-sqa.
    push-IN-MOMENT-PRT

  36 Ina-pti-n-si   pasa-yku-sqa.
    do.like.this-ADVDS-3P-RPT   pass-IN-PRT

34 Then through his cathechist he ordered to have a hole made by five negroes. 35 Then, when this bear passed along the edge of this hole, they pushed him into it. 36 Then he went (fell) into it.

(15)   37 Ina-spa-n-si   chay-manta-s   lloqsi-rpari-mu-n.
          do.like.this-ADV-3P-RPT   this-ABL-RPT   leave-MOMENT-AFAR-3

  38 Ina-spa-n-si   chay   negro-kuna-ta
    do.like.this-ADV-3P-RPT   this   negro-PLUR-OBJ

> chay uchku-pi pampa-rpari-n.
> this hole-LOC bury-MOMENT-3

37 Then after this he left (jumped out) (of the hole). 38 Then he buried all these negroes in this hole.

Although the triplets show the same pattern of three sentences initiated by *ina-pti-n-si*, the internal structure of each sentence, with various sub-units, differs from triplet to triplet and also within the triplets. Some triplets have very simple sentence structures, as can be seen in triplet (11), while others are more complex, like triplet (10).

The sentences 24–29 and 31–36 may seem to be units of six sentences, each initiated by *ina-pti-n-si*, but one will find that both groups of sentences each clearly constitute two different units. The breaks between the units are signalled through both the change of location (although not clearly stated in the surface structure) and the introduction of at least one new participant; each unit in fact constitutes a small episode/scene. Furthermore, the differing internal complexity of sentences 24–29 also clearly divides them into two units, triplets (10) and (11) respectively.

The other triplets are set apart in the surface structure by the intervention of "units" of one to two sentences, usually initiated by the connective clause *ina-spa-n-si* where *-spa* refers to 'same subject'. The nature of these "units"—the bridges—will be discussed below.

The ina-spa- *triplets*

The third and final section of the story is more complex when it comes to surface structure; one reason for this is that it contains the climax and denouement of the story. As can be recalled from chapter 3, Longacre (cf. also Payne, 3.6.2) asserts that the climactic section is often marked in a different way in the surface structure (the peak); he also calls this section the "zone of turbulence" which seems to be a good description of this particular part of the story at hand. The units (25)–(28),[3] in the climactic part of the story, leading up to the culminating point, followed by the denouement, units (29)–(30), are the units that seem to be the most irregular, and it has been difficult to decide where they begin and end; I have followed the overall pattern of triplet units and interspersing bridges in deciding how to group them. What is of greatest interest is that, in the final part—from the culminating point—we find a total reversal of the pattern as seen in section two of the story. The triplets are now composed of

---

[3]See section 5.3.2.2 (Climax and denouement) for more details.

ina-spa-(n)-si sentences, and the focus is longer on one participant at a time. The *(ni-)/ina-pti-n-si* sentences, on the other hand, as well as sentences marked by the connective *chay-pi-s* 'this-LOC-RPT' set the *ina-spa* triplets apart. This seems to be the pattern from unit (29) until the final unit (34). Longacre says that the denouement may be followed by episodes that "keep untangling," called the "final suspense"; these episodes are encoded in the surface structure as pre-peak episodes. However, as noted, in the text at hand all the final episodes, including the denouement, are marked by the same initial *ina-spa*. This may indicate that the Coracora storyteller considers all the material following the culminating point as one major rhetorical unit, whether it be called "denouement" or "final suspense" or something else; this will be discussed in more detail in section 5.3.2.2. See the following excerpt from the text in appendix 1:

(29) 84 Ni-pti-n-si   okumari
          say-ADVDS-3P-RPT   bear

                piña-kacha-ri-ku-spa
                annoy-HERE.AND.THERE-ASP-REF-ADV

                ok-ta   taka-ta   qo-n
                one-OBJ   fist.knock-OBJ   give-3

                wañu-chi-q-lla-ña.
                die-CAUS-AG-LIM-NOW

      85 Ina-pti-n-si   chay   kusillo-qa   api-rpari-n.
           do.like.this-ADVDS-3P-RPT this   little.devil-TOP grip-MOMENT-3

      84 When he said this, the bear, being very angry, gave him a punch, as if to kill him. 85 Then this little devil grabbed him.

(30) 86 Ina-spa-n-si   qapi-rpari-n   qapari-npa-ri-n.
          do.like.this-ADV-3P-RPT strangle-MOMENT-3   scream-AFAR-ASP-3

                87 "Mana-ña-m   chayna-sqayki-ña-chu"
                    not-NOW-DIR   do.this-1FUT2-NOW-NEG

                        ni-spa-n-si
                        say-ADV-3P-RPT

                roqa-pa-rpari-ku-n.
                beg-BEN-MOMENT-REF-3

5.3 The presentational form of the story

88 Ina-spa-s
do.like.this-ADV-RPT

(ina-spa-n-si)   chay   vaca-kuna-ta-pas   qati-rpari-n.
do.like.this-ADV-3P-RPT   this   COW-PLUR-OBJ-ALSO   follow-MOMENT-3

89 Ina-spa-s   chay-pi   deja-rpari-n.
do.like.this-ADV-RPT   this-LOC   leave-MOMENT-3

86 Then he strangles; he screams. 87 And he begs (saying): "I am not going to do like this to you." 88 And his cows also he drives away. 89 And he leaves him (the bear) there.

(31) 90 Ina-pti-n-si   chay   okumari-qa   llaki-sqa
      do.like.this-ADVDS-3P-RPT   this   bear-TOP   get.sad-PRT

         "Kay-cha   kay   kay-pi   allin   apu.
         this-DOUBT   this   this-LOC   good   owner

         91 Imana-saq-taq   kunan-qa?
              what.do-1FUT-QUEST   now-TOP

         92 Imayna-taq   kunan   apa-saq   padreno-y-pa
              how-QUEST   now   take-1FUT   godfather-1P-GEN

                     ni-wa-sqa-n-ta?"
                     say-1O-REL-3P-OBJ

              ni-spa-s
              say-ADV-RPT

              rima-pa-ku-n.
              talk-BEN-REF-3

93 Chay-pi-s   yarqa-y-manta-pas   yaqa+yaqa-lla   wañu-n.
   this-LOC-RPT   be.hungry-INF-ABL-ALSO   almost+almost-LIM   die-3

90 Then very sad, the bear says to himself: This one here is very forceful. 91 What do I do now? 92 How am I going to bring that which my godfather told me to. 93 In this place he almost dies from hunger.

(32) 94 Ina-spa-n-si   chay   ñawpa-q
        do.like.this-ADV-3P-RPT this   go.ahead-AG

              leon-kuna-wan   carga-mu-sqa-n-ta   maska-n.
              lion-PLUR-INSTRM   carry-AFAR-REL-3P-OBJ   seek-3

       95 Ina-spa-s   mana   tari-n-chu.
          do.like.this-ADV-RPT   not   find-3-NEG

       96 Ina-spa-s
          do.like.this-ADV-RPT

              kuti-na-n-paq
              return-NOM-3P-PUR

              ñaka+ñaka-y-ta   tari-ru-n
              suffer+suffer-INF-OBJ   find-ASP-3

              chay ichi-sqa-n   leon-lla-ta.
              this mount-REL-3P   lion-JUST-OBJ

94 And he looks for the lions (being ahead) on which he had (earlier) carried (his things). 95 And he doesn't find them. 96 And in order to return, suffering he finds this lion which he mounts.

(21) 97   Ina-spa-n-si
          do.like.this-ADV-3P-RPT

              chay leon-pi   ichi-ri-ku-spa
              this lion-LOC   mount-ASP-REF-ADV

              maska-n   ok-nin-kuna-ta.
              seek-3   one-3P-PLUR-OBJ

       98 Mana-s   tari-n-chu.
          not-RPT   find-3-NEG

       99 Aswan-si   chay   kusillo-wan   topa-ro-n.
          instead-RPT   this   little.devil-ACCOMP meet-ASP-3

       100 Ina-spa-s   mancha-ri-ku-n.
           do.like.this-ADV-RPT   get.afraid-ASP-REF-3

101 Okumari-qa
    bear-TOP

    "Kunan-qa capaz-cha   wañu-ra-chi-lla-wa-nqa-pas"
    now-TOP almost-DOUBT   die-ASP-CAUS-LIM-1O-3FUT-ALSO

        ni-spa-s
        say-ADV-RPT

    mancha-ri-ku-n.
    get.afraid-ASP-REF-3

102 Lomismu-lla-taq-si   kusillo-pas   mancha-ri-ku-n
    the.same-LIM-EMPH-RPT   little.devil-ALSO get.afraid-ASP-REF-3

    "Kunan-qa   wapu-ya-ru-n-ña-chiki.
    now-TOP   strong-VRBL-ASP-3-NOW-DOUBT

103 Chay-chiki   kay atun   leon-pi   ichi-n"
    eso-DOUBT   this big   lion-LOC   mount-3

        ni-spa-n.
        say-ADV-3P

104 Mancha-ri-sqa   qawa-naku-n.
    get.afraid-ASP-PRT   look-RECIP-3

105 Ina-spa-n-si   rima-paya-naku-y-ta   ati-n-chu.
    do.like.this-ADV-3P-RPT talk-BEN-RECIP-INF-OBJ   can-3-NEG

106 Opalla-lla   muyo-ri-spa-n
    quietly-LIM   turn-ASP-ADV-3P

    ok-nin-pas   ok-nin-pas   pasa-mu-n-ku.
    one-3P-ALSO   one-3P-ALSO   pass-AFAR-3-PL

97 And mounting this lion, he looks for the others. 98 He doesn't find them. 99 Instead he meets this little devil. 100 And he gets scared. 101 He gets scared and says: "Maybe he now will kill me." 102 In the same way the little devil also gets scared and says: "Maybe he has now become big, strong. 103 That is why he is sitting on this big lion." 104 Scared they look at each other. 105 Then (from fear) neither of them is able to talk to the other. 106 Quietly turning, both of them leave.

(34) 107 Chay-pi-s   chay okumari-qa wañu-n   yarqa-y-manta.
         this-LOC-RPT this bear-TOP   die-3   be.hungry-INF-ABL

    108 Ina-spa-s   mana-ña wasi-n-man   chaya-n-chu.
        do.like.this-ADV-RPT   not-NOW house-3P-GOAL arrive-3-NEG

107 In this place the bear dies from hunger. 108 And he is not able to return home.

Bridges

It might seem questionable to use the term "unit" in reference to the interspersed sentences between the *ina-pti-* triplets, because they are often closely attached semantically to the scenic unit in the previous triplet, elaborating its conclusion. Let's consider the section containing the *ina-pti-* triplets where both unit (9) and (15) are elaborations or expanded conclusions in relation to the preceding triplets, (8) and (14), respectively. Also, the use of *-spa* 'same subject' suggests continuity through the repetition of same subject, putting focus on the main participant.[4] Although *-spa* suggests continuity in one respect, it signals discontinuity in another respect; the "units" introduced by *ina-spa-n-si* have multiple functions. They set the triplets apart; sometimes they signal a conclusion of one little episode, as in the cases mentioned above,[5] at other times they provide the "setting," that is, provide background information, for the next (e.g. unit (7) which, by the way, starts off with a different connective, namely *chay-ta-ña-taq-si*). Most often the units seem to signal both at the same time, having a "bridging" function beween episodic units and different locational settings. The pattern also suggests that often a question or statement (introduced by the initial *ina-spa-*) serves as an introduction to the next triplet/episodic unit to come or as a bridge between two such units. Unit (12) is an example of this. On all these occasions one can say that they announce to the hearer the end of one episode/scene and the beginning of a new one, as well as the end of one triplet and the beginning of a new one. From the point of view of Relevance Theory, one can say

---

[4] As already discussed in 4.1.2.2 (see also Stewart 1987), Stewart claims that *-spa* keeps track of the main participant in a discourse. This does not necessarily indicate a repetition of the subject from the previous sentence. At times it does in fact mean a change of previous subject in order to switch the focus to the main participant. Note the use of the term "focus." I use the term in a very general sense, not in an analytical sense, that is, I do not use it in the sense of referring to a specific part of the sentence as "focus," as opposed to the part referred to as the "topic" of the sentence. This is the way the term is used in much of the linguistic literature; see, e.g. Lambrecht (1998) for a discussion on these aspects. In fact, the subjects receiving focus in the text might better be perceived as topics in many of the clauses involved.

[5] *Chay-manta-s* 'this-ABL-RPT' (after this –it is said) in unit (15) suggests a lapse of time.

5.3 The presentational form of the story

that they play a role in "constraining the context," a means used by the speaker to help the listener in his task of construing the context intended by the speaker. The use of *ina-spa,* in all these cases, indicates to the listener that the focus is on the central participant for that particular section of the text, and he is about to change to a new scene, possibly a new location, and a range of new events.

A focus on the central participant is indeed important to the "unit's" bridging function and provides both continuity and points of rest—according to Chafe—before the author propels the listener into further actions. As can be remembered Olrik also talks about "restpoints" in a narrative story.

D. Payne (1992a:378) says that SETTING is a relational notion:

> the term setting as used in structuralist discourse studies suggests that it has primarily been used as referring to a *type* of unit...However, I suggest that setting is better understood as a relation that stands between units, akin to what Mann and Thompson (1986) term a circumstance relation: "a circumstance relationship holds between two parts of a text if one of the parts establishes a circumstance or situation, and the other part is interpreted within or relative to that circumstance or situation" (pp. 64–65). That is, a proposition, or *mutatis mutandis,* a group of propositions, cannot, in and of itself, be analyzed as a setting; it is only when its *relation* to other propositions is evaluated that the term can have any meaning.

In a narrative text, I believe one can see each episodic unit as establishing some circumstantial relationship for the next; circumstantial relationships between various episodes have to do with the coherence of a text as a whole. If we think in terms of Relevance Theory, the context is being construed step by step. This is also the case with the excerpt from the text, where, from the point of view of an analyst, unit (13) has to be interpreted in relation to unit (11), but where unit (12) has to be seen both as a reaction triggered by unit (11) and as a setting for the development in unit (13). Likewise, as already mentioned above, you find the same kind of circumstantial relationships *within* each episodic triplet unit.

However, I do believe that a *setting* can also be considered to be a major type of unit, just as the study of this text clearly shows. These settings, which I refer to as "stage"[6] also have their own particular surface structure (which will be discussed below). They serve to give the introductory background information before the subsequent events of a narrative or a major part of a narrative; but even these establish a circumstantial relationship with other parts of the story.

Although the final section of the text shows a reversal of the pattern, the interspersing units can even there be perceived as having a bridging function in the sense of providing a close semantic tie to the previous and following units, providing a conclusion to one scene and providing the setting for another. On the other hand, the bridging units cause interruption of topic continuity and/or mark crucial turning points in this final part of the story. However, what might at first glance seem to be interruption of topic continuity because of the use of *-pti* (different subject), turns out not to be the case; see, for example, unit (29), sentence 84, where *-pti* is used although there is no change of subject. Why this anomaly? Is it in order to keep to an artistic pattern, reversed at this point, or is there another reason? This will be discussed later.

From what has been said so far, one can conclude that the *ina-pti-* and the *ina-spa-* sentences play very important presentational roles in the creation of a specific pattern that seems to be of artistic nature. One may conclude that they have other specific functions on a discourse level as well, which will be discussed in more detail in section 5.3.2.

Although the *ina-spa-* sentences/"units" between triplets may serve different functions for the reasons discussed above, in need of a common term I choose to call them by the name "bridges." The fact that each sentence is introduced with the initial pro-verb *ina-* with reference to the previous event (which is of course also the case with the triplets), clearly shows that the concept of "bridging" must be prevalent in the Quechua languages—and possibly the Quechua culture. Weber (1989:313) says that clauses formed by switch-reference markers "play a major role in giving discourse cohesion." He continues: "An adverbial clause often recapitulates—in a very summary way—the contents of the preceding sentence."[7] In the text at hand the pro-verb *ina-* serves that function.

---

[6] I use this term in line with Longacre's use of it, as expressed in the 1983 edition of his *Grammar of Discourse*. Longacre uses the term "stage" for the surface structure of the introductory part of a narrative, which he refers to as the "exposition" 'lay it out' in the notional structure. Longacre (1983:29) says the following : "Many times stage is expounded by an expository paragraph or even by a short embedded expository discourse. It may, however, be a subsidiary narrative of some length which is necessary to get the main narrative going."

[7] This is not something peculiar to Quechua; other languages show similar structures.

5.3.1.2 The *ina-* triplet as a poetic unit

The *ina-* triplets are the units that best show the artistic nature of the text. Although the sentences are to a great degree structurally different both within and between units, together they form a consistent pattern. The cleverly arranged pattern is of artistic value to the Coracora Quechua people. Seen from a more traditional point of view, Jakobson (1959 and 1966), who addresses the question "what makes a verbal message a work of art?," claims that verbal art very much rests on the principle of parallelism. Parallelism can operate on various levels within a text, e.g. phonological, morphological, and grammatical. Although many texts are in metric form, the principle of parallelism can be seen to operate in texts that are not metric.

The way the *ina-* triplets are arranged demonstrates a form of parallelism both through their "likeness" and their "unlikeness" (see The *ina-pti-* triplets 5.3.1.1), both phonologically and grammatically (syntactically), although this parallelism is expressed mainly through the repetition of the same initial connective clause. The constant repetition of the same initial connective also creates a rhythm, although rhythm would also depend on how the rest of the sentence is expressed. In conversation with a speaker of Aymara (a language coexisting with Quechua in Southern Peru) concerning this pattern in Quechua, she noted the similarity with Aymara and immediately presented a rhythmic beat. Although the triplets are structurally very different, I think they can be said to give a certain cadence to the text, based on both the sentence-initial repeated connectives and the consistent groupings of the number of sentences containing them. There might be other important rhythmic features on the lower levels but these will not be considered in the present study.

Mannheim (1986:56), as noted in chapter 4, asserts that there are three kinds of parallelism in Southern Peruvian Quechua, to which the Ayacucho Coracora Quechua belongs. He mentions *referential parallelism* "with superimposed parallelism of grammatical categories" in formal rhetoric; but he does not give examples, so it is difficult to know what he means. It could be that he is referring to structures similar to those we have seen in the triplets through the specific use of the switch-reference markers. Another kind of parallelism he mentions is *morphological parallelism* "in derivational and inflectional suffixes" which might also apply to the same kinds of patterns, but might have been seen in the structure of the connective clause as a whole.

Lowth's three kinds of parallelism were listed in chapter 3, one of them being the *synthetic* or *constructive* parallelism. In Jakobson's (1966) terms this is the same as grammatical parallelism where similarity is found in form. This is what has already been discussed above in relation to the triplets and the connective clause. Another parallel structure, according to Lowth, is that of *antithetic* lines which correspond with one another by an opposition, sometimes in expression, sometimes in sense only. Typical antithetic terms would be *black* and *white, light* and *darkness,* to mention but two examples. The different subjects referred to through the *ina-pti-* connectives could be seen as expressing some *antithetic* structure in the sense of *different* and not the *same.* However, I admit that the form for parallelism between the different sentences, through the use of the *ina-* connectives, is weak—if indeed it can be called parallelism from a more traditional point of view.

Another kind of parallelism is found on a different level. The *ina-* triplets clearly display parallelism between different kinds of textual information, in that the triplets parallel an episodic unit—as well as a specific location (a locational unit) in a more subtle way. Also, as already mentioned in relation to the conformity of the triplets, there is a parallelism between triplets in the way the sentential units function in the little episodic unit: the first sentence establishing some circumstance for the second, and the final expressing some kind of result.

5.3.1.3 The sentence as a poetic unit, a verse

In Hymes's analysis the initial particles define the verse (see 3.2.2). If I adopt his analysis, as I introductorily said I would do, I will (at least tentatively) define a "sentence" introduced by the *ina-* connective as a VERSE.

Some of the units so far referred to as sentences are in a rather expanded form and may also include other independent sentences that seem to be of a backgrounding/elaborating nature and as such are sub-units of the *ina-* sentence. By using the term "verse" I avoid the confusion the term "sentence" might create and at the same time I ascribe to this unit some kind of poetic function.

I have already defined the triplet as a poetic unit, partly based on the three times repeated *ina-* sentences. This should support the idea that the *ina-* sentences must also be poetic units of some kind, although they vary greatly as far as internal structure is concerned. Hymes suggests that for the Chinookan language the verses seem to be the pivotal units; the verses are not recognized by counting parts, however, but "by recognizing repetition within a frame, the relation of putative units to each other within a whole" (Hymes 1981:318). This is exactly the way the *ina-* sentences in this Coracora text seem to function. Nevertheless, at this point I do not

5.3 The presentational form of the story

want to commit myself to claiming that what I have now tentatively defined as a verse is the *pivotal* unit in this Coracora Quechua text; the triplet unit might play that role. (I make this tentative suggestion based on previous studies, e.g. that of Stewart (1987) who does not recognize the sentence as an intonational unit, while the paragraph, in this case the triplet—maybe at times with its elaborating conclusion—is recognized as such.)

Leech, as noted in 3.3.5, talks about complementary meanings in terms of poetic deviations from the normal language use. In the case of the text at hand, one possible extended meaning of the *ina-* connectives might be a marker of verse. Leech talks about three different kinds of deviations. In the case of "primary deviation" it has two forms according to Leech, one of them being "Where the language allows a choice, the poet denies himself the freedom to choose, using the same item in successive positions." One question would be whether the storyteller has a choice in regards to the use of the initial *ina-*. I gave an example from Norwegian poetry in 3.3.5, where I pointed to the fact that the poet could easily have chosen a different connective instead of using the same one in initial position throughout the stanza. Considering that the Quechua story in question might have been transmitted from generation to generation and, as such, probably is not an artistic product of the present author, does the language allow for other initial connectives? The verb *ni-* 'say', already noted above, has developed into a regular connective and could have been used instead of the pro-verb, at least on occasion.[8] Weber (1989:313–314) points to this fact for Huanuco Quechua, but the usage of *ni-* seems to be usual across varieties of both Quechua A and B. Carpenter, talks about a construction where "the couplets are tied together in that the independent verb of one couplet becomes the subordinated verb in the next couplet." Instead of using the initial pro-verb *ina-* 'do.like.this' in reference to the previous action, the verb could have been repeated in a subordinated form, followed by the other suffixes typical of the initial *ina-* construction. This "recapitulating" device is, as already noted, very common in Quechua discourse across different varieties (see, e.g. Weber 1989:313ff.). In regards to the text at hand with its constant repetition of *ina-*, it is indeed possible that it is a primary deviation, where the choice of other connectives is being "denied" in order for the connective to function as a poetic device, repeated to introduce verses, as well as giving a certain rhythm or cadence to the text. It is possible that we are here dealing with a poetic canon.

---

[8]This is, in fact, the case for the part referred to as the climactic part which will be discussed in more detail below.

However, there are some heuristic problems if the *ina-* sentence is defined as a verse. Does recognizing the *ina-* sentence within a frame define the verse, or is it the connective clause as a whole that defines the verse? Or is it one part of the connective construction that defines the verse? As we have already seen, the connective clause not only has a linking function as a whole, but individual suffixes within the clause play an independent part, as in the case with *-pti* and *-spa*.

I have grouped the introduction of the story in triplets with interspersing "bridges." Most of these triplets do not have any overt surface marker in the form of *ina-* connectives (although there are a few other connectives), and my grouping of sentences in triplets for this part of the story was mainly based on semantic unity rather than surface characteristics. This needs some modification, because I also took into account one surface feature: the reportative *-si*, which seemed to occur in every sentence in the triplets, as well as in the interspersing bridges, with the exception of sentences 2, 3, and 9; the absence of the reportative in sentence 9 could be explained in terms of apocope with the final *s* in *-pas*.[9] The reportative *-si* is also part of the *ina-* connectives forming the triplets, and furthermore marks sentences in the interspersing bridges and those of the more irregular units of the climactic episodes.

I make the following hypotheses:

- Verses can be recognized on the basis of their regular occurrence within a frame (the triplet equalling a scene).
- *-si* 'reportative' is a formal marker of verse, in addition to other functions it might have. This would also be in line with what Hymes (1992) considers a possible marker of verse.
- *ina-* connectives (containing the reportative *-si*) are markers of verses of episodic nature.

These hypotheses still have their problems: what about the *-si* occurring in clauses that seem to be subordinate both in form and/or in the sense of being hierarchically sub-units of the *ina-* sentences? Does *-si* have different functions in these cases, or does it mark lines within verses? And what about the few cases where you would expect it to occur but where it is absent?

In the previous chapter, it was noted that for Wanka Quechua, among other functions of the evidential *-shi*, Floyd also ascribes to it the function

---

[9] In the case of sentence 3 there might be other markers that also help define the verse, e.g. the suffixes *ña-taq* 'NOW-EMPH' (see analysis of other texts further ahead). In the case of sentence 2 it could be a sub-line of verse 1. If so, the introduction would be a couplet rather than a triplet.

of being a grammaticalized marker of genre; that is, of folktales, legends, and myths. He also states that it occurs in almost every sentence (Floyd 1999:135) and that only *one* is allowed per sentence (p. 30). The latter is not true for Coracora Quechua as just noted above. However, what Floyd describes as a grammaticalized marker of genre might turn out to be a marker of verse, at least for some varieties of Quechua.

At this point in my analysis I will leave these questions unanswered.

5.3.1.4 Verse lines

As said introductorily, I have displayed the text in such a way as to suggest possible lines within verses. This has been done mainly based on subordinate clauses but at times also on independent clauses (sub-units to the *ina-* sentence); and in some cases also based on a predicate or some other feature that seems to set a certain structural unit apart as a possible line. However, the nature of possible lines will not be focused on in this particular study.

Carpenter analyzed the Ecuadorian myths into couplets and based his grouping of couplets on an initial subordinated verb as the first line and the second line containing an independent verb "usually followed by the reportative *nin* 'they say/one says' " (Carpenter 1985:58). In many cases —according to Carpenter (p. 58)—"the independent verb of one couplet becomes the subordinated verb in the next couplet." This subordinated verb would correspond to the *ina-* connective in Coracora Quechua. However, I do not consider this connective clause as a poetic line in itself, as it has no meaning apart from the event it refers back to; I see it rather as introducing the verses that are of episodic nature (as already stated above).

5.3.1.5 The triplet defined as a stanza

Having tentatively defined the sentences marked by the reportative *-si* to be verses, we can now, following Hymes's analysis, conclude that the composition of these form a triplet *stanza*, the stanza corresponding to an episodic unit (a scene) and a more or less specific location. This should be in line with more traditional literature on poetry. Hamer (1966:6) states that "A stanza ideally corresponds with a logical or emotional division of the matter of the poem, to a stage in the thought or narrative, or to a distinct moment of passion or grouping of imagery." A "logical division" might be seen as corresponding to the triplet stanza divisions and the "grouping of imagery" corresponding to the stanza itself forming an episode (scene).[10]

5.3.1.6 Concluding remarks

The point of the discussion above was partly to try to see patterns in relation to already recognized poetological devices, though I recognize the danger in doing so. As expressed by Harrison (1989:22) many of the attempts "to distinguish genres and formal versification of Quechua poetry...stem from a European tradition, with expectations of what poetry should be." However, although languages differ in many respects and the poetological means may be very different, some common underlying universal principles may exist even in the most unusual forms seen from a European tradition. Still, it is important to keep in mind that even some other poetological means specific to individual cultures and/or languages may exist. Further analysis of texts should help refine this initial analysis.

5.3.2 The rhetorical patterns of the text

5.3.2.1 Preliminaries

As stated already in the first chapter, I will be basing this part of the study on the works of various linguists, particularly those of Longacre and Chafe, presented in 3.4 and 3.5.5, respectively. Longacre makes a *profile-salience scheme* distinction in his textual analysis which I have adopted for the present analysis; I have found this approach to be helpful in discovering the various functions of the already discovered patterns described above. For textual *profile* I will mainly be following Longacre's methodology, while for the *salience scheme* I will be drawing on insights from other linguists as well.

It might be helpful at this point to briefly review what the profile-salience scheme distinction entails. The profile has to do with the rhetorical structure of the text in terms of an underlying notional or plot structure (e.g. exposition, developing argument or conflict, climax, denouement, final suspense, and conclusion) and how it is encoded in the surface structure. The salience scheme has to do with different levels of information, e.g. main event line information versus that of background or supportive material.

---

[10] I want to stress here that the "grouping of imagery" most probably also includes elaborating *ina-spa-* verses.

5.3.2.2 The organization redefined—the profile of the text

The rhetorical structure of the text at hand involves several aspects of information. I have talked about the various main sections of the story in rather loose terms; the divisions between the sections are a bit more problematic than it might seem from what has been said above. Three major locational settings have been identified: the cave-site, the village, the woods. The episodic development of the text starts at the end of the first locational setting, that is, the cave-site, and goes on until the end of the story, with the exception of a smaller section that seems to serve as a stage for the very final section.

The last units (units (7)–(9); of appendix 1) of section one,[11] involving the killing of the bear-father, conclude the stage part, but at the same time have a bridging function into the second section, from one major local setting to the next. This "bridging" episode which displays surface features of both stage and episodic development (see below) is the encodement of what Longacre calls the "Inciting Moment" in the notional or plot structure. This kind of episode is reported to have peak-like features (Longacre 1996:37). This does not seem strange considering the text at hand where the inciting moment can be perceived as a climax/denouement to the first part of the story, that is, the stage,[12] at the same time as it sets off the episodic development. The suffix *-rpari* 'sudden action' is used once; this suffix is used several times in the peak-section marking the denouement of the complete story. It also occurs at other times marking crucial moments in the development of the narrative.

Units (20)–(24) of the last section can also be considered to have a bridging function between two major local settings, for the units in question take you from the village to the woods, back to the village, and then back to the woods again for good. These are, in fact, the preclimactic episodes; the climactic episodes show a completely different surface structure, as already stated. At the same time, there are other surface features, like the irregularity of the connective pattern as well as the tense markers (see below) which indicate that unit (20) possibly serves as a stage to some bigger unit. Unit (20) could set the stage for the final major locational setting, the woods; or, it could be the stage to only the preclimactic units. In that case, units (24)–(25) could be seen as bridging units between the preclimactic episodes and the final episodes; that is, the

---

[11]Unit numbers in 5.3.2.2 refer to the numbers in parentheses in appendix 1.

[12]In the beginning of this chapter it was mentioned that the first part of the story also is the only part that exists as a story on its own in some varieties of Quechua; it therefore seems reasonable to think that what is here perceived as the inciting moment originally was the climax of such a short story.

climactic and denouement/final suspense ("wandering") section. In the next chapter, section 6.3.2, we will see how the discovery of the pattern of complementary halves helped in the final analysis of this.

Clearly, we are here dealing with different aspects of information which will be discussed in more detail in the following sections. However, the analysis shows that the story is structured to have a beginning, middle and end, but, as it seems, of different kinds depending on types of information. This contradicts Ong's claim that oral narratives do not have any clear beginning, middle, or end (see 3.4.1).

Divisions based on tense marking

In support of some of the divisions above let us now turn to the tense marking in the text. The introductory part, units (1)–(9), serves as a stage to the second section as well as to the whole story; unit (20) seems to serve as the stage to the final section. These stage units are set apart from the rest of the story through the use of the tense marker -*sqa*, which Soto Ruiz (1976a:99) describes as a narrative past marker (glossed PRT 'participle' in the text, due to its additional function as a nominalizer); the connectives are, moreover, more varied for these units. For the rest of the story (with some modifications) present (or neutral) tense is used. It seems like the narrator sets the stage in the past, then brings you onto the scene through the use of the present tense. This is in line with what several linguists describe for varieties of Peruvian Quechua (Weber 1989, Shaver 1996, Hintz 1996); see also Levinsohn 1991 for Inga, a Columbian Quechua variety. Levinsohn discusses various past tense markers and their usage in relation to the unmarked present tense in five different dialects. One of his claims is that background information, in whichever way it may be marked, "expressed in independent clauses in Inga...may be divided into three categories" (Levinsohn 1991:150). One of these categories is "Events and states which are *preliminary* to the main events of the story...and a rhetorical usage, immediately preceding the climax or 'peak'" (ibid.), referring to Longacre (1976:212ff). (The use of tense markers in the text can be seen in appendix 2; see also discussion on main event line in 5.3.2.3.)

Climax and denouement

Ong, as reported above, claims that narratives in oral cultures do not have a plot structure; I would argue to the contrary for *Juan del Oso* and claim that the final struggle where Osito is confronted with spiritual forces is

5.3 The presentational form of the story

the climactic part (see 5.3.1.1) of the story. The whole story shows a rising tension through the various struggles that Osito is facing and this tension is increasing through units (25)–(28), where Osito is arguing, first with a man, then with the little devil he meets on the road, and which ends units (29)–(30) with the devil grabbing Osito and trying to strangle him, then leading his cows away.

This part of the story is marked in a particular way in the surface structure (cf. Longacre's claims above in regards to climax): units (25–28) have a completely different structure from what has been seen so far for the episodes. Unit (25) has been analyzed as being a couplet. But although the verses of the couplet are introduced by *ina-pti-* connectives, the unit has to be analyzed as a "bridging" unit; Osito is leaving one scene and going on to the next. (Another problem with this unit is that there is uncertainty about the identity of the referents, but both verses seem to be referring to the main participant, Osito, although the unexpected DS marker occurs in both.)[13] Units (26) and (28), interspersed with the bridging unit (27), have been analyzed as being triplets but they do not have the typical markers of the episodic triplets; they also constitute two minor dialogues/conversations displaying the anger of the persons involved until a confrontation is inevitable. Compare Longacre's "shift along the narrative-drama parameter" (3.4). However, dialogues occur at various times; they could be marking crucial points in general.[14] The markings of the triplets are similar in that, unit (26) starts out with a verse marked by *ina-spa-n-ña-taq-si* 'do.like.this-ADV-3P-NOW-EMPH-RPT' while unit (28) starts out with a verse marked by *tarde-ya-ru-pti-n-ña-taq-si* 'as it was getting late', but both links include the final suffixes *-ña-taq-si* 'NOW-EMPH-RPT'. In both triplets the following verses are marked by the

---

[13]Cerrón-Palomino (1987: 278–279) says that according to new data on various varieties *-pti* can in fact be used in cases of coreferentiality. He says that this does not seem to be "...an innovation, but constitutes an intrinsic property of the subordinator in question. One explanation in such a direction, as suggested by Hermon (1985), is that *-pti* assumes a *finite* character, as opposed to the *non-finite* nature of *-shpa/-r*, which supposes obligatory coreferentiality" (translation is mine). It has already been noted (footnote 4 of this chapter) that even in the case of *-spa* for Coracora there is not always strict coreferentiality.

[14]Weber (1989) says that stories (folktales) might consist of only dialogues throughout (see pp.21–22; he also provides an example on p. 22). In her study on Aguaruna discourse, Larson (1978:37) says that "In addition to true dialogue...there are many narrative discourses which have a great deal of dialogue in the surface structure and might at first give the impression of actually being dialogue discourse rather than narrative." However, she asserts, "the structure is truly narrative, but at various points in the narration there are speech exchanges in the deep structure event line. At these points, the surface structure realization consists in a dialogue sentence or a dialogue paragraph...The verbs of saying of such dialogues realize deep structure speech acts which are on the event line of the narrative" (p. 37) and for which she provides a textual example where the narrative mainly consists of "many distinct dialogues between different participants" (p. 38).

connective *ni-pti-n-si* 'say-ADVDS-3P-RPT' and the connective *ina-spa*. However, the lack of the reportative marker *-si* in the final verse of both units may indicate that these are lines within the previous verses, rather than verses on their own. If so, units (26) and (28) would be couplets. It could be that the whole climactic section (excluding the denouement, unit (30)) consists of four couplets, interspersed with the bridging sentence in unit (27). If we still consider (26) and (28) as triplets, these would be framed by two couplets, units (25) and (29), respectively, both considererd also to be of a bridging nature, but with the pattern reversed from what we have seen so far.

The culminating point and the denouement of the story is contained in units (29–30). Unit (30) is marked first of all through a five-times repeated aspect suffix *-rpari*, which indicates sudden actions and also seems to be forming an alliteration game. There are other surface features as well that are significant for the marking of this part, like the two independent verbs in sentence 86. Unit (29), although it is considered to be the culminating point of climax, also has a bridging function, both as a response to the previous event(s) as well as providing the setting for the actions in unit (30) which again picks up the triplet *ina-* pattern but with a significant change. From here on the verses in the triplets all begin with the *ina-spa-n-si* connective and the focus is on the same participant for a longer period of time.[15] What is also significant in the final section—the woods setting—is that the triplets do not show any clear movements between minor locational settings that is typical of the other episodic triplets; the actions can be characterized as aimless wanderings on the part of Osito. We have seen that *ina-spa-* units have served as introductions/conclusions to the *ina-pti-* triplets in the preclimactic episodes; it seems that they here have a function of marking the concluding part of the story as a whole, in the form of stanza triplets. There is a total reversal of the artistic pattern in this final part of the text. I will admit that what I have grouped together as one triplet in (33) might seem questionable; it is certainly very elaborate, particularly the second verse. The focus seems to change from one participant to another and at the same time involve both, clearly focusing on both in the end, marked through the use of the reciprocal

---

[15]Note that in several of these verses the third-person marker *-n* is left out. According to Cerrón-Palomino (1987:279) *-spa* in the Ayacucho dialect allows the third-person marker, which in other dialects is not allowed with the use of *-spa*. In this text the use of the third-person marker seems to be the norm while in these final triplets it is left out in the two final verses of both triplet (30) and (32), and in the second verse of triplet (33). I have no explanation for that at this point. According to David Weber (pers. comm.) the zero person marking always implies same subject, while the use of the third-person marker may imply different subject. I take this to mean different subject but main participant, as has been pointed to earlier. However, there seems to be no strict use of this rule in the text at hand.

5.3 The presentational form of the story

suffix *-naku*. However, the triplet corresponds to one little episode/scene. And, as can be remembered in regards to Chafe's "extended sentence," the length of this could vary a great deal. It could be that we are here dealing with a similar unit, although I am talking about it in different terms. The elaborating nature of triplet (33) may also be due to the triplet being the final and concluding triplet of the story.

It might be argued that units (29)–(30) mark the culminating point and denouement of the story. However, the complete change of surface pattern from the previous units set the latter apart from climax as belonging to or starting off a different rhetorical section of the story. The last section includes the *final suspense*, in Longacre's terminology as well as that of literary scholars. The units (29)–(30) mark a crucial event that makes "resolution possible." "Things begin to loosen up. We see a way out—even if not to a happy ending." The final suspense works out the details of the resolution, "Keeps untangling," which also is characteristic of the final part of the narrative. See further discussion in the following section dedicated to the event line of the text. As noted earlier, the fact that all the final triplets are marked by the same introductory *ina-spa-* connective may indicate that to the Quechua speaker these final triplets constitute one rhetorical unit, whether it be called denouement or final suspense or something else. However, there are other features, like the use of the suffix *-rpari* (discussed above), that may support a differentiation in terms of "denouement" and "final suspense" within this unit. But according to Longacre's findings in various languages, the final suspense is marked in the same way as the preclimactic episodes which is not the case in the text analyzed. This could suggest that the whole final section is the "denouement" of the story. But then, who can tell what is what in the Quechua speaker's mind.

I have analyzed and discussed climax and denouement from Longacre's perspective as far as these rhetorical parts are concerned. Longacre (1996) does not discuss poetry in particular, but talks about language use in general in narrative accounts. Leech, as noted, talks about deviations of language use in poetry. In section 5.3.1.3 "primary deviation" was discussed in relation to the constant repetition of *ina-*, a deviation serving to create a specific poetic pattern; "secondary deviation" would be a departure from a pattern considered an artistic or poetic canon, while "tertiary deviation" would be a deviation from the internal language use of a poem. In the case of the narrative at hand, it has been suggested that it is of a poetic nature, partly based on the repetitive usage of the *ina-* connectives and partly based on repetition within a frame. This constant repetition creates an expectancy on the part of the listener when the poem is recited but which is broken in the climax, denouement and final suspense. In the parts talked about in terms of denouement, and final suspense, it is the general pattern of the triplets that is reversed.

Leech says that deviations serve the purpose of foregrounding, "forming a meaningful pattern in themselves." The break of an internal expectancy chain marks a mounting tension in the poem. In this sense, Leech's tertiary deviation and Longacre's "change in language use" seem to fall together, that is, marking the climactic parts. However, Leech talks about tertiary deviation as a deviation from another deviation, the primary deviation, which is often what makes a poem a poem. Also, the poem need not be a narrative account.

The speaker-hearer relationship was mentioned when discussing Relevance Theory and also in relation to D. Payne with regards to choice of language use. On the one hand, there is the speaker's or author's choice of language use and on the other hand, the audience's or readers' response to the linguistic signals. The grammatical and syntactical parallelisms as perceived in the narrative at hand, through the use of the *ina-* connectives, are deliberate choices of the author (if they're not a poetic canon that must be obeyed). They form an expectancy chain. The change in the pattern is also deliberate, in order to create some mental halt on behalf of the reader or the audience. In Leech's words: "FOREGROUNDING is a term for an effect brought about in the reader by linguistic or other forms of deviation...the normal linguistic features of a poem become the background against which the deviant features are FOREGROUNDED. The degree of deviation varies, and so does the strength of foregrounding" (Leech 1985:47).

As noted earlier, some of the same ideas are inherent in Pilkington, who, from a relevance theoretical viewpoint, approaches the issue of poetry from the perspective of the reader/listener and his/her response. He says that, "verse features, exploited poetically, might be said to encourage the accessing of a wide range of assumptions in the same way as poetic metaphor" (Pilkington 2000:131). Unexpected changes in the pattern may cause a structure to be "thoroughly explored and assumptions within it made to be more highly salient" (p. 134). Pilkington talks about metrical variation, but other unexpected changes relating to grammatical parallelism, for example, would serve the same function. Now, one question here would of course be to what extent certain patterns are expected and as such are part of expected rhetorical patterns. I've earlier claimed that the use of *ina-spa*, for example, announces to the hearer that the principal character is about to leave one scene in order to enter a new one and that the use of *ina-spa* in the final triplets seems to indicate the end of the story.

5.3 The presentational form of the story

One of my claims in chapter 2, with reference to D. Payne, is that a speaker of a specific culture, when producing an oral monologic narrative text and the hearer processing it both have a certain "mental representation of a narrative as a coherent cognitive structure" (D. Payne 1992a:376) and that there will be certain expectations involved as to its structure.

An important point to stress here is that by analyzing grammatical categories in a poetic context, a wide range of new assumptions may be activated; or in terms of our previous perspective, new and extended functions may be discovered regarding the grammatical categories in question. This I have tried to demonstrate through some of my previous examples. Jakobson (1968) says that in studying the grammatical categories one will discover unexpected patterns of both symmetry and asymmetry, creating meaningful, balanced forms as well as contrasts and equivalent forms. He says that the reader/listener senses the poetic effect only unconsciously. I think it is worth stressing, that the grammatical parallelisms, or even the metric ones, are not just ordered adornments pleasing to the ear, but that their functions carry over into the semantics of the poetry, something I hope has been recognized through my discussion so far.

In concluding this section I would suggest that the main divisions of the text can be seen as operating on several interacting and partly overlapping "levels," that of the underlying notional or semantic structure, manifested in the surface structure in terms of stage, episodic development before climax, episodic development within climax, and episodic development after climax (which is also the concluding section). The semantic structure can also be divided in terms of three major locational settings, as well as in terms of the movements within these settings. In marking of the divisions, both tense and the different kinds of triplets play a major role.

The various aspects of the text discussed above are graphically shown in figure 1. It is important to note that the levels shown do not indicate any particular order, but rather the various strands of information that play a role in the structuring of this text. I do, however, recognize some underlying semantic structure, shown at the bottom of the figure, and it might be that the minor locations connected with the episodic units belong here.[16]

---

[16] Isbell (2004:250) says, "...for Andean people, the earth is a living being and localities...are animated."

	LOC I: cave-site	LOC II: village	LOC III: woods
Tense:	-------- -sqa ---------	---------------------- -n ----------------------------------	-sqa -------- -n ---------------------
	Triplets: -si---------	-----------Triplets: ina-pti-n-si -----------------------	(Stg)----Drama---------Triplets: ina-spa-n-si------
	Introduct/ Stage	--------------EPISODIC UNITS----------------------	(Stg)----EPISODIC UNITS---- (Peak)
	Exposition	----------------minor locations-- --------DEVELOPING CONFLICT----------------------	--wanderings-------------- (Ex)---Climax/Denouem./ Final suspense---------

Figure 1: The profile of the text

5.3.2.3 The salience scheme of the text

As stated in section 3.5, various linguists recognize a distinction between main event line information versus that of supportive information. This distinction is often highlighted through the use of different tense/aspect markers.

Payne (1992a:379)—as noted in 3.5.2—identifies "a clause as part of the 'semantic main event line (MEL)' if it has two properties: (a) It must report an event as actually occurring. The 'event' cannot be a hypothetical one that is presented as possibly occurring in the future or one that might have occurred in the past. States, which are nonevents by definition, are also excluded. (b) The actual reporting of the event must advance the action of the narrative along a chronological time line." Simultaneous and partly overlapping events, as well as repetition are also excluded, from what Payne considers to be the main event line.

Considering tense

Considering the Coracora text, there are two tense markers: -n 'present tense' and -sqa 'narrative past' (as defined by Soto Ruiz 1976). The 'narrative past' suffix -sqa can be excluded right away as a main event line

5.3 The presentational form of the story

marker because it typically occurs in material of introductory nature,[17] as already discussed above (see also sentence 33 where -*sqa* is used in reference to an earlier event—a flashback serving as a clarifying piece of background information).

The other tense marker to consider is -*n* 'present tense'. Weber (1989:99) says: "...in a narrative—after establishing the time as past, the text may continue in the 'historical' present." According to Hintz (1996) -*n* marks the main events in both Corongo Quechua (a Quechua B variety) and Lambayeque Quechua (a Quechua A variety from northern Peru). If one adopts Payne's definition of main event line, Hintz's claim does not seem to hold true for the Coracora text, where -*n* 'present tense' also seems to mark events excluded by the definition, such as simultaneous and partly overlapping events (e.g. sentences (21)–(23)) as well as some non-events (states, irrealis, and negations).[18]

I do realize that the utilization of the tense system is very simple for this text; it might be different in other texts. Also, I know that the tense systems for both of the "dialects" Hintz is referring to are much more complicated, and I am in no way suggesting that her analysis is incorrect.

Considering the ina- *connectives*

As stated earlier, *ina-* is a pro-verb referring back to the previous event. Considering the text at hand and the regular repetition of the *ina-* connectives with what (at least at first glance) seems to be the semantic main line events, *ina-* is a good candidate for being a main event line marker. But there is obviously some distinction between the *ina-pti-*

---

[17]Introductory material can also have an event line; the fact that the first part of the *Juan del Oso* story is considered a story on its own in some varieties of Quechua strongly supports this. However, in the present text I do not consider any event in this part as a main line event because the whole section is set apart from the rest through the consistent use of -*sqa* and obviously serves as a stage to the rest of the story. In any text I would consider the events referred to in the stage as events of background information and as such not main line events.

[18]According to Soto Ruiz (1976:156), -*spa* may indicate action simultaneous to that of the principal verb. This is contrary to Longacre's "naturalness assumption" (1983:198), referred to in Stirling (1993:44). According to the "naturalness assumption," "SS [same subject] marking tends to be taken to imply sequentiality of the eventualities described, which seemingly reflects an expectation that actions performed by the same person will normally be performed in succession. Conversely, DS [different subject] marking tends to be taken to imply simultaneity, which apparently reflects an assumption that actions which overlap are performed by different people." Stirling continues to say that the "naturalness assumption" is not "an absolute universal" as in many languages "both temporal orders are marked for each of SS and DS," though she says that she knows of no language" in which the opposite association is made, i.e. of simultaneity with SS and sequentiality with DS" (Stirling 1993:45). However, the latter seems to be true regarding the text at hand.

connectives and the *ina-spa-* connectives as to their function on text level apart from that of marking same or different subject for the independent clause.

The events of the main verbs (with some modifications) in the *ina-pti-* triplets seem to stand out in a way that the events connected with *ina-spa-* do not. Also, the use of *ina-pti-* constantly makes us alert to a change of referent. It appears that the events and the change of referent together play a role in the marking of the more important events. The events connected with *ina-spa-* and with focus on the same subject—or main participant of a section—have a more backgrounding function in some subtle way, in terms of Payne's definitions above (e.g. simultaneous and partially overlapping events) as well as in terms of their bridging and concluding functions. However, there are some problematic verses that obviously contain background information and for other reasons, according to Payne's definition, do not comply with the definitions made for a main event, but still are introduced by an *ina-pti-* connective (e.g. sentence 33, already mentioned above).

Looking at the patterns from a cognitive perspective and the concept of "centers of interest" in narrative production—as suggested by Chafe (1980b:40–41)—one could see an *ina-pti-* triplet stanza as a center of interest corresponding to a "single mental image." This center of interest, in turn, contains several "foci of interest"; e.g. each single *ina-pti-* event being "a focal component with high acuity." The interspersing bridges consisting of peripheral components "with lesser acuity" serve as "a context for the focus"—or "resting places," as suggested earlier, leading us from one "perch" to another "perch" in the narrative (in fact, from one location to another in case of this story). According to Chafe, the concept of a mental image also allows for some change or movement between information levels within an "imaginal unity." The triplets themselves can be perceived as macro-events which take us along in a chronological order in the narrative account. This could explain some irregularities as far as the order of events is concerned in some of the triplets in the text. Another explanation could be the overriding importance of keeping strictly to an artistic triplet pattern.

Considering what has been said so far in relation to the *ina-pti-* triplets, one could conclude that the *ina-spa-* units are not main line events to the Coracora Quechua speaker, but are establishing stage/circumstantial or concluding/elaborating relationships with respect to the triplet episodes.

On the other hand, it might be a bit difficult to defend this hypothesis in view of the *ina-spa-* triplets in the final part of the story. But, although the events/units seem to belong to the main event line, the actions are

5.3 The presentational form of the story

somehow in low relief, which can also be seen through the choice of verbs in the final triplets (e.g. *seek*, did not *find*, etc.). There is a marked slowing down of the speed of actions, and the focus is on just one participant for a longer period of time. Also, this final section as the denouement/final suspense is in a concluding relationship to the story as a whole. According to Longacre's salience scheme, the *ina-spa-* verses may mark a secondary storyline, that is, "happenings of lesser importance (often preparatory to or resultant from happenings reported on the primary storyline)...Clauses on the secondary storyline report happenings that, as it were, fill in the *chinks* between those which are reported on the primary storyline" (Longacre 1996:27).

Still, the suggested culmination and denouement, (units (29)–(30)), is a problem. Although the *ina-spa-* actions referred to in unit (30) are due to the same referent throughout, they cannot be said to be in low relief due to the significance they carry to Osito. It has also been stated above that this unit contains other markers that set it apart as crucial. However, unit (30) is an elaboration of what happens in unit (29), the "grabbing" of Osito, and could even be considered a concluding elaboration of three verses to a main unit (29), that has changed into a couplet—that is, the artistic pattern is reversed within the episodic unit, due to its climactic nature. Nevertheless, the final triplets cannot be said to be elaborating stanzas to some previous *ina-pti-* unit; rather they seem quite independent. It could be that from a cultural point of view, the "grabbing" of Osito by the little devil (29) also tells the listener what the final outcome is and as such the following triplets are all part of the unwinding of the story, even though unit (30) seems to stand out through the change of surface pattern.

Another problem is presented by the *ina-pti-n-si* verses in the final section, which I have claimed to have a bridging function in this section. Have they changed their nature from marking high acuity events? Unit (29) is not in low relief, while unit (31) seems to be. Although unit (31) does not contain action verbs, the verbs portray the deep despair of Osito and as such are very significant to the final development. It could be that units (29) and (31) should not be talked about in terms of bridges, in the sense previously used; they rather mark important points in the story. Their nature has not changed from what we have witnessed in the preclimactic episodes; they still mark high acuity events. They do, however, through the switch-reference markers and the use of *ni-/ina-*, have a bridging function that here serves to set apart a new triplet pattern. Could it be that units (29)–(30) serve a similar function toward the end of the text, like the inciting moment serves at the beginning of the text, namely as "bridging" episodes between the stage and the episodic development and between the episodic development and the final suspense/conclusion respectively? (See the final analysis of this text toward the end of chapter 6.)

Unit (29), introduced by *ni-pti-n-si*, shows another interesting change: it is marked by the different subject switch-reference marker rather than the expected same subject marker, but semantically there is no switch of subject. (We saw the same kind of anomaly in unit (25).) Is it due to the change of the final pattern of the story? Is the different subject marker *-pti* necessary in order to match the following verse creating a unit by setting the following *ina-spa* triplet apart? In other words, does the change serve an artistic function? Stirling (1993), who discusses switch-reference markers and their nature and various functions in some detail, suggests (based on the works of various linguists, e.g. Roberts, Payne, and Woodbury) that different subject switch-reference marking is sometimes used for marking a new rhetorical unit indicating a switch in the spatio-temporal setting, even though there is no switch of subject. Unit (29) cannot be said to indicate a switch in the spatio-temporal setting, but the use of the *ni-pti-n-si* does serve some specific foregrounding function, in terms of both Leech and Longacre. It could be marking a new rhetorical unit (the final one), or it could be marking the culminating point—or possibly both![19] The interplay between an artistic patterning and other rhetorical functions may be merged in this final part of the text. This could in fact also be the case with unit (25). This unit is certainly a bridging unit as it relates Osito's walking on to another scene. Osito as the main participant is still marked through the use of *ina-pti* when one would expect *ina-spa*. The use of the switch-reference marker here would comply with Stirling's suggestion above. However, the unit is also the introduction to the climactic section and a new turn in the development as far as Osito is concerned.[20]

---

[19]Stirling (1993:114) notes that Roberts (1988) "suggests that DS in Amele may also be used when there is 'a surprise change', some unexpected turn in the narrated events..." It is possible that this is in accord with what I talk about in terms of climactic events.

[20]Kindberg and Kindberg (1996) in a grammatical sketch (ms.) of the Caylloma variety of Quechua, also a southern Quechua A variety, note that in a rather lengthy text, *"Aras Bien y Aras Mal,"* there are three unexpected occurrences of the different subject switch-reference marker where one would expect same subject marking. They do not give any suggestion as to the reason for this. However, having studied the text myself, the use of the different subject switch-reference marker occurs at what seem to be very important points in the text, that is, when the king (at three different times) promises Aras Bien certain future blessings. These do not necessarily mark new rhetorical units in the text, but rather convey some important future changes in Aras Bien's circumstance of life. Having studied several texts from different varieties of Quechua, it looks as if the different subject switch-reference markers, in general, even when marking a switch of referent, often occur in subordinated clauses with climactic or other important events. Although there is switch of reference in other parts of the text this is not marked through the use of the switch-reference marker *-pti*. This could, however, also suggest that the anomalies referred to are due to the need to comply with an artistic pattern in this particular text.

As far as event line marking is concerned, according to Longacre and other scholars, one would expect changes in the parts referred to as climactic. Unit (29) has been analyzed as the culminating point, the event that leads up to a resolution and the final suspense of the story. The preceding climactic episodes, as discussed earlier, also have different patterns than seen in previous triplets, e.g. through other connectives than what previously has been the case. Longacre says that in the climactic sections the main event line may be "phased out," that is, it may show various changes, even contradictory to what has been noticed in the preclimactic episodic development. Therefore the changes seen in the patterns can best be explained in terms of deviations from the expected internal pattern of the poem or narrative, serving some foregrounding function, in terms of Leech, or marking the climax/denouement in the story in terms of Longacre. This also shows how the profile and the salience scheme of a text overlap in various ways.

According to Fabb, Stirling (1993) says that

> SS marking may sometimes characterize storyline ('foregrounded') clauses. This is partly because SS marking can function as a signal of narrative continuity, and also because there is a correlation between SS marking and temporal sequentiality between clauses (while DS marking correlates with simultaneity between clauses). Stirling also shows that DS morphology in particular is sometimes used in a language to mark the shifting between storyline and non-storyline material. (Fabb 1997:187–188)

Stirling's insights seem to correspond with Stewart's views. Stewart (1987:289) claims that for Conchucos Quechua "same-subject switch-reference in narrative is reserved for central participants," which the analysis of this text supports. Stewart does not explicitly assert, though, that this equals the marking of the main event/story line, although that might be implied, for she claims that different-subject switch-reference marking "is reserved for clauses which refer to discontinuous or not-yet-continuous participants and events...[that is] for less central adverbial kinds of reference ('background' in the sense of Hopper 1979)" (Stewart 1987:301–302). However, my analysis does not support these claims. On the one hand, the different-subject switch-reference marking in the text creates discontinuity through the constant change of participants and events, but on the other hand, I find that it is part of creating a pattern of unity which marks events of high acuity and not just some kind of background information. Although same-subject switch-reference marking is reserved for the central participants and most often signals continuity of referent, it is also part of a pattern that signals discontinuity, in terms of announcing to the hearer a change of an episodic unit (as earlier defined), as well as setting triplets apart; in this sense same-subject switch-reference serves more as a backgrounding function, although the final conclusion of the story as a whole could imply something else. As suggested above, SS marking may correspond to Longacre's secondary storyline. In my findings, the marking of SS is not likely to mark the main eventline, at least not in the case where there are other human or human-like participants involved; it is the interaction between participants that is of interest and creates tension in the development of the story.

5.3.2.4 Paragraphs, stanzas, and sentences

Related to the above, there are also a few other points to consider. As already discussed, within an artistic pattern one could treat stanzas as fitting some "grouping of imagery" or "logical division" in a poetic text. Seen from a traditional grammatical point of view that observes the clues for paragraph marking in the texts, one could indeed question some of the stanzas as legitimate episodes, as some of them may contain a so-called paragraph marker in the middle of the stanza and these may even suggest a lapse of time. This applies, for example to stanza (8), verse 20, which contains the temporal marker *ok vez* 'once', implying that some time had passed between the statement expressed in the previous verse and its subsequent action. Nevertheless, I do not think it can be denied that the verses in question can all be perceived as a "grouping of imagery," and as such constitute a poetic unit or unity. There need not be isomorphism between a poetic unit and what is traditionally perceived as a grammatical unit.[21] I believe the poetic concept of "grouping of imagery" (cf. Hamer 1966:6) in a poem complies well with Chafe's insights (section 3.5.5) and the concept of "centers of interest" corresponding to a "single mental image." Hymes, in a more recent article (2002), says that, "We have long recognized the need to be as accurate as possible in hearing and representing spoken words and sentences. We have taken for granted that the territory between the sentence and the whole consists of paragraphs....During the last 40 years or so, some of us have come to realize that paragraphs are about as natural a unit in telling stories as high heels

---

[21]Another example of poetic and grammatical units not being isomorphic is found in stanza (23), where the final verse contains *kaq* 'again', which according to many linguists would imply a paragraph break. However, the verse can best be analyzed as belonging to the stanza, in terms of creating a "mental image" or "grouping of imagery" (cf. Hamer referred to below; also referred to in section 5.3.1.5). According to Givón "the correlation between structure and function in language is not absolute, but rather an approximation" (1984:34). There need not be complete isomorphism between a code and a message. This applies to linguistic structures on lower levels as well.

are in swimming" (p. 23); and he goes on to say that texts are rather organized in terms of lines and verses according to an implicit cultural patterning; that is, in terms of smaller rhetorical and/or episodic units. It is not my intention to argue for the non-existence of paragraphs in ordinary discourse, and, as has been seen, there are markers in the text that indicate, for example, lapse of time through temporal markers, and as such indicate a grammatical paragraph break in the traditional sense. Even in a poetic narrative these play an important role in the development of the story. However, as discussed above, "the centers of interest" and/or the "groupings of imagery" may play just as important a role in the organization of a text, specifically, if the text is organized according to some implicit cultural pattern, such as in terms of specific poetic units.[22]

In the Quechua text at hand, the idea of the triplet stanza—the little episodic unit—as a "center of interest" or macro-event, that moves the story forwards makes sense in view of several linguists' claim (e.g. Stewart 1987) that the paragraph and not the sentence is a marked intonational unit, or as Burns and Alcócer Hinostrosa (1975:44) express it: "the paragraph is a legitimate element of the grammatical structure of Quechua" (translation mine). The question is whether such intonational paragraphs correspond to what I have termed stanzas in this text.[23] At any rate, the paragraphs—or stanzas—still have their own internal structures in forms of well-marked units (verses, in my analysis) within the stanzas, which the analysis of this text clearly demonstrates. These I have analyzed as "focal components of high acuity," in terms of Chafe, and they play a part in the moving forward of the story. I believe it would be a fatal mistake not to recognize these structural units due to the lack of some final pauses.

In the literature on European epics, several authors have mentioned the Serbian epic break which is subject to very strict rules in their metrics. According to Jakobson (1960:364–365), quoted in Hymes (1981:339),

> Any line of Serbian epics contains precisely ten syllables and is followed by a syntactic pause. There is furthermore a compulsory absence of word boundary before the fifth syllable and a compulsory absence of word boundary before the fourth and tenth syllable....

---

[22]Cf. Wendland's statement in section 2.6.2.

[23]Since I have not received the text orally delivered, I have to admit that intonational paragraphs might not exactly correspond to the triplet stanzas, although it seems likely, considering that the stanza corresponds to a little scene. However, it might be that some of the *ina-spa-* verses considered as conclusions of a scene would also be included in such an intonational paragraph. Still, considering what has just been discussed in the previous paragraph, the mentioned linguists may perceive "paragraphs" differently from the stanzas; that is, introduced through some of the more traditionally accepted paragraph markers.

This Serbian epic break, along with many similar examples presented by comparative metrics, is a persuasive warning against the erroneous identification of a break with a syntactic pause. The obligatory word boundary must not be combined with pause and is not even meant to be...perceptible by the ear. The analysis of Serbian epic songs phonographically recorded proves that there are no compulsory audible clues to the break, and yet any attempt to abolish the word boundary before the fifth syllable by a mere insignificant change in word order is immediately comdemned by the narrator. The grammatical fact that the fourth and fifth syllables pertain to two different word units is sufficient for the appraisal of the break.

What applies to the Serbian epics may apply in a similar way to Quechua, if not on the same syntactical level. The absence of a pause after the verse (sentence) might be compulsory and still the verse (sentence) is a very real structural unit within the stanza formation in the Quechua speaker's mind.

Some of the functions already discussed regarding the triplets are summarized below; a few other possible functions are also mentioned.

5.3.2.5 Other functions of the triplets in the text

First, each little episode is contained in the form of the triplet (with some modification because at times the "bridges" are included when occurring as a conclusion), which could be a center of interest (or mental image) to move the story forward. Each episode occurs in a slightly different location and transitioning the activity from location to location is an important part of the underlying structure of the story. This also gives a feeling of rapid pace to the underlying developing conflict. It is only in the final setting in the woods that the locations become very fuzzy; the movements between triplets here seem more to indicate aimless wanderings, possibly a symbolic expression of the hopelessness of Osito's situation (see below).

Second, the triplets in the second section all mark constant change of subject which also adds to the rapid pace of the developing conflict; there is only a pause of rest between each triplet when an *ina-spa-n-si* verse(s) is introduced. Looking at the *ina-pti-n-si* connective from a slightly different perspective than before, one can see it both as an anaphoric and a cataphoric expression; anaphoric in the sense of the pro-verb *ina-* (as well as *-pti*) referring back to the previous event, cataphoric in the sense of *-pti* signalling a change of subject to come, but which is not known to the hearer until he is informed in the following superordinate clause.[24] De Beaugrande and Dressler (1981:61) say, "The cataphora raises a momentory problem in the surface text and helps to propel the readers into the story." (For an oral performance this applies to the hearer.)

Third, the very final part of the story (the final suspense), is marked by triplets of *ina-spa-n-si* verses, which also underlines the slowing down of pace, both through events in low relief and also because the units refer to the actions of the same participant (with some modifications, according to previous discussions).

In relation to the above, I want to quote de Beaugrande and Dressler:

> In poetic texts, the surface organization of the text is often motivated by special correspondencies to the meaning and purpose of the whole communication....Frost (1969:224) closes a poem with the lines:
>
> [26] And miles to go before I sleep
>   And miles to go before I sleep.
>
> in order to evoke the even, continual motion of the speaker's journey in a sleigh through a snowy landscape at night. Uses like the above are instances of ICONICITY: an outward resemblance between surface expressions and their content. (1981:56)

Whether the features of the present text are conscious choices on the part of the author or conventional markers for the kind of functions the various parts in the text have on text level, is a question that cannot be answered on the basis of the study of this one text. The features typical of this text do, however, tell us something about the possible functions the various parts considered may have on text level, whether they be sentence-level grammatical features or features belonging to higher-level units, like the triplets. If these features are found in the texts yet to be analyzed they will be a substantial confirmation of my analysis so far and the idea of conventional Quechua rhetorical patterns of poetic nature.

5.3.2.6 Cultural patterns in the text

As has been seen in the discussion above, the pattern number three is very salient. This was one of the pattern numbers mentioned in chapter 4 as one of several pattern numbers in the Quechua culture. However, three seems to be a universal pattern number in folklore and, at this point, I could not relate it to anything peculiar to Quechua.

---

[24]Cf. the discussion of Weber (1989) and the relationship between switch-reference clauses in section 4.1.2.2.

Other pattern numbers—or other cultural organizational patterns—will be discussed after the analyses of the other Coracora texts, because I was not able to discover these until after the analysis of these texts had been done. (In the present text I noticed, for example, the two triplets forming one big chunk of six lines—this occurs twice; it seemed to have some significance which I was not able to perceive at the time.)

It is conceivable that transitioning from location to location is a metaphorical expression for some underlying cultural pattern. To get from one location to the next was an important task for the *chasquis*, the messengers of the old Inca empire. The internal rapid pace of the *ina-pti-* triplets might also be significant in this respect. Weber (1989:314) says that "Quechua seems to have an intense preoccupation with getting people to where they are going." (He says this in reference to grammatical patterns.)[25] This might also be of significance to the way the Coracora story ends: "In this place the bear dies from hunger. *And he is not able to return home.*"

The aspect of moving or walking is in general a very important feature of Quechua culture, something which has been stressed by, for example, Schechter (1987) in his article "Harp Music as Structural Metaphor on Purina" (*purina* 'walking') for Ecuadorian Quechua. (See chapter 8 for a more complete discussion of cultural patterns.)

5.3.3 In conclusion

The study of the Coracora text shows that the text is highly structured according to certain principles of organization. This is seen in regards to several aspects of information.

It has been of particular interest to discover the functions that patterns, such as the different kinds of triplets, have in the formation of the text as a whole. They mark the rhetorical cohesion of the different parts of the story.

Another very interesting discovery has been the important role that the switch-reference markers *-pti* and *-spa* play in the pattern formations, as well as in the marking of events as to their acuity (or as being, or not being, on the main event line) (See chapter 8 for a further discussion on this).

What the analysis of this text has not been able to give an answer to yet is "how the text can be divided into bigger parts based on unity of triplets forming some specific pattern, such as a specific number of scenes to an act." So far it has been difficult to see any clear pattern in this respect. The texts that I am now going to turn to will hopefully give some further insights.

---

[25]For example, Weber says that a Quechua speaker normally would say something like: ...he went to Pillku. Upon *arriving* he did such and such a thing...; 'John went to the store and bought a shirt' is strange to a Quechua; rather: 'Having gone to the store, John bought a shirt' or 'John went to the store. Having arrived, he bought a shirt'.

6

Textual Patterns (II)—Ayacucho Coracora Quechua

6.1 Preliminaries

My next challenge is to compare the analysis just presented with the analysis of a few other texts from the same variety of Quechua—Ayacucho Coracora Quechua. The texts were all collected by Lauriault and published in 1957 and 1958.

I will present the analysis of four texts, three of which are typical of the genre "folktales," involving animals where the fox plays a major role. As will be seen, the patterns of these texts are somewhat different but at the same time will confirm my analysis above, as well as provide some additional insights. The texts are not analyzed morpheme-by-morpheme but have a semiliteral translation given by the Quechua-speaking authors, and they are not always in good Spanish. In a few places I have made some changes in the translation to harmonize it with my present interpretation. In the appendices to this book all of the texts except the first one appear in their complete form with a Spanish translation. An English translation is given for any examples given here.

6.2 Analysis of smaller texts

6.2.1 The presentational forms of *Ampatopa Cuenton*

The short text *Ampatopa Cuenton* is considered first. This complete text is provided below so as to reveal the patterning as it is perceived by me. The original published version does not show any patternings. Each verse is numbered and each stanza (couplet) is marked.

6.2.1.1 Artistic patterns

On the whole, the text of *Ampatopa Cuenton* shows verses introduced by *ina-pti-n-si* throughout the episodic development; verses 4 and 7 are exceptions. Verse 4 does, however, comply with the semantic pattern of switch of referent and, in addition, the introductory word is marked by the reportative *-si,* while 7 as a "bridge" complies with the pattern of no switch of referent. One might argue that verse 4 contains two sentences/verses rather than one, since the second clause begins with *chay-pi* and also contains the evidential *-si*. However, I believe that the *chay-pi* clause is an embedded clause.[1] The stanzas in this text consist of two rather than three verses, and there are two stanzas to each episodic scene. Why do I not rather consider the scene to consist of one stanza of four verses, corresponding to one "center of interest" or a "grouping of imagery"? The answer is that the somewhat different introductory constructions in verses 3 and 4, both with the final parallel construction *ña-taq-si,* set them apart as a stanza different from the next. Considering verses 8 and 9 and verses 10 and 11, they constitute two different units, based on the concluding statement in 9, which also foreshadows what happens in verse 11; also, verse 10 starts out focusing on the fox as opposed to the frog(s) in verses 8 and 9. Artistically I believe we have here stanzas of two verses, and maybe smaller groupings of imagery within a bigger one.

Moreover, there are only two episodic scenes to the whole text. This suggests an interesting parallel pattern of two to a part, that is, two verses to a stanza, two stanzas to a scene, and two scenes to the whole text. The pattern divides the text into two more or less equal parts.

---

[1] Compare verse 31 in the *Watuchi II* text (section 6.2.4) and see the analysis of the rhetorical structure for more details on this.

Ampatopa Cuenton[2]
(Story about the Frog)

Stage
Stanza I
		SS/DS	ASP	TNS
1	Ok punchawkunas ok atoq purikusqa orgon orgon			-sqa
2	Sikia pataman chayaruspanñataqsi chaypi purikuchkasqa	SS	-chka	-sqa

1 Some day(s) a fox was walking from hill to hill
2 When he arrived at the border/limits of the irrigation channel he was walking along (there)

Scene I
Stanza II

3	Inaptinñataqsi ok sapo latako sotiyoq puñokuchkasqa	DS	-chka	-sqa
4	Atoqñataqsi sutin kasqa akako, chaypi puñokuchkaptinsi latakutaqa sarurparin	DS	-rpari	-n

3 Now a frog called latako was sleeping there
4 The fox called akako, while he (the frog) was sleeping, stepped on the latako

Stanza III

5	Inaptinsi latakuqa nin: "ama chaynakuchawaycho alli maqta punicho kanki ako apuestachkason pim ganaqmi alli maqta kanqa" nispansi nin	DS		-n
6	Inaptinsi nin akakoqa: "munaptillaykiqa ganaruspaymi mikurusqayki" nispas ninakun	DS		-n

5 Then the latako said: "Don't do like that to me. Are you a good guy, akako? Let us make a bet; the one who wins, he will be the good guy"
6 Then the akako said: "And if you like, if I win, I'm going to eat you" (saying) they said (they agreed on this)

---
[2]Lauriault (1958:55)

Bridge

    7 Chaynas apuestanku   SS   -n
      ok orqo wichay correchina
      kunankupaq

7 Like this they made the bet, in order to run down to the foot of the hill (to see who would arrive first)

Scene II
Stanza IV

    8 Inaptinñataqsi llapa latakukuna oñonarukuspa
      seqeslla churachinarukuspa
        correnku   DS   -n

    9 Inaptinsi latakuqa ganan chayna   DS   -n

8 Then all the frogs got together and they made a line and began to run
9 Then like this the frog won

Stanza V

    10 Inaptinsi akakullaqa
      chawpi qatallapi quedarparin,   DS   -rpari   -n
      akakos "lataku" nispa,
      qayaptinsi latakuqa
      "akaku akaku" nispa
      nimun orqopatamantaña

    11 Inaptinsi, chaypi ganan akakutaqa   DS   -n
      latakuqa

10 Then the fox was left in the middle of the slope of the hill, the fox calling "lataku," and the frog calling "akaku, akaku," from the foot of the hill already
11 Then like this the frog beat the fox

Conclusion

    12 Inaspansi piñasqa pasakun   SS   -n
      "yanqam imanarowanmampas"
      nispa

12 Then he (the frog) left annoyed: "Something might happen to me here" (saying)

The discovery of the pattern as laid out in the presentation of the text intrigued me, especially since I found similar patterns in the other texts which will be discussed below. The patterns show how rigidly the texts are put together according to some principle of organization. The text *Ampatopa Cuenton* can be graphically displayed as follows:

6.2 Analysis of smaller texts

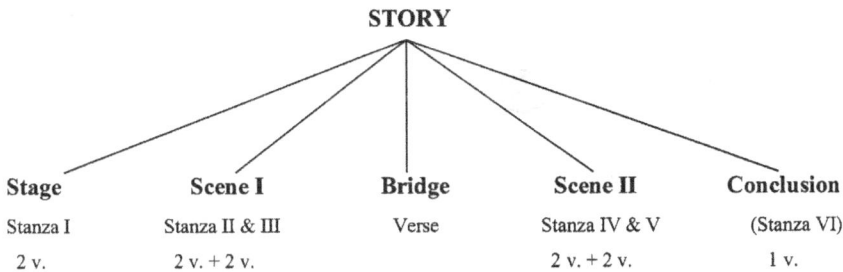

Figure 2: Structure of *Ampatopa Cuenton*

The main body of the text shows a pattern of four stanzas to the episodic scenes, plus an introductory (stage). The conclusion is not a complete stanza as it contains only one verse. If one looks at the level above the stanza listings, there are five parts to the whole story containing stage, scene I, bridge, scene II, and conclusion. The bridge divides the story into two more or less equal parts (or halves) in almost a mirror image where the conclusion differs from the introduction by having only one verse instead of a couplet.

In section 4.3, it was noted that both López-Baralt and Rostworowski think duality is a basic pattern underlying the Andean social, ritual, and spatial organization. Moreover, Rostworowski suggested that all cultural numbers represent "multiples of the dual and quadripartite divisions." According to her, the number eight is also of "great significance in the Inka social structure" and the duality is seen in both opposition and complementary halves, e.g. in the sense of upper and lower, left and right.

The two episodic scenes can be perceived as forming two complementary halves, each one representing multiples of dual divisions and the two scenes together consisting of as many as eight verses, divided by the bridging verse. Whether the complementary parts are perceived in the sense of left and right as in the graphic example or in the sense of upper and lower as shown in the presentation of the whole text in its printed form, I am not able to answer at this point as I do not have any idea about how the oral Quechua-speaking mind organizes a text.

López-Baralt also suggests that the cosmic pattern consists of a total of $4+1=5$, which is a pattern also seen in the text—as the graphic presentation in figure 2 suggests—where the pattern number 5 appears in the upper level division of the text. Although the observed number of parts might just be a coincidence and have nothing to do with any specific cultural pattern number, one can indeed truly talk about a dual patterning of this text, as well as hierarchical levels of the story containing two episodic scenes, the scenes containing two stanzas, and the stanzas containing two verses. But if one were to consider the conclusion to equal a stanza, then we have a pattern of three stanzas to each complementary half, the first being the introduction and the last being the conclusion.

6.2.1.2 Rhetorical patterns: The profile of the text

The upper level in the graphic presentation in figure 2 gives only a hint of the rhetorical pattern of the text. The presentation is an artistic division in terms of scenes and stanzas. The first stanza has been analyzed as stage and introduces one of the main participants, the fox, walking along in the hills and introduces the location for the future events to happen. The fox receives the major attention in the first part of the story, whereas there is a switch of vantage point in the latter part to the frog. However, the frog is already introduced in the second stanza as the other main participant important to the story. The first stanza also provides some background information which helps set the stage for the story as a whole.

The use of tense markers is the same as in *Juan del Oso*; *-sqa* 'narrative past' marks the stage, then in the rest of the story *-n* 'present tense' is used. Stanza II displays the use of both tense markers. Longacre (1983:31) says that the stage "may run into Inciting Moment in a very brief narrative. Inciting moment is, however, set off from stage by virtue of the onset of the event line with its characteristic tense." However, the two Quechua texts thus far analyzed both show a mix of the two tense markers in question; in the latter text the first verse of the stanza is marked as stage, and the second is marked as part of the episodic development. This fact underlines the bridging function of this unit.[3] A similar pattern will also be perceived in the other stories.

It is difficult to discover any clearly marked climax; this is probably due to the shortness of the story. I analyze stanza V to be the climax (including the culminating point) of the story, containing a very irregular verse (verse 10) with a switch of participants marked through the use of *-pti* within the verse and a miniature dialogue where the two participants are calling to each other. The switch of participants marked through the use of *-pti* is also observed within verse 4 (due to the embedded clause) and could be a feature belonging to both climax and the inciting moment. As noted earlier, Longacre (1983) reports that in other languages features of climax have been observed also in the inciting moment (cf. the analysis of *Juan del Oso*). Verse 11 concludes with who won the bet; however, this is

---

[3]As can be remembered from *Juan del Oso*, there was a "bridging" stanza there that seemed to be part of the stage and at the same time started off the episodic development—the "Inciting Moment," according to Longacre (see section 5.3.2.2).

6.2 Analysis of smaller texts 131

already announced in verse 9 of the previous stanza. An outstanding feature of stanza V is the use of *-rpari* 'sudden action' which I view to be an attention-drawing device, like we have seen in *Juan del Oso*; it also occurs at the end of the first stanza of scene I, namely verse 4, and could be marking the very event within "Inciting Moment" which triggers the subsequent events of the story, similar to the *Juan del Oso* text. This means another climactic feature observed in the inciting moment.

The final verse brings the story to conclusion. The focus is on the previous referent, the frog, who has taken the lead in this latter part of the story.

From this rhetorical *profile* analysis one can see features similar to those of the *Juan del Oso* text. The big difference is of course the length of the latter which also provides for a well-marked climax, a denouement/final suspense.

6.2.1.3 Rhetorical patterns: The salience scheme of the text

This text shows a main event line pattern similar to that of *Juan del Oso* in that the *ina-pti-* stanzas with the constant change of participant is marking the main event line—in Chafe's terms, the events of higher acuity. Or, as already discussed in relation to *Juan del Oso*, the whole episode/scene might in itself be a big macro-event (center of interest in terms of Chafe), moving the narrative forward in a chronological order. Such an explanation, however, seems strange when applied to this short text; a more likely interpretation would be to consider each stanza as a minor macro-event or "grouping of imagery," moving the story forward.

There is only one *ina-spa-* verse, which occurs in the conclusion of the story. Its focus is on the previous referent, the frog. (As noted, in the last scene of the story the major focus has switched from the fox to the frog.) The only bridging verse refers to the previous participant, which in this case means both participants. The first part of the verse serves as the bridge through the use of *chayna* 'like this' in the clause "like this they made the bet" which concludes the preceding scene; at the same time, through its purpose clause in the latter part of the verse, it announces the events to come in the following scene. The bridge marks a change of vantage point because in the latter part of the story the frog is in focus. The following events, which propel the audience forward through the constant switch of referent, also include the most pivotal events of the story, the climax, as already discussed above. I will return to this issue later, after the analysis of other texts.

The suffix-construction *-ña-taq* 'NOW-EMPH' occurs with the introductory words in the bridging introductory stanza—stanza II—of scene I (the inciting moment)[4] as well as at the very beginning of scene II. It could be treated as an attention drawing device, maybe even marking the introduction of the scenes in this text. I did not focus on this structure in *Juan del Oso* because it normally occurred with the *ina-* connectives. However, in *Juan del Oso* as well as in other texts analyzed, it is difficult to regard the marking of new scenes as the only function of *-ña-taq*, although the suffixes often but not consistently occur in such parts of the text.

6.2.1.4 Final remarks

It can be concluded that although this text shows the use of couplets rather than triplets and is also much shorter than *Juan del Oso*, one sees that the same features have the same kind of functions in both. Moreover, this text also shows some artistic patterns on higher levels in the grouping of two more or less complementary halves in some kind of mirror image.

6.2.2 The presentational forms of the *Mankapa Cuenton*

Mankapa Cuenton (found in appendix 3) is also short. It relates the story of a travelling salesman and his speaking kettle. On one of his journeys the kettle advises its owner that something is amiss at home. The man returns home and finds his wife with another man. A conflict arises from this, and a final resolution is achieved by his killing the intruder.

6.2.2.1 Artistic patterns

One can detect five main divisions of the story: stage, three episodic scenes, and conclusion. It could be that both the stage and the conclusion should be considered scenes in which case the story consists of five scenes. However, both the stage and the conclusion are different in their use of verse markers.

We have seen in the presentation of *Ampatopa Cuenton* that there are two stanza couplets to each scene and there are two verses to each stanza; this applies to *Mankapa Cuenton* (Story about the Kettle) as well. The stanzas are based on smaller groupings of imagery, as well as on parallel surface structures, mainly seen in the introductory connectives. The latter is not so obvious in the middle scene. In scene I, in the first stanza, the verses are introduced by *ina-pti-* 'do.like.this-ADVDS' connectives; the second stanza

---

[4]It should be remembered that Longacre refers to the inciting moment as the *episode* that starts off the episodic development.

6.2 Analysis of smaller texts

contains a dialogue with the verses introduced by *ni-pti-* 'say-ADVDS'. The middle scene, scene II, shows a mixed use of the *ina-* connectives and as such is irregular. The scene that follows, scene III, has a very regular patterning with the use of *ina-pti-* in all verses in the two stanzas. The story can be graphically shown as in figure 3:

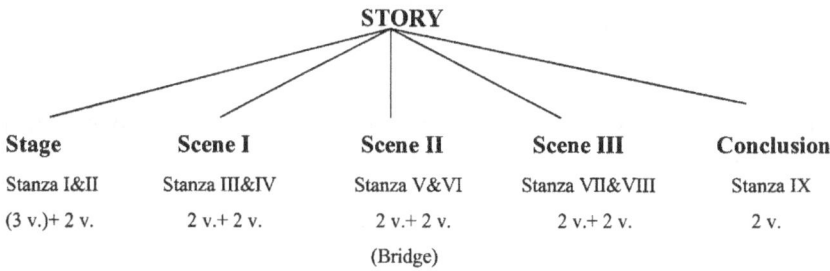

Stage	Scene I	Scene II	Scene III	Conclusion
Stanza I&II	Stanza III&IV	Stanza V&VI	Stanza VII&VIII	Stanza IX
(3 v.)+ 2 v.	2 v.+ 2 v.	2 v.+ 2 v.	2 v.+ 2 v.	2 v.
		(Bridge)		

Figure 3: Structure of *Mankapa Cuenton*

The introductory part is a bit tricky. It can be seen as consisting of two parts, where the first one consists of three very short verses describing the main participant. Maybe the first part is of a more general nature in the sense of being some kind of formal opening and as such not really part of the story, although each sentence is marked by the reportative *si-* (tentatively defined as a formal verse marker). The other text (*Amatopa Cuenton*) has no description of the main participant except for indicating his location; in some sense it shows an almost "jumping directly" into the action of the story.

The way *Mankapa Cuenton* is displayed in the graph, it creates an even pattern, both as far as verses and stanzas are concerned, if the first three verses are considered as being outside the story itself. One obtains a neat pattern of multiples of two with the highest number being sixteen (a number that is also mentioned by Rostworowski). However, this might be stretching the analysis to fit it into a pattern that is not warranted from the point of view of the author. It is not likely that a person telling a story would be able to keep track of numbers of verses. But certainly, keeping track of numbers on the upper levels would automatically multiply the lower levels in the way we have seen the patterning so far, in this text up to sixteen. And, as Weber suggests (pers. comm.), the story as oral literature may reflect some conscious design that is now fixed. The narrators would not have to remember any number, just be faithful to a tradition that was handed on to them and to which they might want to add a bit to, like the descriptive introduction. The graph also shows that the story can be perceived as consisting of two complementary halves in a mirror image

—maybe two different acts. As noted, the introduction is longer than the conclusion.

6.2.2.2 Rhetorical patterns: The profile of the text

The *profile* pattern is very similar to what we have witnessed in the *Amatopa Cuenton* text, but a few characteristics specific to this text will be discussed in the following.

The stage has been analyzed as having two introductory stanzas. The first has three verses and is a description of the man. The second stanza has a bridging function between the introduction of the man and the beginning episodic development in the first scene which follows, as we have seen in an analogous way in the other texts. The use of tense markers supports this, and we can conclude that this stanza is encoding the "Inciting Moment," although it is not marked by *-rpari*—the attention drawing device—as is the case in the texts analyzed above. However, it is only here that two other aspectual markers occur. The first one only indicates the duration of the event; the second one may have some specific significance by helping mark the stanza as being the "Inciting Moment." According to Soto Ruiz (1976a:106), *-yku* "indicates an action performed in a manner different from what is normal" (translation mine). The meaning depends on context: surprise, fright, severity, cordiality.

The bridge is a scene—scene II—consisting of two stanzas instead of a single verse, which is different from the *Amatopa Cuenton* text. This middle scene, I consider to entail many different functions at the same time, accounting for the irregularity of the pattern. The scene can be perceived as a first climax, or the beginning of the climactic part, as it relates the man's return home and the situation that he is faced with. The use of the attention drawing device, *-rpari*, occurs no less than three times. On the one hand, the pattern underlines the cohesive, bridging nature of the scene; every event or event cluster ties into a previous or a following event, being the circumstance or setting to one and a conclusion to another. Yet the bridging scene can also easily be perceived as two halves, where the first stanza forms a conclusion to the first part of the story (maybe of a first act) and the second stanza functions as a setting to the last part of the story (maybe to a second act), but at the same time forming a unit (scene).

Verse 10 (Scene II, Stanza V) 'and he entered his house', creates a problem because the evidential *-si* as a formal marker of verse is missing, although the verse is introduced by *ina-spa*. The marker could be missing by accident, or its absence could suggest a close tie to the previous *kutin* 'he returned' in verse 9. However, the translation of verse 11 suggests that the author[5] considers verses 10 and 11 to belong together. But why does verse 11 use *ina-pti-* when there is seemingly no change of subject? As suggested above, the whole scene may serve as a first climax to the story. Verse 11 tells that the man encounters a very delicate situation, his wife sleeping with another man. According to Leech, a break in the internal expectancy pattern of a poem serves a foregrounding function. And according to Longacre, the climactic section of a narrative is marked in specific, often unexpected ways. This unexpected change in the switch-reference pattern was also noted in the culminating part of *Juan del Oso*, in unit (29). As also noted earlier, Stirling (1993) suggests that in narratives, the unexpected use of the different subject switch-reference marker suggests a new rhetorical unit indicating a switch in the spatio-temporal setting. According to my analysis of other Quechua texts, it does not necessarily indicate a new rhetorical unit but signals crucial points in a story. In this text also the unexpected use of the switch-reference marker indicates a crucial event and moreover happens in what I perceive to be the second verse in the stanza, based on the grounds discussed above, as well as on the fact that it is the previous verse that indicates a change of location. This part of the story is irregular, as suggested by the unusual combination of suffixes in the *ina*-connective in verse 13. Although this scene has a bridging function, it may be better to talk about it in terms of being a "turning point" (different from the "bridge" in the previous text analyzed, where the bridge marks a change of vantage point).

Though the story is short, it includes several tense climactic points. The third scene shows a mounting tension through the angry interaction between man and woman, which results in the killing of the intruder, and the culminating point of the story marked in the surface structure by the use of *-rpari* in the second stanza. Yet, the verses in this scene are all marked by the *ina-pti-* connective, normal for the episodic development of *Juan del Oso*, but similar to the pattern seen in the previous short text.

After the third scene there is a concluding stanza which can be perceived as a short final suspense of the story. However, the stanza shows several switches of reference and even a new participant occurring (possibly the people of the town or the town authorities) in the final verse. This is a departure from what has been noticed in the other texts. The final verse includes a new switch of referent and the focus back to the main participant who concludes the story through a minor monologue, blaming his speaking kettle for the killing of his rival. The switch does not make use of *ina-spa*, but the way the story ends, one is left with a feeling of something missing, e.g. what is the reaction of the people to the man's

---
[5]The author has also translated the text into Spanish.

response. In some way the story is not quite finished, but that may be my perception, based on my own cultural experiences of how a story ought to end.

6.2.2.3 Rhetorical patterns: The salience scheme of the text

As stated in the section on artistic patternings, the stanzas are based on the notion of "groupings of imagery," as well as on surface structure patterns. Like in the previous text analyzed, the stanzas do not correspond to a little scene, and it was suggested that a possible interpretation would be to consider each stanza as a minor macro-event or "grouping of imagery" moving the story forward. A question is, do these stanzas correspond to a "center of interest," in terms of Chafe, or are they artistic groupings within a "center of interest," corresponding to a little scene? The "resting places" in terms of the kind of "bridges" we have perceived in *Juan del Oso*, are also missing. The bridging unit, as suggested above, rather creates some climax (or turning point) and also involves more than one person.

6.2.2.4 Final remarks

Although the discussion above has pointed out various problems and difficulties in the structuring of the text, both in regards to the artistic patterning as well as the rhetorical structuring, one can also conclude that there is an obvious regularity in the verse and stanza formations. Although the patterns in the texts analyzed so far suggest a poetic canon of some sort where the switch-reference markers play an important role, there would always be room for personal creativity by each storyteller. And there is also the possibility of a storyteller not being able to handle both rhetorical stylistic features and artistic patterns at the same time. However, the irregularities may also be conscious choices from the storyteller's side, deviations from the internal expectancy chain of artistic patterning, as well as a poetic canon, in order "to encourage the accessing of a wide range of assumptions in the same way as poetic metaphor" (Pilkington 2000:131). The unexpected use of the different subject switch-reference marker where one would expect same subject switch-reference marker has been observed in two texts. In both instances, although they may be marking new rhetorical sections, those sections are also of a crucial nature to the further development of the story, because they are climactic.

6.2.3 The presentational forms of *Watuchi I*

Watuchi I[6] is longer than the last texts analyzed, though not as long as *Juan del Oso*. In addition to dividing the text into stanzas and scenes, I have also divided it into ACTS. In doing so, certain patterns emerged. It has to be admitted though, that there are several problems with the divisions in this text, some of which will be discussed below. Although I have tried to keep the discussion of the various presentational forms apart, it has been necessary at times to discuss certain features at once in order to show the possible major divisions of the text.

6.2.3.1 Major divisions of the text

I have divided the text into three different ACTS, where act I is the stage for the whole story and relates how the fox and the condor go to celebrate a mass; the condor disappears and the fox is looking for him without result.

Act II contains the crucial episodic development with climax. It relates the fox's actions as he approaches God himself but fails to enter heaven by the means of a rope God has told him to make; the cause for this is a bird (a kind of parrot) which chews on the cord and causes the fox to fall down and be fatally injured. It is interesting to see that this act has been included as the major episodic part of this text because it really belongs to another famous tale (myth) from the Andes (the *Achkay* story—see Weber and Meier 2008), although not with the fox as the main character. This shows how storytellers may make use of different modules in composing their texts, not only modules pertaining to one and the same story, but even modules pertaining to other stories; we see that such intertextuality is a feature not only characteristic of literate societies but also of oral societies.

Act III contains the episodic development referred to as the denouement and/or final suspense. It puts focus on the misery of the fox and on the other participants involved; first the condor (his *compadre* 'godfather')

---

[6]According to Gnerre (2004:372) *watuchi* is "the most common name used to refer to "riddles" in southern Peruvian Quechua—to which also Ayacucho Quechua belongs. "Riddle" is also the translation given for *watuchi* by Soto Ruiz in his *Diccionario Quechua: Ayacucho-Chanca* (1976b). However, for the published texts concerned, *Watuchi I* and *II* from the Coracora area, the translation given for both is "cuento". Although the texts could be riddles of some kind from a Quechua point of view, this does not seem likely. Gnerre (2004:371) says that "Riddling, as a dialogical enterprise, relies on both speaker and hearer's abilities, as well as on the audience's supportive participation. Riddles are positioned half-way between extremely short narratives, with some internal rhetorical structuring, and question games triggering an abductive effort by the hearer(s)- participant(s)."

who fails to help him; then a relative who has mercy on him and takes him to a relative's home (the very final part of the final stanza). Significant to this section is that the scenes all contain long monologues related to the fox's misery.

The complete text is in appendix 4. The transition between act I and act II has a problem. The final *manaña tarisqachu* 'he didn't find him' in stanza/scene III could conclude act I. A final *mana* 'negation' line often appears to mark a conclusion. However, this final line carries the tense marker *-sqa* 'narrative past', as also does the next stanza, which has been analyzed as typical of the stage as seen in the other stories. The content of stanza IV suggests that it has a bridging function between the first two acts, because it refers back to what has happened previously and at the same time sets the stage for the episodic development of act II, introducing a new participant, *Dios* 'God'. This double function has been noted in the analysis of the previous texts as well. (Compare this with what has been said above in regards to the "Inciting Moment.") The use of two different tense markers has been a characteristic of this stanza in the other texts so far analyzed, and I have pointed to the ambiguity of this scene. In this particular text, however, there is no switch of tense within the stanza.

The facts considered above suggest that there are two different levels of the text, the artistic grouping and the plot/profile structure, that may need to be kept apart even if they normally overlap. For the text at hand there are two possible analyses of its artistic structuring which will be discussed below.

First, if I decide to consider stanza IV as part of the introductory stage—that is, act I—based on the use of *-sqa*, it makes for a very consistent pattern as seen in the graphic presentation in figure 4.

In the graphs all the stanzas (St) correspond to a little scene (Sc). As can be seen there is a 1:1 correlation between Sc and St; one seems to be a redundant layer of the other but by displaying both, the figures show how closely the stanzas and scenes correlate. Also, it compares with *Juan del Oso* in the way each stanza corresponds to both a little scene and/or episode, as well as some location in a more subtle way for acts I and II. (Figures 4 and 5 do not show that each stanza contains two verses, unlike the other graphs.)

Act I is also followed by a single verse (verse 11) which could imply a "bridge" between act I and act II, providing the setting for the latter. This would match earlier analyses where "bridges" occur between specific units. Bridging verses, however, do not create any consistent pattern in this text; there are only two of them.

6.2 Analysis of smaller texts

Second, there is an element in act II, viz. *chaymanta kaq* 'afterwards again', which I could analyze as dividing act II into two different complementary halves by choosing to analyze stanza IV as part of act II. Analyzing stanza IV as the stage of act II seems reasonable because it introduces a new participant. (Verse 11 could also be a "bridge" between the stage and the rest of act II.) This analysis does not create a parallel pattern for the three acts as seen in figure 4 but it will show a nice pattern for act II, similar to the patterns presented in the graphs for the previous texts. The preferred analysis is presented in graphic form in figure 5.

6.2.3.2 Artistic patterning

Watuchi I does not show as consistent a surface pattern as what we have witnessed in the other texts, although the underlying semantic pattern based on switch of referent is the same. However, both connectives as well as the evidential *-si* have played a major role in identifying the verses and the grouping of stanzas (see appendix 4). The differences in the surface pattern are particularly noticeable because of the use of the suffix construction *-ña-taq* 'NOW-EMPH'. In the previous texts analyzed it normally occurs with the *ina-* connectives. In this text and also in the following text, however, *-ña-taq* occurs with other elements, often with the expressed subject occurring at the beginning of the sentence, thereby putting focus on the subject.

The acts contain stanzas, each stanza corresponding to a small scene in a slightly different location and/or the introduction of some new participant, much as seen in *Juan del Oso*, for the major episodic development. Then the final act, a denouement and final suspense, has the focus on the fox in one location until he is taken off the scene in the final stanza. Temporal lapses also play a role in the formation of scenes. The scenes differ, however, in the number of verses to the scenes, for in this text there are only two to a scene while in *Juan del Oso* there are three to a scene. Two verses to a stanza correspond well with the stanzas in the texts analyzed previously. However, I have analyzed this text as having only one stanza to a scene in contradistinction to the patterning of those texts, which have been analyzed as having two stanzas to the scene. The grouping of two stanzas to some kind of a scene would be quite possible, if not corresponding to a locational scene for the first two acts; in fact, the grouping of two stanzas to a scene might be better for act III. Nevertheless, I have followed the general pattern and feel most comfortable with the analysis as shown in figure 5. According to Hymes, when there are pairs of verses to a scene, the first can be "complication," the second "resolution." I'm not sure though that this is how the scenes in this text can be perceived. Nevertheless, I think they can be perceived as "groupings of imagery" or possibly "centers of interest" moving the story forward.

In one stanza (stanza VII) *ina-spa* sentences have been interpreted as sub-lines of the verse (verse 17) because they are not marked by a following evidential which so far has been considered the norm for the marking of a verse, with some variations. The verses also show a very close semantic connection to the previous event as elaborating and/or expanding on it; moreover this stanza belongs to the climax, leading up to the culminating events in stanza VIII (see a more detailed discussion on these issues in chapter 8).

The pattern shows three acts. For the graph in figure 4 each act contains four scenes consisting of four stanzas, each stanza containing two verses, the latter are not included in the graph. The "bridges" are not shown in the graphic presentation. As has been noted, they do not play a part in creating a specific pattern in this text. Verse 11 as a bridge has been discussed in relation to the possible divisions between the first acts. If we assume the organization shown in figure 4, verse 26 (the second bridge) does not favor the division into acts because it occurs in the middle of act III. It could still mark the transition to the concluding scenes of the story as a whole.

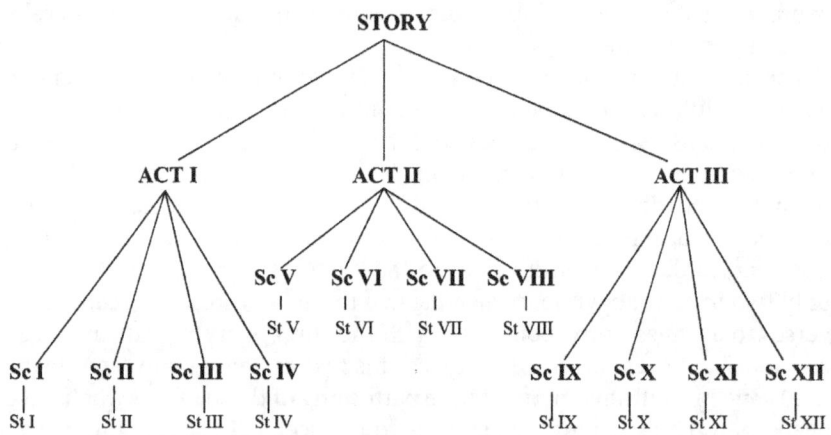

Figure 4: Structure I of *Watuchi I*

The alternative analysis for this text is presented in figure 5. From the graphic representation it can be seen that act I and act III turn out to have three and four scenes, respectively, and do not display the parallel pattern of figure 4. However, in this view, act II turns out to have an interesting

6.2 Analysis of smaller texts

organization where scene VI with its initial *chaymanta kaq* 'afterwards again' serves the function of a bridging scene between the two scenes occurring before it and the two following it; this scene also has the focus on the main character, while the other scenes keep to a pretty consistent change of referent pattern except in the conclusion. The initial verse of scene VI lacks the evidential marker, but this might have to do with the quality of *chaymanta kaq* as being a major division marker. In an analysis by Shaver for Lambayeque Quechua—a Quechua A variety in northern Peru—Shaver suggests that *chaymanta* "signals important changes within an episode" (1996:74, translation mine). I think his "episode" might correspond to what I have called an act in the present text.

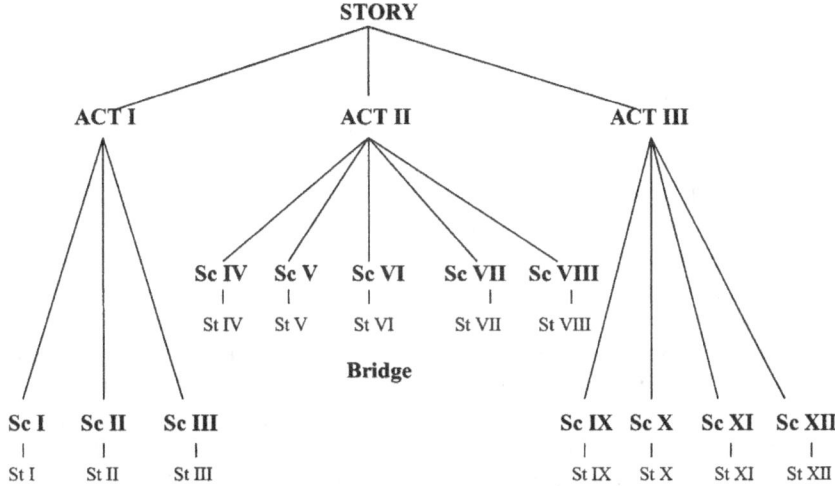

Figure 5: Structure II of *Watuchi I*

Watuchi I differs from the shorter stories by having a long introductory act as well as a long final concluding act. The main body is act II which displays the same pattern as the two shorter stories above, in the way of having five parts to it and with the bridging scene setting apart two more or less complementary halves.

Both figures 4 and 5 show nice patternings, although the "bridging" verses create some problems for both, verse 26 for the analysis presented in figure 4 (as noted above), and both verses 11 and 26 for this final analysis (figure 5). The latter with the following verse also contain -*rpari*. It is possible that neither of the presentations above show the correct analysis. I may be trying to "force" the text into a dualistic pattern that does not exist. However, considering the texts so far analyzed, I believe such a pattern to be basic to the stories. It is quite possible that the storyteller/author does not handle so well the often overlapping intricate patterns of poetic texts, and/or the text has been changing over the years through multiple tellings and some of the original patterns have been lost.

6.2.3.3 Rhetorical patterns: The profile of the text

The use of -*sqa* 'narrative past' supports my previous analyses as regards its use in the introductory scenes, but in this text it also marks the climactic scenes (scenes VII and VIII). The climax is, in addition, marked by the nonverbal dialogue between the two participants, as well as the use of -*rpari* 'sudden action', in the breaking of the rope to heaven (scene VII), and in the culminating event (scene VIII) where the fox is lying "splashed" on the ground. The climactic scenes really mark a reversal of fortune. Diane Hintz (1996:260–262) suggests that -*ñaq* 'narrative past' for the Quechua B varieties has this function, in addition to marking settings (stage). According to Soto Ruíz (1976) -*sqa* marks past events that are surprising and unexpected. Weber (pers. comm.) thinks that this is the principal function of -*ñaq* in the Huallaga variety, although he ascribes to it the function of marking stage as well. There is no conflict between these insights as one could easily conceive of a reversal of fortune as something causing surprise.[7]

Most of the stanzas in the denouement/final suspense have an introductory *ina-pti*- verse, followed by an *ina-spa*- verse; there is a switch of referent between stanzas but the referent stays the same within the stanza, that is, the focus is longer on one participant at a time—although the pattern here is not as obvious as in *Juan del Oso*, where the denouement and final suspense are marked by triplet *ina-spa*- verses. Verse (23) is a bit confusing in this regard because it is marked by *ina-spa*- but shows switch of referent; however, it refers to the main participant who is brought back on stage. The surface pattern of this particular stanza (stanza IX) complies with the rest of the stanzas belonging to the final part of the text.

Verse 22 may be seen as introducing a first denouement, while verse 26 (the "bridge") and the following stanza, stanza XI, might be seen as introducing a second denouement in the story, marked through the attention drawing device, -*rpari*. The first "compadre" arriving on the scene in verse 22 would be expected to help him—an expected denouement—but fails to do so. The state of the fox is worsening, and now his relative arrives on the scene, stanza XI, providing the much needed help—the final

---

[7]Weber (pers. comm.) also says that there is probably not a single use across Quechua languages. The farther south (within QB) one goes, the more the meaning is 'sudden discovery'; farther north within QB (e.g. Huaylas and Dos de Mayo), it can be simply the main narrative tense, showing up on event line verbs. But this varies from speaker to speaker or text to text. No one has studied it well, nor assembled enough data across varieties.

denouement. It is difficult to know the exact nature of what is considered the climax, denouement or final suspense; sometimes this is based on subjective feelings but also on knowledge of a specific culture. According to Longacre, climax and denouement may be marked in similar ways in the surface structure, while the final suspense would be marked in the same way as the preclimactic episodes. As noted before, the final section of *Juan del Oso* (after the climax with its culminating point) showed one and the same connective pattern which also applies to this text, although the patterning otherwise show some nuances, e.g. in the use of *-rpari*. This suggests one final rhetorical unit of some kind in the longer texts so far analyzed. (See previous discussions on this issue in chapter 5.)

Levinsohn (pers. comm.) thinks that the final part of the story is the major one and also the most important. The story is first of all a story about the *compadre* 'godfather' relationship which receives specific focus in this latter part of the story. Levinsohn sees scenes IX–X as the climax of the story, all the rest leading up to this point. In his view it is the pre-climactic events that are marked with *-sqa*.[8] However, according to the analyses of the other texts so far considered, *-sqa* is rather used with stages and background information, and on occasion with possibly surprising and pivotal events.[9] There are also other features that occur in the section viewed as the climax in my analysis which correspond with features of climax in the analyses of the other texts.

6.2.3.4 Rhetorical patterns: The salience scheme of the text

We can conclude that this text shows a somewhat different surface structure pattern of main events than we have witnessed in the previous texts.

---

[8]Levinsohn's view on climax does not correspond with Longacre's. According to Longacre, climax can be one or more episodic units leading to a "confrontation" (culminating point, according to the terminology I use) and followed by a resolution/denouement. According to Levinsohn and Dooley (2001), climax can be identified within the resolution of the story and which they define, along with the *Oxford English Dictionary*, as "the event or point of greatest intensity or interest; a culmination or apex." They further state "Immediately prior to the climax, it is common to find one or more devices whose rhetorical effect is to slow down the story and create the expectation that the climax is about to be presented" (p. 105). Levinsohn and Dooley's rhetorical devices prior to their perception of climax (or culminating point) seem to correspond to what Longacre defines as climax and a "zone of turbulence" leading up to a "confrontation" (culminating point, in my terminology) and a denouement.

[9]This seems to be the usage of *-sqa* in triplet (14) of *Juan del Oso*. These events can be perceived as climactic, followed by the concluding events, unit (15), that have been analyzed as constituting a "bridge," with the focus on the main participant. The "bridge" here might be seen as a denouement to this act, the act constituting one of the minor stories within *Juan del Oso* (cf. the analysis of the final part of *Juan del Oso* where the pattern is reversed and the denouement is a triplet rather than a couplet).

However, the pattern strongly suggests that the constant change of participant, or, as already noted above, the "groupings of imagery" or "centers of interest" containing these changes, is what moves the story forward. This is not so obviously marked through the use of *ina-pti-*. Interestingly, the *ina-pti-* connective is seen more in the denouement/final suspense, but always followed by an *ina-spa* verse as has been discussed above.

6.2.4 The presentational forms of Watuchi II

6.2.4.1 Major divisions of the text

Except for *Juan del Oso*, *Watuchi II* (see appendix 5) is the longest of the texts analyzed, having a total number of eighteen stanzas. It consists of act I setting the stage; act II and act III being the main body with the crucial episodic development; act IV as the denouement/final suspense. There is a conclusion that might be considered part of act IV. As with the final analysis of *Watuchi I*, the introductory act and the final act are the ones that show uneven patterning, while the two middle acts, acts II and III, form two complementary halves separated by a bridging verse. *Chaymanta* 'afterwards' also occurs, but in this text it starts off the first scene of act II, thus setting the stage for the act and clearly marking a major change in the episodic development, not within an episode but between episodes.

Act I (the stage for the story as a whole) is somehow strange because it is not closely related to the rest of the story. However, it introduces two of the main characters, the fox and the rat, while a third, the condor, is introduced in act III. In act II the fox and the rat are the only participants; at the end the rat moves off scene and does not reappear until the final act, act IV.

6.2.4.2 Artistic patterns

Although parts of the text have a fairly consistent grouping of the *ina-pti-* and *ina-spa-* connectives and the semantic "grouping of imagery," other surface features such as *ña-taq-si* help in making decisions about dividing the text into stanzas. These stanzas have been analyzed as consisting of two verses like we have seen in the texts already analyzed. Even if four verses to the stanza might be a better analysis for some parts (e.g. scene III, stanzas VI and VII), I have followed the overall pattern of two verses to the stanza.

The stanzas of the two middle acts, acts II and III, do show a pretty consistent pattern, in a way similar to *Juan del Oso*, but at the same time different. In *Juan del Oso* there were three verses to the scene, while in this there are three stanzas to the scene. The scenes are very much like the

6.2 Analysis of smaller texts

scenes in *Juan del Oso* in the way the first stanza functions as an introduction to the next and the final stanza functions as a conclusion of the scene. The difference is seen in the number of verses and the grouping of these within each scene. The units marked by the *ina-spa-* verses (or some other connective) at first seem to set the others apart but under closer scrutiny the units are very closely related to the previous stanza(s) in functioning as a conclusion or elaboration of previous events.[10] Nevertheless, the stanzas serving as conclusions would announce to the hearer the end of one unit as well as the beginning of a new, in a way similar to what has been suggested earlier.

Act I contains a scene of two stanzas only, whereas act IV can be seen as having four stanzas if the final concluding stanza is considered part of it. However, the patterning is uneven for these acts, much like the final analysis of *Watuchi I*. The total number of stanzas is eighteen, six of them corresponding to the first and final acts, the other twelve corresponding to the two middle acts with exactly six to each act.

The text is shown graphically in figure 6. For the stanzas I have had to exclude the numbers due to lack of space. However, the numbers pertaining to each scene should be obvious.

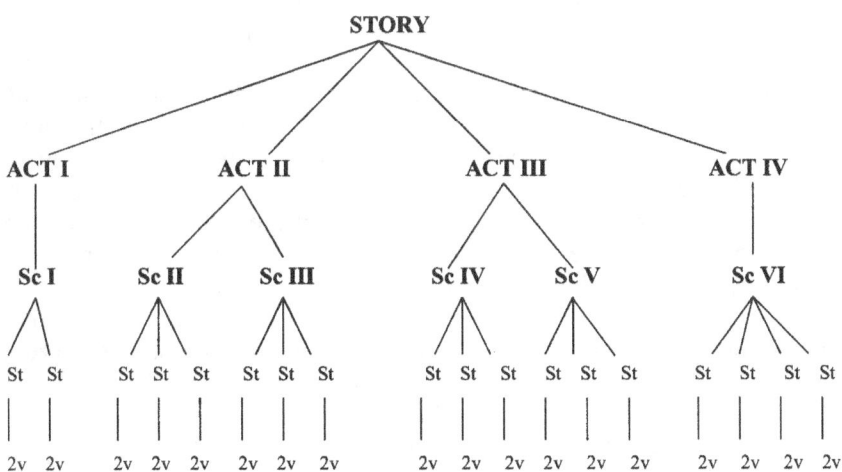

Figure 6: Structure of *Watuchi II*

---

[10]Only a couple of times does an *ina-spa-* verse occur in an introductory function. On these occasions, however, such a verse occurs as the second verse in the stanza, the first verse being introduced by another connective.

6.2.4.3 Rhetorical patterns: The profile of the text

This text shows a rhetorical *profile* structure very similar to the profile of *Watuchi I*. The use of *-sqa* 'narrative past' occurs as expected in the stage. Its use is consistent in all the texts analyzed. But with this text as with *Watuchi I*, *-sqa* is not limited to stage portions of the text; it occurs also in the climactic scenes. However, *-sqa* occurs in other stanzas; possibly having a backgrounding function in verse 12, stanza V, and a setting/introductory function in verse 32, stanza XV. But since it is attached to the suffix *-rpari* 'sudden action', it might rather be seen as marking something surprising or crucial or have a double function. (See the text in appendix 5.) Another feature that also occurs in some introductory stanzas is that the verses are marked by *-ña-taq-si* 'NOW-EMPH-RPT', yet the same construction also occurs with verses that are not introductory. The suffix *-rpari* occurs several times in the more crucial sections of the story; act II contains a first climax of the story (scene III), while act III contains what could be regarded as a second climax or denouement (scene V). However, if one considers the patterns observed in *Juan del Oso* and *Watuchi I*, it could be that from a cultural point of view, scene V is another climax, followed by the denouement and/or final suspense in act IV, which would nicely correspond with the previous analyses. In act IV the fox is dead, but there is a lot of activity around the dead body of the fox, indicating first a hope of resurrection by the rat, then the hope dwindles off in a lamenting monologue by the same participant. The final part is marked in the same way as *Watuchi I* with the stanzas starting off with *ina-pti-* and change of referent, but switching to *ina-spa-* in the next verse, indicating 'same referent as in previous verse'; that is, the focus is on the same referent within each stanza (with some modifications). Stanzas XVI and XVII might also include some minor climax related to the rat. There are, for example, two occurrences of *-rpari* and some other factors that suggest this. A final monologue of some sort is part of the pattern of the other texts analyzed, although the length of it varies a great deal.

6.2.4.4 Rhetorical patterns: The salience scheme of the text

The salience scheme (the main event line patternings) is similar to that of *Juan del Oso*, although more varied in the use of the connectives that introduce the verses. The stanzas have to be regarded as "groupings of imagery" or "centers of interest," moving the story forward. These are also at times irregular in the sense that they do not always show a constant change of participant even when the surface pattern suggests so.

Occasionally *ina-pti-* is used, although semantically the verse refers to the same subject as the previous verse. This has been discussed earlier as possibly being related to a change of a rhetorical unit, according to Stirling's view, or possibly marking a climactic point, which may also happen to be a change of a rhetorical unit, as my analyses suggest. It could, however, be the need to conform to a specific surface pattern that causes this discrepancy between the grammatical form and the underlying semantics of the text. It could very well be that the author is not able to coordinate surface patterns and semantic content quickly enough at certain points in the story. An example of this is seen in verse 10. Another example is seen in verse 34; this verse does not start a rhetorical unit, but rather, as suggested above, is part of some minor, final climax within the latter part of the story. The verse even includes a sub-line with another *ina-pti-* connective (not marked with *-si*), yet the participant is the same. The pattern in stanzas XVI and XVII does show a neat surface pattern that corresponds to the first stanza of the scene, stanza XV, and which also corresponds to the pattern of the denouement and/or final suspense, as perceived in *Watuchi I*. This suggests that verse 34 is within a major rhetorical unit, although the verse implies movement within the unit. The surface pattern of switch reference does not correspond well with the underlying semantics, unless we think in terms of Stewart that *ina-spa* is "reserved" for the main participant of a story or main section of a story. Here, in the latter part, it is the rat that is main participant. This discrepancy between sentence grammaticality and discourse "grammar" has been discussed before in relation to the analysis of *Juan del Oso*. However, stanza II in the stage is confusing in this regard. The referent of the first verse, verse 4, has to be understood as the *pericote* (the rat) in order for the second verse to make sense. The analysis of the use of two *ina-spa-* clauses here must be based on other grounds as marking the end of the scene, as in other texts. It could also be that the fox is considered as the main participant of this stage scene, and for this reason the scene has to end referring to him through the use of *ina-spa-*, but that wouldn't explain the usage of *ina-spa-* in verse 4. The switch-reference markers also show discrepancies in other respects as well. For example, at times a verse starts out with one participant, then includes in the end a second one through the use of the reciprocal *-naku*; the grammatical markings show indeterminacy in this respect. This is noticed in other texts.[11] This could also suggest that its ambiguous grammatical markings are due to the need to keep to an original artistic

---

[11] My research is not on the nature of the switch-reference markers, but the use of these in the artistic structuring of the texts has forced me to consider some literature related to these. There are many aspects related to the use of the switch-reference markers that I cannot deal with at the time but which merit further research in the Quechua languages.

patterning which had precedence over grammatical functions on the sentence level. Some of the original patterns (e.g. stanza II) may be better preserved than others that have slightly changed due to multiple tellings and various changes over the course of time.

6.2.5 Typical features in the texts

It can be concluded that on the whole the texts show very similar rhetorical patterns, although they have to differ to some extent due to the different length of the stories. Some texts also show their own specific features in the use of the suffix -*sqa* 'narrative past' as well as in the use of connectives, which also bear on the artistic structuring.

Artistically, the latter texts do not show a triplet pattern as seen in *Juan del Oso*. Yet there is a clear pattern of stanzas based on verses introduced by various connectives and the evidential -*si*. In all the texts the *ina-pti-* and *ina-spa-* connectives play a major role but there are a few connective suffixes like -*ña-taq* 'NOW-EMPH' that also play an important role in the pattern formation; this applies specifically to the two *Watuchi* texts. These might have been told by the same author, or be peculiar to a slightly different variety of Corocora Quechua. However the underlying semantic pattern of switch or no-switch of referents (depending on the nature of the rhetorical units) is significant and generally the same. Sometimes -*ña-taq* occurs with the *ina-* connectives as is also seen in *Juan del Oso*, but in the latter texts normally this construction occurs with other elements, usually with the expressed subject at the very beginning of the verse and almost always with the evidential -*si* attached. The nature of *ña-taq* is not clear. Maybe it is used in two different senses; as a discourse rhetorical feature and as an artistic verse marker.

All the texts can easily be grouped into *couplet* stanzas of two verses, although there are parts even in these texts that are a bit more tricky to make grouping decisions on. The couplets, however, correspond one to a scene in just one of the texts; in the others there are two or three of them together to the scene. At times it might be more reasonable to group four verses together as *one* stanza corresponding to a scene, but the overall pattern suggests that the stanzas are couplets which can be grouped in pairs corresponding to scenes.

The most interesting discovery in the smaller texts analyzed has been the patterning of the texts into two complementary halves. This discovery led me to return to *Juan del Oso* for further analysis which will be presented in the following section.

6.3 Other patterns seen in *Juan del Oso*

6.3.1 Acts

On the basis of the analysis above, it was to be expected that similar patterns would be found in *Juan del Oso*, apart from those already described in the previous chapter. In charting out the text according to different acts, I discovered that each act had its own organized parallel pattern. Because of the length of the text the graphic presentations have to be done act by act (figures 9–14), although I will initially provide an overall pattern of the story based on the number of acts (figure 7).

In this text, as with the other texts, the stage and the bridging stanza(s) between the stage of the story and the beginning episodic development create an irregular artistic patterning. The patterning breaks from an otherwise very nice parallel pattern for all the acts. In the case of *Juan del Oso*, the units (29)–(30) referred to as the culminating point and the denouement also create a problem. This was discussed when analyzing the text. I have decided to regard act Ib and act Va as tiny "sub-acts." Act Ib (figure 9) is the climactic conclusion of the background information in the stage (act Ia)—a story on its own in some varieties (see 5.2)—and at the same time it serves as the inciting moment for the episodic development in act II, as well as to the story as a whole. In a parallel way, act Va concludes the climactic act IV and sets off the final suspense of the story. Although it is considered a "bridging act," it has the same surface pattern as the final act Vb, showing a complete change in the triplet surface pattern. The units are not marked in the overall structure as presented in figure 7. (See also appendices 1 and 2.)

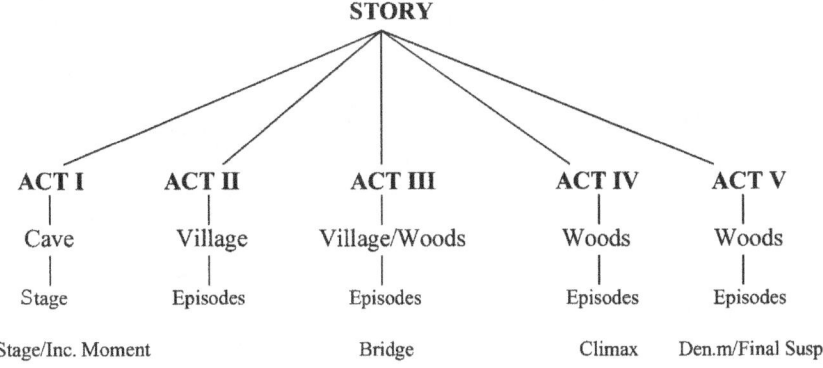

Figure 7: Overall structure of *Juan del Oso*

The graphic presentation shows that act III forms a bridge between acts II and IV in that it entails movement between two major local settings (see section 5.3.2.2). This bridging act will be discussed in more detail in section 6.3.2 with reference to the graphic presentation to be presented as figure 11.

It should be noted that the final and beginning couplets marked as bridges may be the same for two different graphs. That is, the final unit marked as bridge for act IV is the same as the initial unit marked as bridge for act V (see, for example, figure 10). When the same unit is marked twice it is indicated by the " = " mark before or after it, depending on the order of the units. The numbers in parenthesis refer to the various stanzas as numbered in the text in appendix 1. I indicate in parenthesis when the bridges consist of couplets; when nothing is indicated the bridge consists of only one verse. At the beginning of act Ia (see figure 9) the broken line indicates that the initial triplet may not be considered part of the pattern of act I; it introduces the main participant for this act and behaves in an irregular way, similar to what we have seen in some of the smaller texts; for example, the *Mankapa Cuenton*.

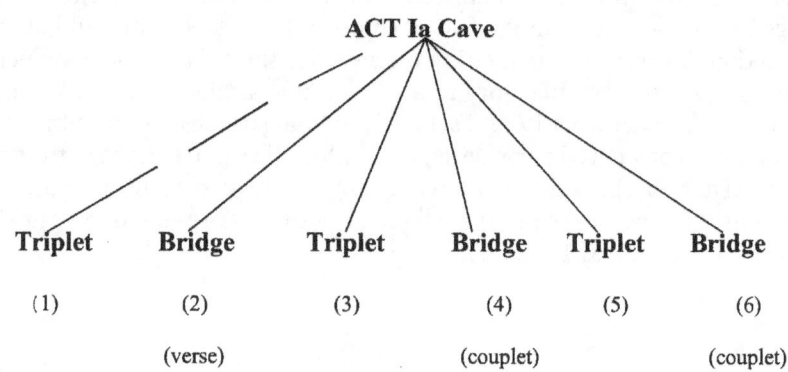

Figure 8: Act constituting the major part of the stage

6.3 Other patterns seen in Juan del Oso

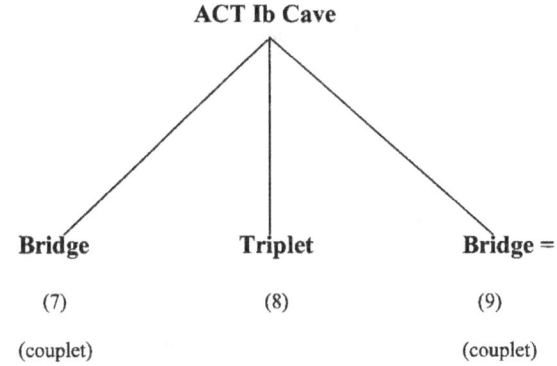

Figure 9: Act serving as part of the inciting moment

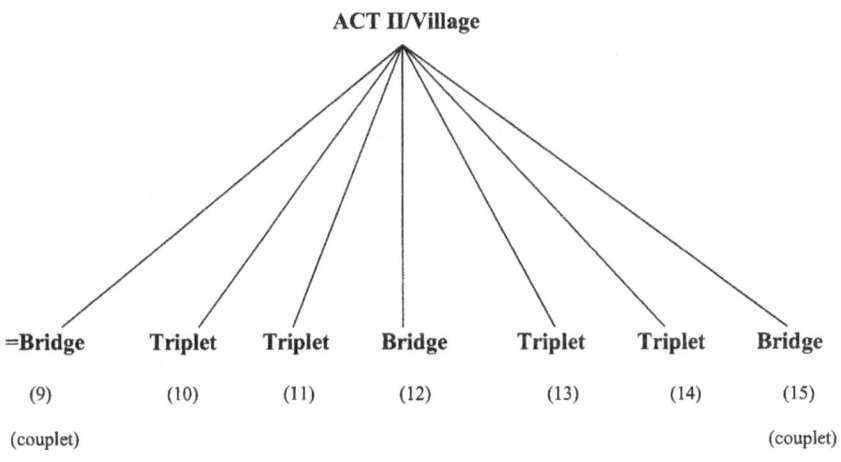

Figure 10: Act containing episodic development

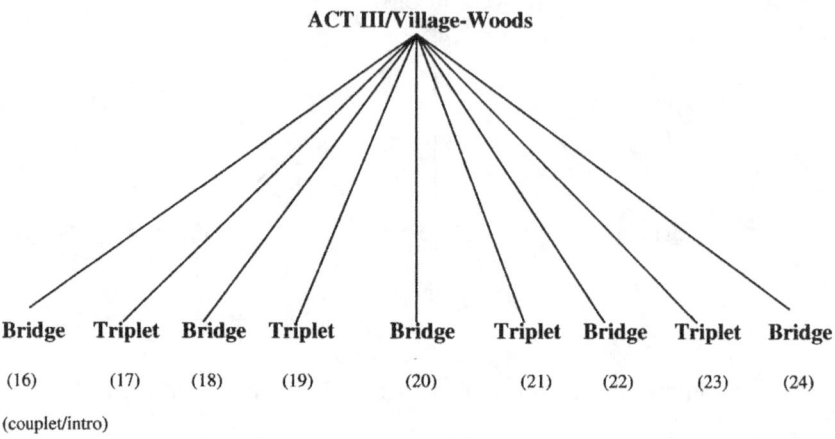

Figure 11: Bridging act containing episodic development

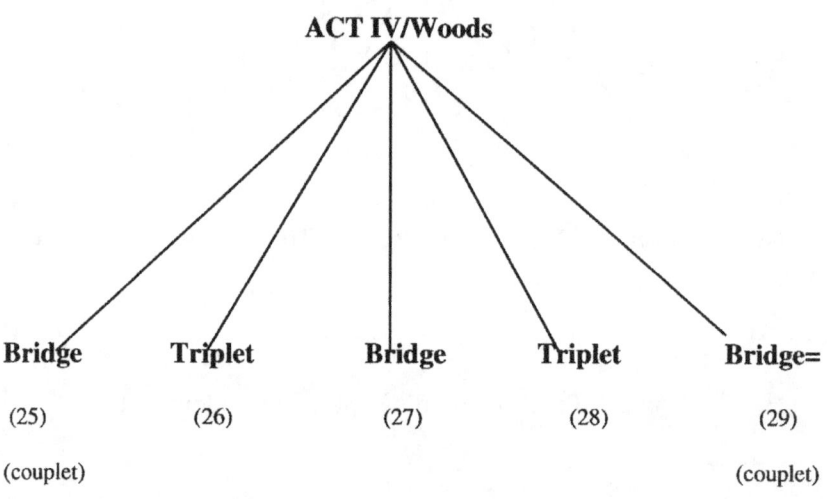

Figure 12: Act containing climax (and culminating point)

6.3 Other patterns seen in Juan del Oso

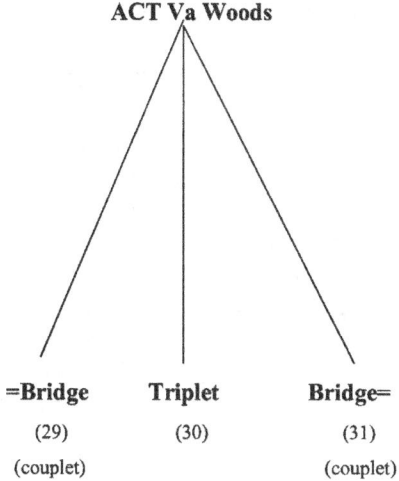

Figure 13: Act containing culminating point and denouement

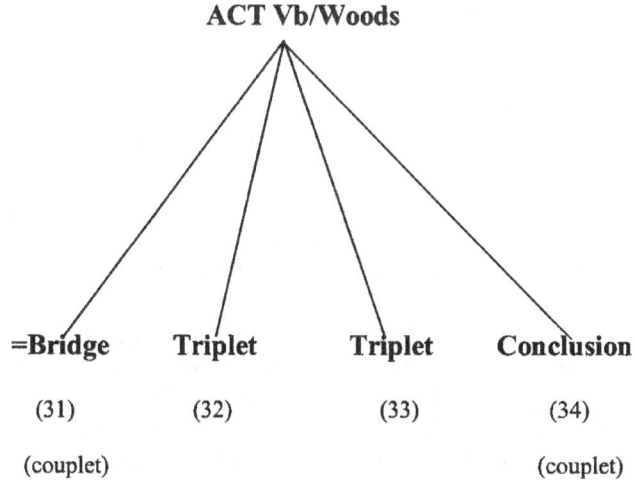

Figure 14: Act containing final suspense

6.3.2 Complementary halves

After making the graphic figures of each individual act based on my previous analysis[12] into triplets and bridges of *Juan del Oso*, I observed the emergence of a very interesting system: each act shows a clear pattern of complementary halves in a mirror image. The pattern almost fell into place, and it solved the problems I had had in deciding where some of the acts began or ended. Only the bridges that at times consist of one verse, and at times two (couplets), display a few irregularities,[13] but not irregularities in the order they occur in the formation of the pattern. As can be noticed the acts, even the tiny subacts are consistently framed by couplets. However, each act has its own internal structure. None of them are quite alike.

The problem of the parts called act Ib and act Va has already been discussed. However, the initial triplet of the story (if indeed it can be called a triplet, as the pattern is very different from the rest and also lacks two evidentials) does not seem to fit in with the rest of act I. The very first description of the bear-father could be analyzed as not belonging to the story itself; it is presumably a general introduction by the storyteller, much like what we witnessed in the case of *Mankapa Cuenton*. If that is the case, the pattern of acts Ia and Ib will turn out to be very similar to that of the final acts Va and Vb. The two units, act Ib and act Va which are the inciting moment and the culmination and denouement, show very similar patterns and also demonstrate an interesting parallelism between the crucial beginning and the crucial end of the story.

It was mentioned in section 5.2 that in some areas various parts of this story may exist as several separate stories. This might have been the case originally in the Coracora area as well, which could explain the fact that each act is so different in structure. However, from a rhetorical point of view, the story is considered as one, where each act plays an individual role, such as stage, episodic development, climax, and denouement/final suspense.

Act III caused some questions in my previous analysis (see 5.3.2.2) where I discussed what the function of the different stanzas might be in relation to moving back and forth between the village and the woods. I analyzed unit (20) as setting the stage for the final part. However, in making the graphic presentation I realized that this unit serves as a bridge between two complementary halves of act III. It probably also sets the stage for the final part of act III but at the same time marks the introduction to

---

[12]The only part that has been adjusted according to the pattern I saw is the climactic part for which I had a hard time discovering any patterns; making the graphic presentations helped me see how to group this section, too.

[13]This applies specifically to act Ia. As noted earlier I am uncertain about my analysis of this act into verses and stanzas. There might be a pattern that is more consistent than what my analysis shows.

life in the woods and the various struggles that Juan del Oso will be facing in the latter part of the narrative. It could be that what I have referred to as bridges on the upper level are rather marking major "turning points" in the story (cf. my analysis of the Shawsha *Juan del Oso* text in 7.3.2.3). According to Hallberg (1992), the ancient tragedy, consisting of five acts, should mark a turning point more or less in the middle of the third act. This concept (in Greek *peripe'teia*) had already been introduced by Aristotle. The Coracora *Juan del Oso* story could be conceived of as a tragedy of five acts. If the story is consciously constructed with such an idea in mind, one can assume that the storyteller or some earlier author of the story had been exposed to some teaching on how to compose a European tragedy according to ancient patterns. On the other hand, if the story is of European (Spanish) origin, as earlier discussed, it may be part of the original structure of the story. The latter does not seem reasonable, however, considering that the story has been "stitched together" in various ways in different Quechua languages. As already alluded to, the analyses of the smaller texts discussed above also reveal bridges that might better be perceived as major turning points in the middle of the story.

The structure of the texts in parallel complementary halves in some kind of a mirror image is what is referred to as CHIASTIC structure in literary circles. Usually chiastic structures are seen on lower levels of text, like reversed structures of sentences in different verses or verse lines. In the texts analyzed they may be used as a means of foregrounding, a "turning point" as mentioned above. However, they could also reflect an underlying cultural pattern, as discussed in chapter 4. As noted there, the idea of complementary halves was quite fundamental in the ancient Andean societies. Complementary halves are also seen in the textile patterns. These issues will be further discussed in chapter 8.

The analysis of all the texts, particularly the pattern that emerged from the graphic presentation of *Juan del Oso*, also seems to confirm that my second analysis of *Watuchi I* as shown in figure 5 is the better one.

6.4 Patterns pertaining in general to the texts

6.4.1 Specific units

From the results of the analysis of the Coracora texts one can conclude that each individual act represents a pattern of two complementary halves in a mirror image. In the two shortest texts I did not talk about acts, only scenes, but admittedly these scenes formed complementary halves around a "bridge" and can, as such, be seen as stories of one act only. *Mankapa Cuenton* could be analyzed as having two acts.

If one considers the story as a whole, the patterns consist of complementary halves. This is clearly expressed in *Juan del Oso* with the bridging middle act (act III) where the events occur in two different places. There is a switching back and forth between locations. However, although the beginning and final acts are quite similar as far as artistic structuring is concerned, according to the discussion above, acts II and IV do not show parallel structures.

It is reasonable to conclude that the *act* is a very real cognitive unit in the Coracora Quechua speaker's mind. Texts are formed through the stitching together of acts of similar or different patterns (at times different shorter stories) into a patterned unified whole, a complete story, whose narrative account in its complete form also obeys rhetorical rules in the marking of plot and event line in the surface structure, which the analyses of all the texts show.

At times there is a complete overlap of different kinds of functions, as in the case of the stanzas showing constant switch of referents in a creative artistic pattern which at the same time is part of the marking of the main event line of the story, as well as corresponding to a scene in most texts. In some texts the stanzas, although not corresponding to a scene, still play a significant function within the scene, e.g. serving as introduction, middle, or conclusion to the scene, as seen in *Watuchi II*. From this one can conclude that the scene is also a very real cognitive unit in the Coracora Quechua speaker's mind.

It is also possible to see the scenes comprising two stanzas as forming complementary halves, and the stanza couplets as forming complementary halves, that is, one verse to each part (see the *Ampatopa Cuenton* text in 6.2). It is probably better, though, to talk about these in terms of being binary patterns.

The units which I have called "bridges" play an important role in the pattern formation. However, this is more obvious in some texts than in others —*Watuchi I* and *II* are different in this regard, and the "bridges" do not form a specific pattern on the lower levels, as they do in some of the other texts.

When I started my analysis of *Juan del Oso* and discovered its structure in terms of *ina-pti-* triplets and interspersing units, the term "bridge" seemed to me to be a very relevant term for the kind of function I perceived the units to have. As also stated earlier, even the *ina*-connectives with their switch-reference markers certainly have a bridging function between verses in the way they always refer to the past event(s) and the subject or major referent involved, and at the same time guide your focus toward future event(s) and referent(s). Little did I know at the time that

6.4 Patterns pertaining in general to the texts

the concept of "bridging" is very relevant to the Quechua speaker in the creation of texts. Ralph Toliver, who specializes in Ambo-Pasco Quechua, told me (in personal conversation) about instances where the Quechua co-translators insisted on the need of a "bridge" between certain textual units. This was a very interesting discovery to me and lends support to my analysis. That the concept of "bridging" is so prevalent in the structuring of the texts on various levels has also been an interesting discovery which has become obvious in the course of the analysis of the texts, and not based on any preconceived idea of mine.

6.4.2 Other parallel patterns

The parallel patterning is also seen between levels in the way each level—except for the very lowest, the verse—creates a story unit in terms of stage,[14] body, and conclusion. Figure 15 gives an example of this kind of parallel patterning which is manifest in different ways in the texts at hand, though the bottom level is not obvious in *Watuchi I*.

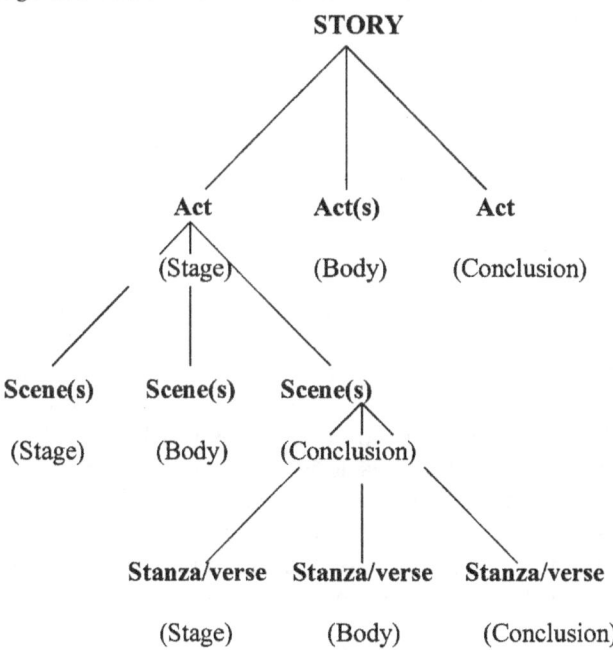

Figure 15: Parallel patterning at different levels

---

[14]Chapter 5 deals with the concepts "stage" and "setting." For the graphic illustration here I have chosen to use the term "stage" for all levels, in order to show the parallel pattern between levels.

The most important surface structure tools in creating the patterns that have been seen so far are the connectives, the evidential -*si* 'reportative', and the switch of reference through the use of switch-reference markers. There are a few inconsistencies, but not enough to hide the patterns that must be very real to the Coracora Quechua speaker's mind, whether they operate on the conscious level or not (see chapter 8, particularly 8.3.2).

6.4.3 Numeric patterns

From the patterns of the text one can conclude that, if one excludes the bridges, there are never more than five major parts to any unit on the upper levels. On the lower levels we find patterns of twos and threes; that is, two or three parts to a scene and two or three parts to a stanza. In the case of *Juan del Oso*, three verses to a stanza as well as the scene; in the case of *Watuchi II*, three couplet stanzas to a scene.

The analysis reveals three pattern numbers that play an important part in the patternings of the text: the numbers five, three and two. At times these numbers link to form other numbers in multiples of two, as in the case of the shorter texts analyzed. In the case of both the Juan del Oso text and the Watuchi II text, even multiples of three are introduced.

In any case, the principle of duality in the way of forming complementary halves is seen to be the basic underlying principle that creates a parallel pattern between different levels of the text.

6.4.4 In conclusion

We are left with one important question: if the patterns are not operating on a conscious level, how is the speaker able to handle all these patterns orally without any reference to some specific visible structure as he goes along in his creative construction of a story? This is a question that will be considered in chapter 8. Another question is whether similar textual structures are found in other varieties of Quechua. Considering the general homogeneity of the Quechua people and culture, it is to be expected that similar basic patterns and principles can be found, although the nature of the different language varieties would necessarily create different surface structures on the lower levels. It is to be hoped that the present study will be able to give some further insight into this as we turn to chapter 7 and the analysis of the Shausha Quechua texts which come from a variety belonging to the Quechua B branch.

7

Quechua Textual Patterns—Shausha

7.1 Preliminaries

The Shausha texts were collected by John R. Wroughton working under the auspices of SIL during the years of 1986–1987, and published in 1996 with a grammatical sketch of the language. As stated earlier, Shausha Quechua belongs to Quechua B. It is one of three varieties spoken in the Mantaro valley in central Peru.

The Shausha area has over the years undergone a change from a typical Quechua culture toward a more Hispanic-Andean culture. According to Wroughton, the Hispanic influence is more marked in this area compared to other Andean areas, and this is particularly noticeable in the sociolinguistic situation. In most Shausha Quechua areas, the children no longer speak Quechua and their parents do not use it as their primary vehicle of communication. In some more remote communities, Wroughton (1996:11–12) noticed that people above the age of fifty spoke Quechua and Spanish with equal frequency; only the older women seemed to prefer to speak Quechua. According to Wroughton this is a natural consequence of contact with Spanish since the time of colonization in the sixteenth century. Considering the many years of contact with the high-prestige Spanish-speaking population it is remarkable that the language is still in use. Resistance to Spanish is proof of the importance that Quechua has had over the years.

The texts, according to Wroughton, were provided by people who still speak Quechua or spoke it in their childhood. Given the facts above one may wonder whether typical rhetorical Quechua patterns still exist in the texts at hand. However, Beyersdorff (1986) found that Quechua rhetorical patterns are transforming "literary genres constituting the Hispanic tradition" in the urban areas with a major influx of Andean people. In view of her findings, it is not unlikely that typical Quechua rhetorical patterns still persist in the texts told in Quechua. Moreover, the texts to be analyzed are typically the kind that persist over time in oral form. Nevertheless, it is to be expected that some characteristic features typical of Quechua rhetorical patterns have gotten lost due to the Spanish influence in the area.

7.2 Language specifics

For the Coracora texts analyzed in chapters 5 and 6, it was noticed that the sentence-initial connective *ina-* followed by a switch-reference marker played a significant role in the pattern formation, as did the evidential marker *-si* 'reportative'. The latter was also normally attached to the sentence-initial connective, at least when it was part of marking the verse as I have defined above.

In Shausha Quechua the sentence-initial connective is typically *chay-pita* 'that-ABL' which is almost always followed by the reportative *-sh(i)* 'RPT', the phonological manifestation of the suffix in this variety of Quechua. Although the switch-reference markers also exist in Shausha Quechua, they never co-occur with *chay-pita*. It is interesting to notice that when there is an initial *chay-pita* followed by a subordinate clause marked for switch reference (often with reference to a previous event), it is normally the subordinate clause, and not the initial connective, that is followed by the reportative *-shi* (shown in sentences 2 and 7 in the text analyzed in 7.3.1).

7.3 Patterns found in the Shausha texts

To aid the discussion of patterns found in the Shausha Quechua texts, a more detailed analysis of one text will first be presented. The text—one of several smaller texts involving the fox as one of the main participants—is a version of the 'Fox and the Frog' (*Ampatopa Cuenton*) story that was presented in its complete form in chapter 6, the Ayacucho Coracora version.

7.3.1 The presentational forms of 'The Fox and the Frog'

7.3.1.1 Artistic patterns

The text is artistically structured. It is one act (possibly two acts) consisting of four scenes, each scene a triplet stanza. In the case of the Coracora version presented in chapter 6, there are only two episodes, each consisting of two couplet stanzas. One major difference, which also makes the Shausha text longer, is that it focuses on the fox's final destiny, something that is altogether missing in the Coracora version. The text consists of two complementary parts in a mirror image, divided by a bridging verse in the middle. There is an initial sentence serving as an introduction to the story, more as a kind of heading than a stage; it is not marked by the reportative -*shi*. The first scene includes both main participants; the second focuses on the frog; the third, on the fox; the last includes both. There is a final author comment about the fox always losing, which as one would expect, does not have the reportative marker.

According to the tentative definition given in chapter 5, I consider the evidential -*shi* to be a marker of verse and its combination with *chay-pita* to be a marker of verse of episodic nature, though not consistently so; see, e.g. v. 13. Scenes II and III show clear triplet patterns through three verses all introduced by the connective *chay-pita*. Some scenes do, however, obscure the patterning. In the stage, scene I, *chay-pita* is lacking in verses 2 and 3. One might ask, on what grounds has this unit been considered a triplet stanza? Neither initial connectives nor the switch of subject follow our criteria. The answer is that semantically it creates a scene, forming a triplet in the same way as the scenes that follow. The verses are also marked through the use of the evidential -*shi*. However, verse 3 is a bit tricky. It contains a direct quote, but without the expected quote margin (with *ni-* 'say') preceding or following it. Verse 3 could be regarded as part of the previous verse. We might contend that the use of -*shi* in this context is not to indicate reported or secondhand information; it is normal for expressions like "Let's see which...." On the other hand, the use of -*shi* could serve to indicate that this quotation is a separate verse, for it would then fit into the pattern of a triplet stanza. The same use of -*shi* in a quote is also noticed in another text—see appendix 6, verse 10 (the bridge). The last triplet also constitutes a semantic unit, but each *chay-pita* seems to introduce two independent verses, both being sentences marked by the reportative -*shi*. However, I have chosen to regard the second sentence as a sub-line of the first line because semantically it is an elaboration of the former. The last verse lacks the initial connective, an issue to which we will return below when discussing rhetorical structuring.

The complete text is provided in the following pages, indicating the different scenes; a graphic representation of the text follows in figure 16.

The Fox and the Frog
(El Zorro y el Sapo[1])

               SS/DS ASP TENSE

Intro
(1) 1 Unay timpu atuh-kah
   time time fox-DEF

    prupwista-ta lula-pa:ku-ñah sa:pu-kah-wan.   -ñah
    proposal-OBJ do-PL-NARPST   frog-DEF-ACCOMP

Scene I
(2) 2 Hatun lu:ma-ta altu-ta   hishpi-lku-l-shi
   big   hill-OBJ altitude-OBJ escape-ABOVE-ADVSS-RPT

    chay-traw apusta-lka-ñah   SS   -ñah
    that-LOC make.a.bet-PLIMPFR-NARPST

    sa:pu-kah-wan   atuh-kah.
    frog-DEF-ACCOMP fox-DEF

  3 "Mayhan-ninchik-shi tra-lpu-ña-nchik
    who-12P-RPT   arrive-BELOW-NARPST-12

    uklu   pampa-kah-ta primiru?"
    bottom pampa-DEF-OBJ first

  4 Chay-pita-sh
    that-ABL-RPT

    "Ñuha ga:na-lu-shayki-tra: ham-ta-ha.
    I   win-OUT-1FUT2-CONJ.THEN you-OBJ-TOP

    Imay u:ra-tra: ham usyusu tra-lpu-nki?"
    when hour-CONJ.THEN you lazy.one arrive-BELOW-2

    ni-ñah   atuh-kah a:pu-kah-ta.   DS   -ñah
    say-NARPST fox-DEF   frog-DEF-OBJ

1 Once upon a time the fox made a bet with the frog. 2 It was, as they arrived on a big hill, that the fox made the bet with the frog (both sentences plural—reciprocal action). 3 "Let's see who gets first to the bottom of the hill."4 Then "I'll beat you! At what time would you arrive, you lazy one?" said the fox.

---

[1]Wroughton (1996:86–89).

Scene II
(3) 5 Chay-pita-sh   sabidu sa:pu-kah trula-naku-lu-ñah
     that-ABL-RPT   wise   frog-DEF put-RECIP-OUT-NARPST

          kalu   kalu-man   pasah asta
          afar   afar-GOAL much until   DS   -lu   -ñah

          pampa-kah   lu:ma-kah-pita.
          pampa-DEF   hill-DEF-ABL

   6 Chay-pita-sh
     that-ABL-RPT

          "Kimsa biyahi yupa-l-mi
          three   time   count-ADVSS-DIR

          patrka-shun suk-ta."
          jump-12FUT   one-OBJ

              ni-ñah   sa:pu-kah.
              say-NARPST   frog-DEF   DS?   -ñah

   7 Chay-pita
     that-ABL

          "Buynu" ni-ñah   DS   -ñah
          well   say-NARPST

          "unu,... dus,... tris,..." ni-pti-n-**shi**
          one   two   three   say-ADVDS-3P-RPT

          sa:pu-kah   patrka-lu-ñah   DS   -ñah
          frog-DEF   jump-OUT-NARPST

          pasah   trula-naku-sha-n-man
          much   put-RECIP-REL-3P-GOAL

          kada   patrka-y-traw-**shi**
          each   jump-INF-LOC-RPT

          sa:pu-kah   "troh" "troh" "troh"
          frog-DEF   (onom. for sound of frog)

          luli-traw-ña.
          inside-LOC-NOW

5 Then the wise frogs placed themselves (in a line) from the top of the hill down to the pampa. 6 Then "Let's count to three, then let us start," said the frog. 7 Then "OK, one, two, three," they said and each jumped to where the next frog had placed himself, "croak, croak, croak" with each jump, the frog was already in!

Bridge

(4) 8 Atuh-kah   panay-lah-shi
       fox-DEF   gradually-YET-RPT

        tra-lpu-ya-n
        arrive-BELOW-IMPFV-3

        tra-lpu-ya-n
        arrive-BELOW-IMPFV-3

        tra-lpu-ya-n
        arrive-BELOW-IMPFV-3   DS   -ya   -n

Scene III

(5) 9 Chay-pita-sh   atuh-kah   pasah
      that-ABL-RPT   fox-DEF   much

        hallu-n-ta   ahta-ku-lu-n   pasah. SS   -n
        tongue-3P-OBJ hang.out.of.mouth-REF-OUT-3 much

   10 Chay-pita-sh   ña   pampa-kah-man
      that-ABL-RPT   now   pampa-DEF-GOAL

        tralpu-lpu-ya-pti-n-shi
        arrive.below-BELOW-IMPFV-ADVDS-3P-RPT

        sa:pu-kah   ña   pampa-kah-traw
        frog-DEF   now   pampa-DEF-LOC

        trukiya-la-mu-n.   DS   -lu   -n
        onom.frog-OUT-AFAR-3

   11 Chay-pita-sh   atuh-kah
      that-ABL-RPT   fox-DEF

        pata-m   patrya-lu-ñah   DS   -lu   -ñah
        stomach-DIR   burst-OUT-NARPST

        tra-lpu-ya-pti-n.
        arrive-BELOW-IMPFV-ADVDS-3P

8 Little by little the fox is descending. 9 Then his tongue is totally outside (from exhaustion). 10 Then while he is descending to the pampa, the frog is already croaking there in the pampa. 11 Then, while descending, the fox's stomach bursts.

Scene IV

(6) 12 Chay-pita-sh   ga:na-lu-n   sa:pu-kah   DS   -lu   -n
       that-ABL-RPT   win-OUT-3   frog-DEF

        midalla   di   uru-ta-sh
        medal   o   gold-OBJ-RPT

        wallha-ku-lu-n   sa:pu   SS   -lu   -n
        put.neck-REF-OUT-3   frog

7.3 *Patterns found in the Shausha texts* 165

13 Chay-pita-sh asta kanan-kama-pis that-ABL-RPT until now-LIM-ALSO	DS? (generic)	Ø
sa:pu-kah bininusu frog-DEF poisonous		
Midalla-n-shi chay bininu ki:da-lu-n medal-3P-RPT that poison be.left-OUT-3	DS (poison)	-n
sa:pu-kah-pah frog-DEF-PUR		
14 Atuh pubri-kah-pah fox poor-DEF-PUR	DS	-lu -n
ki:da-lu-n pata-n lashwa-paku-sha-sh be.left-OUT-3 stomach-3P crushed-?-PRT-RPT		
midya falda-traw middle hill-LOC		
Pirdi-lu-n chay pubri atuh-kah. lose-OUT-3 that poor fox-DEF	DS	-lu -n

12 Then the frog won and he put on a gold medal. 13 Then until this day the frog is poisonous; he is left with his poisonous medal. 14 As for the fox, he was left "spread out" in the middle of the hill; he lost, the poor fox.

Author comment
15 Ima-traw-pis ma: chay atuh-kah pirdidu?
what?-LOC-ALSO well... that fox-DEF lost (the.lost.one)

15 Well, in whatever circumstances has he not lost, the fox (a bit unclear).

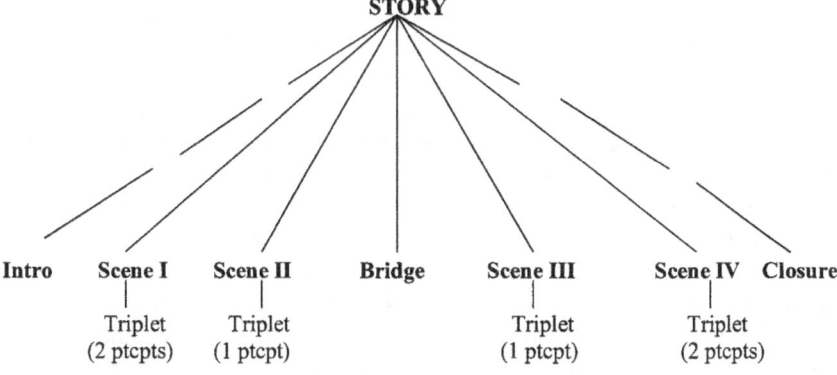

Figure 16: Structure of *The Fox and the Frog*

As already noted, the text shows a clear pattern of complementary halves, each half a combination of units (triplet stanzas). The introductory sentence and the closing statement are not considered part of the story itself (both sentences lack *-shi*) although these units form part of a pattern of complementary halves in this particular text. It is interesting that the number of participants in the triplets also plays a part in creating the pattern but this could be a coincidence. The bridging verse is closely tied to the first verse of scene three (verse 9), providing the setting for the next episode of the text. The lack of an initial *chay-pita-sh* right away announces to the hearer that the previous scene (triplet) has ended and a new scene (triplet) begins. In other words, it thereby indicates a walking off and on scene; the former not expressed overtly but implied; the latter expressed both through the fronted *atuh-kah*, changing focus of interest, as well as providing the setting for the climactic scene through the three times repeated *tra-lpu-ya-n*. The fact that the so-called bridging verse divides the text into two complementary halves also indicates that to the Quechua speaker the two units are considered to be specific rhetorical or cognitive units; that is, the two complementary halves are not just an artistic expression but also overlap with two major rhetorical units, whether they be called "acts" or something else.

7.3.1.2 Rhetorical patterns: The profile of the text

It is interesting to notice that in the first part, *-ñah* the 'narrative past' (the equivalent of *-sqa* in Coracora and *-naq* in some other varieties of Quechua B) is used consistently throughout. As pointed out earlier (chapter 5), the use of this suffix varies a lot across varieties, as well as between individuals of the same variety. Here it looks like the whole first part is setting the stage for the third scene where the fox is in focus. This scene, which is the climactic part of the story, is also introduced in the bridge, with three repetitions of the fox's descending the hill, drawing the listeners' attention to what is to come. The narrator seems to have chosen to use *-ñah* for the episodic development until he arrives to the most crucial event(s).[2] The use of *-ñah* then occurs only once more, marking the culminating point (verse 11) which relates the sad fate of the fox.

Scene I is an irregular triplet for the use of connectives. It sets the stage as well as starts off the episodic development; its function is that of the inciting moment. Verses 2 and 3 seem to keep the focus on the same subject —both participants—although it could be that the fox alone is the one

---

[2]Could it be that the narrator has learned the first part of the story, while the second part is his creative continuation of it? See also 6.2.3.3, specifically the last paragraph and footnote 7.

7.3 Patterns found in the Shausha texts 167

speaking in verse 3. Moreover the same verses are not marked by the connective *chay-pita*. The connective occurs in the next verse, verse 4, setting off the episodic development of the story through the use of the connective (and possibly also through the change of subject). In the Coracora texts I mentioned the ambiguity of this scene caused by the use of the different tense markers and its bridging nature as being both stage and setting off the episodic development. This is seen in a similar way in this text. Although the tense marker is the same, the connective or the lack of it seems to play a similar role. As can also be remembered, Longacre says that in a shorter text, stage "may run into Inciting Moment."

Scenes II and III, the major episodic units, each contain three verses, each beginning with the sentence-initial *chay-pita*, each with a change of subject. Verse 7 in scene II is lengthy and elaborate: it includes two reportatives, both within the same grammatical sentence but marking two different events. This is a crucial point in the story, possibly a climax of the first part, relating that the frog has already arrived at the bottom of the hill. Verse 11, on the other hand, is the culminating event of a second climax, telling of the fox's death. Tension has been building through the frogs' croaking already in the pampa (v.10), as opposed to the fox's struggle coming downhill, verses 8–9, with the burst of tension in verse 11. Verse 11, as already noted, also has the tense marker *-ñah*, which may indicate a reversal of fortune. Interestingly both in verses 10 and 11, as well as in verse 7 the different-subject switch-reference marker *-pti* occurs, while it is absent in all other verses of the text implying a semantic switch of referent (cf. the information in footnote 3).

Verse 11 signals that this is the way out of the predicament for the frog who would have been eaten by the fox. This is not clearly expressed in this text, but it is probably a fact known to the Quechua people. It is clearly expressed in the same story in the Coracora text displayed in chapter 6. However, it is the following scene, scene IV—the denouement and the conclusion—which states that the frog has won, the frog is being honored with a golden medal, as opposed to the sad fate of the fox. The latter is said to be lying in the middle of the hill with his stomach burst, (verse 14, which concludes the story). This verse also lacks *chay-pita* and indicates the conclusion of the story. What is significant for this scene is the elaboration within verses 12 and 13, each verse containing two independent clauses; both marked through the use of *-shi*. It is unclear to me why *-shi* occurs in the elaborations in these verses except that *-shi*, as already noted, seems to have a function in the marking of sub-lines in certain sections of the story. It is possible that the use of *-shi* in these lines indicates that they are considered crucial by the narrator and as such are pragmatically marked, receiving a higher status in the hierarchical ordering than what would normally be expected. It could also be that the lines are necessary in order to create a rhetorical pattern typical of the denouement and/or final suspense of a story, as was suggested in the discussion of the Coracora texts in the previous chapters.

The final scene, scene IV, as noticed in most of the Coracora texts, shows a longer focus on each referent. There is a possible change of referent between verses 12 and 13 so that verse 12 focuses on the frog making the bet with the fox, while the reference to a frog in verse 13 might be to any frog in general. The elaborations in verses 13 (the poisonous medal) and 14 (a crushed stomach) include a switch of subject referent; but these subjects are not animate, but body parts of the animate participants involved. On observing the pattern for the final suspense found in the Coracora Watuchi texts and the same-subject (SS) switch-reference marking for the latter part of the texts, I am prompted to note that Stirling (1993) claims that in many languages they would use SS marking for body parts, although according to sentence grammaticality you would expect different-subject switch-reference marking. I do not know whether this applies as a general rule to Shausha Quechua or any other variety of Quechua.[3]

The reportative (-*shi*) is of course also ascribed other functions in the Quechua languages (Weber 1989, section 21.1.2 and section 21.2; and Floyd 1999, section 6.3), apart from my definition of it as also a possible marker of verse, explained in chapter 4. It is likely that different functions overlap. In fact, given that artistic patterning is encoded by the speaker and discerned by the hearer, it is natural that differing artistic abilities between hearer and speaker will at times result in differences of communicated artistic patterns. The result can be a mismatch, or ambiguity, or a failure to communicate any pattern.

The very final sentence—not marked by the reportative—was a comment/reflection by the speaker.

7.3.1.3 Rhetorical patterns: The salience scheme of the text

As has already been stated above, the Shausha texts operate with different connectives than those used in the Coracora texts, typically *chay-pita* which does not carry explicit switch-reference markers. However, there is

---

[3]Verse 11 could imply something different though since there is a marked switch of referent (through the use of -*pti*) although one of the referents is a body part. However, this verse has been analyzed as the culminating point and, as has been noted, -*pti* tends to occur at such points (in some texts even when the referent is the same). Nevertheless, the switch of referent here accounts for a regular pattern of switch of referent for the whole stanza.

7.3 Patterns found in the Shausha texts

a quite regular rotation of subject in consecutive verses so that the resulting pattern is similar to that of the Coracora Quechua texts. The rotation of subjects generally goes hand in hand with the use of the connective *chay-pita*.

The parts that differ from the pattern are the scenes containing the stage (scene I) and the denouement (scene IV), a pattern also observed in the Coracora texts.

The bridge (verse 8) does not keep the focus on the previous participant, the frog, but changes to the fox. Verses 8 and 9 could be considered one structural unit where chay-pita occurs in the middle of a longer sentence structure.[4] The part of the sentence that I've analyzed as verse 8 has been fronted, I believe, in order to function as a bridge between two complementary halves, as well as enhancing the triplet patterning. The fronting also serves to change focus and provide the setting for the climactic events to follow and could be considered to mark a turning point or a change of vantage point in the story. I have chosen to regard the unit as constituting two verses, 8 and 9. By doing so, the neatness of the triplet pattern stands out. However, the pattern of rotated subjects might be slightly obscured.

From the discussion above, one could conclude that the rotation of subject, normally going along with the connective *chay-pita*, is what gives the text its forward motion. This pattern is most typical of the major episodic units. However, in the last scene, scene IV, verse 13 shows both markers but cannot be said to be an event; it is rather a piece of important information. Similar irregularities were noticed in the Coracora texts. A proposed justification of this fact was the need to conform to an artistic pattern, considering the stanza as a big macro-event moving the story forward. According to Chafe, as noted in chapter 5, it is not unusual that aspects from other information levels (or other centers of interest) occur within a given center of interest corresponding to a mental image activated at the time.

7.3.1.4 In conclusion

As with the Coracora texts, the Shausha texts show departure from expected general patterns. It seems as if the text at times complies first of all with rhetorical needs and excludes a parallel patterned stanza of repeated initial connectives in non-episodic material, and at other times complies with an artistic pattern through the use of *chay-pita* with non-episodic material. I do not attempt to explain each departure, but the form in which the text is displayed in figure 16 demonstrates a very obvious pattern,

---

[4]The original publication shows verses 8 and 9 as one long sentence. The text in its original publication is, however, not displayed as having artistic patternings.

structured in a way that suggests artistic refinement. This is particularly noticeable in the case of the triplet scenes, the repeated connectives in the two middle stanzas, as well as the dual composition of the story as a whole, signaled by a bridging verse. This verse introduces the climactic scene and as suggested with the Coracora texts, by occurring in the middle of the text, it might be marking a turning point in the story. Its bridging function may not be so obvious in this text, as we leave one major participant behind in order to focus on a new one already introduced in the very beginning of the text.

7.3.2 Patterns of other texts

The text provided in 7.3.1 showed a neat pattern of triplets. It also showed an obvious pattern of complementary halves. However, not all the Shausha texts at hand readily demonstrate such a pattern. In the following I will present the graphic representations of two texts with a few additional comments. In order to avoid repeating myself, the rhetorical patterns will only be discussed in section 7.3.3 where the Shausha texts and the Coracora texts are compared.

7.3.2.1 *The text* El Zorro y la Vizcacha I

There is no real stage to this story. There is a concluding verse, followed by a narrator's comment (which is not, strictly speaking, part of the story; see appendix 6). Apart from the final verse which has no matching introduction or stage at the beginning, artistically the story displays a nice pattern of three triplets, between which occur two bridging verses. But is it possible to detect any complementary halves in this structure? As can be remembered from the analysis of the *Mankapa Cuenton* in chapter 6, the middle scene seemed to serve various functions at the same time; although forming a unit—a scene—there was some movement between different locations involved. Specifically, the scene involved moving from one scene to another. The first part of the scene (a couplet stanza) served as a conclusion to the previous scene, while the last part of the scene (also a couplet stanza) served to provide the setting for the following scene. At the same time the two stanzas formed a scene or a "center of interest" in Chafe's terms. A similar pattern can be perceived in this middle scene, which is regularly marked through the repeated connective in consecutive verses and as such also displays a neat triplet pattern complying with the pattern of the previous and following scenes.

7.3 Patterns found in the Shausha texts

Although it is hard to make complementary halves of a triplet pattern, on closer scrutiny, the last verse (9) of scene II seems to consist of two lines. It might be stretching the analysis to say that another connective, *chay-traw* 'that-LOC (location)' followed by *-shi*, plays a role in this verse forming a complementary half to the first two and at the same time providing the setting for the next scene. The events of this final scene are at a different location but are viewed from afar, up above on a hill, at the location to which *chay-traw* refers. In fact, bridging scenes involving movements between locations within the scenes seem to occur in the middle of a story to divide the text into two consistently patterned complementary halves. We saw this occur in several of the texts so far examined, including the Coracora *Juan del Oso* text. It has also been observed that these bridging scenes or bridging verses occurring in the middle of the story might rather be treated as major "turning points" in the story. They can of course serve a double function. In the discussion of the previous text it was also seen that each of the two complementary halves also may constitute a rhetorical unit, a possible "act." Figure 17 shows the structure of the text *El zorro y la vizcacha I*.

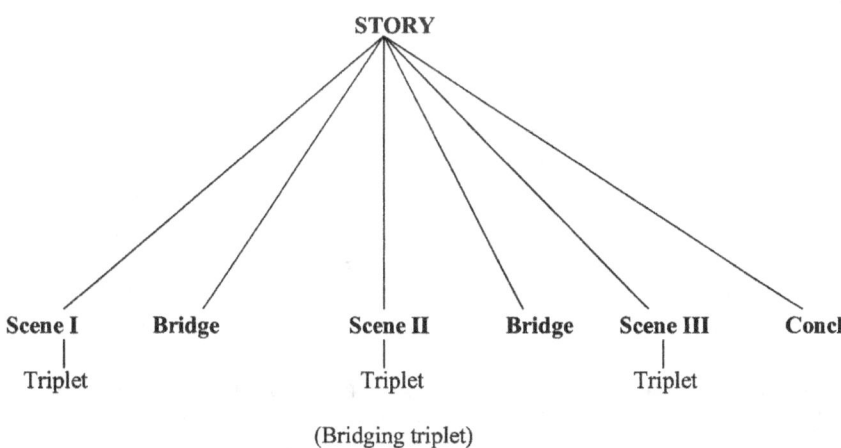

Figure 17: Structure of *El Zorro y la Vizcacha I*

7.3.2.2 The text El Zorro y la Vizcacha II

The text *El zorro y la vizcacha II* (appendix 7) is different from the ones we have looked at so far and is less consistent with respect to both structure and rotation of subjects. There is a triplet pattern to the scenes but it is not as obvious as in the other texts because the initial *chay-pita* is not as consistently used. The scene that is most consistent in the use of the initial *chay-pita* is the final scene which one would expect to be less consistent than the rest according to the analyses of the other texts.

The story consists of four scenes. The narrator takes us right into the story in the first scene; the second scene gives background information and carries the features of stage; it is as if the narrator forgot the stage and adds it as an afterthought. Interestingly the second verse of scene I lacks the sentence-initial connective *chay-pita* but the subordinated verb referring back to the previous action carries the switch-reference marker *-pti*, announcing a change of subject or referent. However, this structure breaks with the pattern found in the other texts.[5] In scene III, the final verse, there is an inverted word order where the subject occurs before *chay-pita*. This might serve to draw specific attention to the fox. If so, it is evidence that such a textual function (focus of interest) may supersede the artistic pattern, at least as far as this narrator is concerned.[6] Another possibility would be that the verse is marked as a setting to the next scene at the same time as it is part of the actual scene, scene III. It is reasonable to believe that the word order both serves to draw attention as well as indicating that a new unit is coming up.

The text can be graphically represented as in figure 18. Does this text show an artistic pattern of complementary halves? Four scenes should make that easier, but scene III seems to be the scene indicating movement between the scenes involved as well as a switching of focus on the participants involved. Yet, this scene occurs as the third scene with only one more following it, and as such is not dividing the text into two halves, except for its being itself the first part of the second half of the story. It is a possibility that the narrator at the time of telling the story did not consider the background information in scene II as part of the story; the information could have been added as a specific explanation to the linguist collecting the story; a Quechua audience might already have this knowledge fixed in their minds. If this is the case, the pattern of this story would turn out to be similar to the one above but missing the interspersing bridges. The textual structure would consist of three consecutive triplets

---

[5]It could be that the use of the different-subject switch-reference marker here indicates the inciting moment. As noted, for some of the other texts analyzed, the use of the different-subject switch-reference marker seems to occur with climactic points and has also been noted to occur with inciting moment. Cf. previous discussions on the nature of climax and inciting moment.

[6]This was alluded to in the analysis of the first Shausha text. It could be that the narrator of all these texts about the fox is the same and that the stories were told one after the other during the same setting, which could also explain the lack of proper stages in the latter texts.

as shown in figure 19. The reader can also see that the final verse of scene II, (scene III in figure 18), contains two clauses marked by the reportative *-shi* and shows similarities with the final verse of scene II in the text represented in figure 17. It is possible to treat this scene as having a bridging function, concluding the previous scene by departing the scene and providing the setting for the next through a switch of focus in the last verse. However, the last scene also displays a switching of focus between different locations, if not exactly a bodily moving between them.

Although all the stories show some artistic refinement, it has to be remembered that the stories have been handed down through generations. They might originally have been created according to a previous artistic canon but not perceived as such by the present generation, at least not on the conscious level. This might also explain why pragmatic-rhetorical functions seem to supercede the artistic patterning on several occasions, as alluded to earlier. It can also be remembered from the introduction to this chapter that the Shausha area has been greatly influenced by Spanish language and culture for generations, and some of the missing artistic features may be due to the influence of Spanish. Another explanation is that individuals have different gifts as far as artistic presentations are concerned. In the previous analyses it has been suggested that the storyteller might not have been able to handle both artistic and rhetorical-pragmatic functions at the same time.

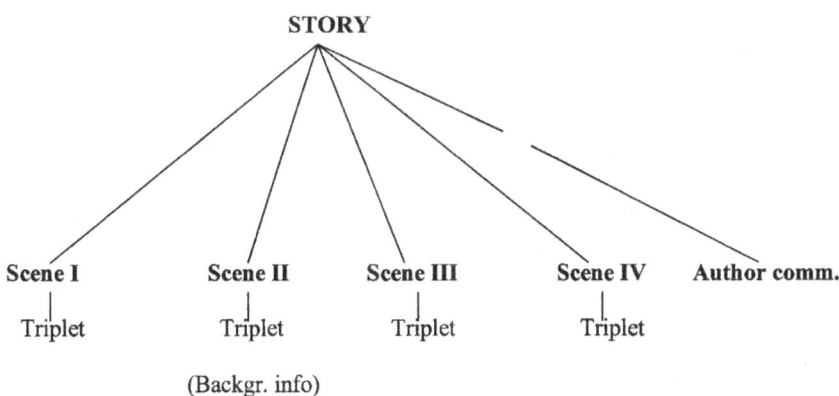

Figure 18: Actual structure of *El Zorro y la Vizcacha II*

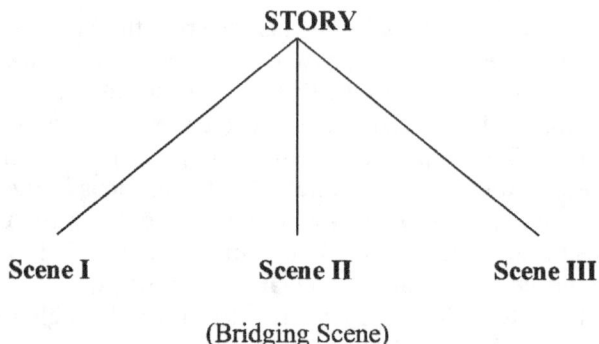

(Bridging Scene)

Figure 19: Possible structure of *El Zorro y la Vizcacha II*

7.3.2.3 The text Juan del Oso

Artistic patterning

At first glance the *Juan del Oso* text does not demonstrate any clear surface patterns that structure the text into stanzas of three, as we have seen in the other Shausha texts analyzed; there is only one triplet stanza that makes a consistent use of the initial *chay-pita*. Yet the verses are marked by the use of the reportative *-shi* and a very consistent rotation of subjects, sometimes marked through the use of switch-reference suffixes. However, since there are few bridging verses, there is no easily detected grouping of three based on the change of subject. The triplet units can best be discovered based on their semantic unity, that of forming a little scene. According to Hymes (1981:319), when units/patterns are first discovered based on surface features you can also discover them where the surface features are absent. The lack of surface patterns in the present text may be due to the influence of Spanish. As mentioned in the introduction to this chapter some of the storytellers have known Quechua since childhood but have not necessarily spoken it much. The use of Spanish in a couple of instances in the text may indicate that the storyteller is not completely confident in the Quechua language. The storyteller might have excluded the repetitious connectives on grounds that such "tedious" repetition would not be considered good literary style in Spanish. He might also have chosen to tell the story his own way, but obviously has obeyed underlying semantic and artistic patterning, as the analysis of the text shows.

The text is easily divided into three acts, based on both semantic unity and major locations (the cave, the village, the city). Moreover, each act consists of exactly three scenes. The final scene in the first two acts (scene

7.3 Patterns found in the Shausha texts

III and scene VI) indicates a moving off from a major location and alerts the audience of a new major rhetorical unit where new events will be taking place in another major location. Between the acts there are also bridging verses that likewise serve to emphasize the changes already alluded to in the final scenes. In the case of the bridges, they refer back to the previous events as well as point forward to following events. In the text at hand, bridging verses do not play a role in setting smaller scenic units apart but rather indicate transitions to bigger rhetorical units (and major locations), referred to as acts. The final scene of act III is the final suspense and a short concluding verse telling that *Juan del Oso* has become rich.

In order to comply with the basic triplet patterning for the scenes, I have considered a short introductory sentence marked by the narrative past as part of the first act, although not part of the first triplet scene. It functions both as a heading for act I (possibly the whole story), as well as setting the scene for the same act. In a parallel way I have considered the two final verses as part of the final act, although not part of a scene. These concluding verses both conclude the act as well as the whole story. However, the two verses do not hang together well and seem a bit confusing. The first brings *Juan del Oso*'s mother back on stage as he shows his gained riches to her, while the next is a repetition of the promises as expressed by the priest in the final scene. The story ends with an author comment, which is, as expected, not marked with *-shi*.

Apart from a neat division into acts of three scenes, the text can also be conceived of as two complementary halves, where scene V, rather than being of a bridging nature, indicates a turning point in the story and possibly marks a reversal of fortune (e.g. the event that forces Osito (and his mother) to leave the village) through the use of *-ñah* as well as the focus on one and the same referent, that is, Osito. However, the following scene indicates a moving on to a new location, the city, and a new act in the rhetorical, as well as the artistic, structuring of the text. A bridging scene, referred to as a possible "turning point" was also noticed in the middle act of the Coracora *Juan del Oso* story (as well as in some of the other stories discussed earlier). The pattern which can be seen in figure 7 turns out to be very similar to that of the Coracora text, although the Coracora version is much longer.

The major structure of the text can be graphically represented as in figure 20; the introductory sentence and the conclusion are not shown.

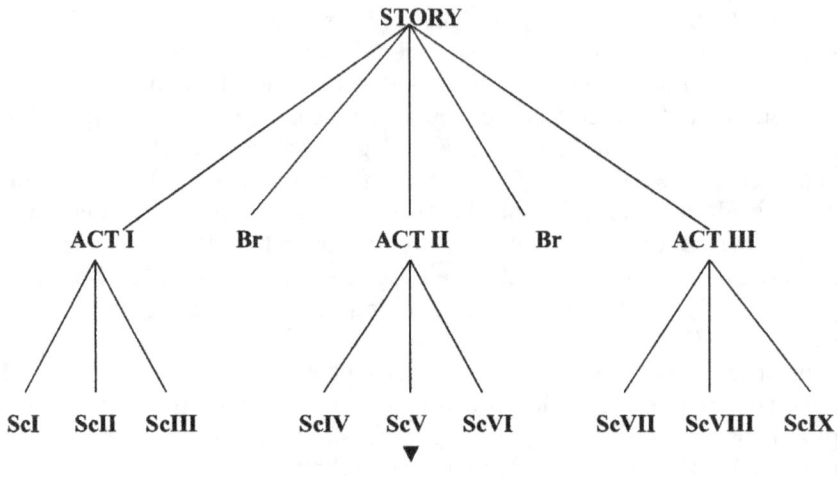

Figure 20: Structure of *Juan del Oso*

The graphic presentation does not show that each scene equals a triplet stanza. Apart from a pattern of complementary halves, the text shows nice parallel patterns between different levels, in that the story consists of three acts, each act consists of three scenes (stanzas), and each scene consists of three verses. Moreover, there is a horizontal parallel pattern in the consecutive three scenes of the same structure within each act, as well as on the level below, where you find three consecutive verses in each scene.

Rhetorical patterns: The profile of the text

An examination of the plot structure of the text does not reveal any specific surface structure features that determine the different parts of the text, except for what was mentioned in relation to the artistic patterning, e.g. the use of *-ñah* in the introduction and in scene V, the turning point of the story.

Scene II is the only scene that shows a consistent surface pattern. It uses the initial connective *chay-pita*, followed by the reportative *-shi*, and shows rotation of subjects. But the semantic main event line of this unit is most irregular. Possibly scene I sets the stage, while this unit marks the inciting moment, the birth and the coming of age of the son of the woman. The second verse also foreshadows the next stanza and in addition carries the tense marker *-ñah* which could be marking the setting for scene III as

7.3 Patterns found in the Shausha texts

well as the crucial event of Juan del Oso turning eight years of age; it is at this moment in time that things start happening in order to change their situation. As noted, *-ñah*, is also a marker of crucial and climactic events (see also 7.3.3) and as discussed with the Coracora texts, features of climax also occurred with the inciting moment.[7] The last verse, however, is not an event but a description of their situation in the cave. I am not able at this point to give any satisfactory explanation for the irregularity of this scene, except that it seems as if the author is lumping together a lot of information at once from different centers of interest.

As noted, scene V marks a turning point in the story. The following scenes, scenes VI and VII, seem to lead up to the climactic part, building tension. The first scene contains a dialogue where mother and son are sent away from the village; the second concludes with a very long monologue by the priest of the church in the capital, giving promises to Osito if he succeeds in killing the condemned priest (spirit).

Scene VIII, relating how Osito succeeds at his task, includes the very climax of the story with the culminating point in verse 30. Verse 29 shows a repetition of events (marking the introduction to the climactic part in some of the texts analyzed above), the repeated event also including an elaboration as well as a switch of referent and the use of the different-subject switch-reference marker in the final line; the use of the different-subject switch-reference marker also occurs in verse 28 introducing the scene (cf. footnote 7). Verse 30 concludes with the fact that the condemned spirit is beaten to pieces. This event is marked by the punctiliar *-li*, which also occurs a few other places in the text, in relation to events that might be of crucial nature seen from the perspective of the narrator (see scenes IV and V). This is, however, only a guess on my part.

The denouement is a long monologue where the priest is fulfilling his promises to Osito thereby resolving Osito's situation. The focus is on Osito and his deeds, noted through the way the priest is addressing him in vocative form a couple of times. However, this fact cannot be said to be an indication of the denouement, for the same features occur in the monologue of scene VII. I am sure there is more to discover in the structure of this text, but as far as the connectives and the rotation of subjects are concerned, they cannot be said to mark this unit in any specific way, contrasting with the Coracora texts.

---

[7]However, verse 9 in scene III makes use of the DS marker which, as noted, for some of the other texts seems to have occurred with climactic points as well as the inciting moment in some cases. The DS marker in this text is used more frequently. Sometimes it seems to start off new scenes and functions in a similar way as *ina-pti-* in the Coracora texts, although not marking each verse of the scene. But it could be that its function in the Shausha texts analyzed is primarily to mark crucial scenes or events. See the following discussion on the perceived climax of the story.

Rhetorical patterns: The salience scheme of the text

The lack of a consistent use of sentence-initial connectives makes it difficult to discover rhetorical patterns. However, there are features similar to those of other texts, particularly in regards to the salience scheme of the text and the rotation of subjects advancing the event line. This suggests that the rotation of subject apart from the use of connectives is what indicates which events belong to the main event line (or, maybe better, using Chafe's terminology, which events are of higher acuity versus those of less acuity). But, as was noticed in some of the earlier texts analyzed, there are events or states of a backgrounding nature that are marked as main events according to the surface criteria given earlier, and this may be due to some traditional artistic pattern where such features were prevalent, but which at the present time has gotten lost for the text in general. Also, according to Chafe, background information may be just as important to narrative processing as events on the main event line; and according to Kalmár one needs to think in terms of important information, rather than in terms of events. It has also been suggested (see 7.3.1.3) that the stanzas as units (centers of interest) are moving the story forward, and that these may contain information from different centers of interest, for example pieces of background information.

This could, however, also suggest that neither the connectives nor the switch of reference serve the function of indicating the main event line in general, but rather that both are first of all markers of a specific artistically patterned skeletal structure, and as a consequence, they also quite consistently turn out to be marking what seem to be main events—or at times important information. Weber (pers. comm.) believes that it is the other way round, that the sequence of events gives rise to the use of the connective *chay-pita* and the rotation of subject antagonist, protagonist, gives rise to the switch-reference or the rotation of subject. Chapter VIII provides a further discussion of this issue.

In conclusion

Although the connectives do not play a specific role in structuring the text at hand into triplets, the text nonetheless displays a structure much like that identified in the other texts. Here the essential criteria are rotation of subject and the semantic unity of verses in stanza triplets comprising a small scene.

On a higher level one can detect a division of the text into complementary halves, much like that noticed before in the other texts. Finally, the story shows a parallel pattern based on the number three, hierarchically between levels, as well as horizontally on one and the same level.

7.3.3 Shausha texts and Coracora texts compared

The texts at hand show clear corresponding patterns with the Coracora texts, both on the artistic level as well as on the rhetorical levels. In the following sections the more typical patterns of the Shausha texts will be discussed and compared with those of the Coracora texts.

7.3.3.1 Artistic patterns

Following my analysis of the Coracora texts in chapters 5 and 6, most of the Shausha texts can be analyzed into quite clear structures of stanzas. In the case of the Shausha texts, these are always triplets corresponding to little scenes—much like the Coracora *Juan del Oso* text—interspersed occasionally with bridging verses. Movements between different locations are also noticeable, although maybe not so consistently related to each switching of the triplet scenes.

The triplet verses are nearly always marked by the reportative *-shi*. Apart from *Juan del Oso*, the verses of episodic nature are generally introduced by the sentence-initial connective *chay-pita* 'that-ABL'. In most instances *chay-pita* and *-shi* co-occur. The very few instances where a verse or verses in the triplet stanza are marked only through the occurrence of *-shi* 'RPT' happen particularly to stanzas constituting a stage. However, a semantic theme unites the verses in clusters of three to a scene, that is, a stanza triplet, which suggests that also to the Shausha Quechua speaker the scene is a very real cognitive unit.

Although switch-reference markers occasionally occur, they do not seem to play the major role in the artistic pattern formation that we noticed in the Coracora texts. But interestingly, in the texts at hand the regular change (rotation) of subjects between verses also plays a role in the structuring of the texts. In most texts the rotation of subjects plays a part in creating the triplet pattern, much as in the Coracora *Juan del Oso* text. In the Shausha *Juan del Oso* text, the rotation of subjects—as well as the notion of a scene—plays the major role in the pattern formation.[8] Other surface features do not so consistently occur as in the other texts.

---

[8]As mentioned earlier, in the book *Tradición oral andina y amazónica*, Hornberger (1999) has analyzed two lengthy texts from two other Southern Quechua varieties. Although she does not discuss rotation of subject in regards to the artistic patterning or in terms of rhetorical structuring in "my" terms, she nonetheless shows in display of the second act of the two texts that there is a constant rotation of subject, or in her terms *cambio de actor* or *cambio de locutor* ('change of actor' or 'change of speaker').

However, the general pattern suggests the same kind of patterning as in the Coracora texts, albeit with different surface manifestations.

In the Coracora texts the bridging verses were typically identified through the use of the same-subject switch-reference marker attached to the connective word *ina-*, the focus staying on the previous referent. The switch-reference markers are not attached to the string *chay-pita* in the Shausha texts; however, the bridging verses keep the focus on the previous referent. On a few occasions, focus was on the next referent to occur, providing the setting for what comes next, as was seen in the 'Fox and the Frog' text in section 7.3.1. Moreover, the bridging verses typically lack the sentence-initial connective *chay-pita;* occasionally there is a reversal of order where the connective occurs within the verse, not at the beginning of it. However, often there are no bridges between stanzas.[9] As noted, in the Shausha *Juan del Oso* text the bridges rather occur between major rhetorical units—the acts—and mark transitions between major locations.

One can also conclude from the patterns observed that the act is a real cognitive unit to the Shausha Quechua speaker's mind, much in the same way as for the Coracora Quechua speaker. This is particularly noticeable in *Juan del Oso*, which forms a pattern of three acts divided by interspersing bridges, each act consisting of three scenes. And as discussed in relation to the analyses of some of the shorter Coracora texts, it is also a question whether the bridges or bridging scenes in some of them mark divisions between acts rather than scenes, as perceived by the Quechua speaker.

The patterning of complementary halves is not so readily perceived in the Shausha texts as in the case of the Coracora texts, although on closer scrutiny this principle of patterning plays a role in the formation of most of the texts displayed in the graphic representations and the discussions of the texts analyzed.[10]

7.3.3.2 Rhetorical patterns: The salience scheme of the texts

In the Coracora texts it was noticed that the *ina-* connectives played an important role in marking the event line. The analysis showed a difference beween the *ina-pti-* and *ina-spa-* verses as they functioned to mark main events versus events of a more backgrounding nature. The latter typically occurred in what was analyzed as bridging verses between scenes (that is, introductions and conclusions, or serving as both) and

---

[9]This is also observed in a couple of other Shausha texts which are not focused on here but referred to in chapter 8.

[10]This same feature can also be noticed in the texts referred to in footnote 9, although not talked about in the same terms in the analyses of the texts.

could be perceived as secondary storyline events, according to Longacre's salience scheme.[11] The former always played a part in the development of the main events (events of high acuity) through a constant switch of reference within what was perceived as centers of interest moving the story forward.

In *Juan del Oso*, we saw that the *ina-spa-* verses were typical of the conclusion of the story as a whole. As such, the *ina-* connectives seemed to play a role in both marking the salience scheme of the text as well as specific parts within the plot structure or profile of the text—in addition to the role of forming a specific artistic pattern.

According to the discussion on the artistic pattern formation and the similarities pointed to between the texts from the two varieties of Quechua considered, one can conclude that the rotation (switching) of subjects also plays a part in the Shausha texts to mark the salience scheme of the texts, since the rotation of subjects generally marks the main events (events with higher acuity or alternatively, the stanzas containing these). However, the discovery of this pattern in the Shausha texts is based on the already discovered patterning marked in the surface structure of the Coracora texts.

In sum, it has been noted:

- The connective *chay-pita* normally goes along with the rotation of subjects.
- It is reasonable to conclude that *chay-pita* is a surface marker of the main event line, even though there are exceptions.
- The bridging verses keep the focus on the same referent and typically also lack *chay-pita*.
- Within the triplets, when *chay-pita* is missing, its absence often happens in what is considered stage (background) information.

Questions in regards to the salience scheme/main event line will be discussed in more detail in chapter 8.

7.3.3.3 Rhetorical patterns: The profile of the texts

The last statement in the previous section relates to the profile of the texts as well, which has to do with the plot structure of the texts in terms of stage, inciting moment, episodic development, climax, denouement/final suspense, and conclusion. As discussed in previous chapters, the salience

---

[11]As discussed previously, at times these also marked non-events, which could be due to the need to conform to an artistic patterning, as well as marking important information.

scheme, profile, and artistic structuring are intervowen, but not always isomorphic.

In the Coracora texts analyzed, certain features were noted as characteristic of specific parts of the plot structure just mentioned. The stages were set apart from the main episodic development in various ways, e.g. by (1) the failure to use sentence-initial connectives consistently, (2) the use of the same-subject switch-reference marker, and (3) the use of the tense marker -*sqa* 'narrative past' (whose equivalent is -*ñah/-nah* in the Shausha Quechua).

In the case of the Shausha texts, there is no consistent use of the narrative past tense across texts in the parts that seem to serve as stages for the stories.[12] However, as alluded to above, there is also a tendency for the stages to keep focus on one referent in consecutive verses, which also lack the initial *chay-pita*. These facts are very general because the texts vary in how they begin. In fact, certain expressions in the texts about the fox suggest that the stories might have been told one after the other at the same time and as a consequence proper stages are missing. (See the individual texts as they are displayed in the appendices, as well as the text displayed in section 7.3.1.)

The episodic development, as already noted, is a result of the constant change of subject, and in most texts it occurs in conjunction with the use of *chay-pita*. According to Longacre, the part of the episodic development pertaining to the climax is often marked in a different way in the surface structure (the "peak" of the story), usually with less regularity, a "zone of turbulence."

It was noted in regards to the Coracora texts that the climactic parts showed irregular surface structure features, through extensive use of dialogues and the lack of the regular triplet markers (in the case of *Juan del Oso*), as well as the switching of participants within the same verse marked through the use of the different-subject switch-reference marker, as seen in some of the other texts. A specific aspectual suffix (-*rpari* 'sudden action') occurred as a marker of climactic points (the denouement in *Juan del Oso*), as well as marking other crucial events; otherwise there was no specific outstanding feature marking the climax of all the texts in

---

[12]*Juan del Oso* makes use of -*ñah* in the very first introductory sentence, setting the stage (the location) for the story, or at least the first part of it. The story about the fox and the frog, as noticed, makes use of the narrative past -*ñah* throughout the whole first part of the story, possibly setting the stage for the most important parts of the story, the climactic scenes. Levinsohn (pers. comm.) thinks that -*ñah* is used with events prior to or leading up to the climax, a claim that does not seem to hold true considering the analysis of the present texts (see also discussion below). Hintz (1996) says that for the texts she has analyzed, -*ñah* is used with settings, explanatory information, as well as a reversal of fortune. As mentioned earlier, Weber claims that the use of -*ñah* differs a lot across varieties of Quechua, as well as between individuals within one and the same variety.

7.3 Patterns found in the Shausha texts

the same way. In the Shausha texts at hand, the climactic part is introduced through repetitions of various kinds, in two of them through a twice and three times repeated sentence-initial connective (which can be seen in appendices 6 and 7). In *Juan del Oso* the aspectual suffix *-li* 'PNCT' occurs in the climax and with other crucial events of the story. As has been noted, also in the Shausha texts there have been switching of participants within verses of climactic nature, marked through the use of the different-subject switch-reference marker.

In some of the Coracora texts the climactic parts were also marked through the use of *-sqa,* possibly also indicating a reversal of fortune (seen in chapter 6 and the analysis of *Watuchi I*). According to previous studies (Hintz 1996), *-ñah,* the equivalent of *-sqa* for Quechua B varieties, seems to be marking a reversal of fortune. This could be said to be true of the use of *-ñah* in several of the shorter Shausha texts at hand, in the parts where the final unlucky fate of the fox is related. In some of the texts the culminating point falls together with the conclusion of the story, seen in the stories about the fox and the vizcacha in appendices 6 and 7. In the first fox story, displayed in figure 16, there is one use of *-ñah*, apart from its use in the whole first part of the story, which occurs in the sentence relating that the fox's stomach bursts. In the other two fox stories (in appendices 6 and 7), the first makes use of *-ñah* no less than four times in the same verse, the verse relating that the fox is crushed by a stone and as a consequence the fox's stomach also bursts. The last shows the same use; *-ñah* occurs no less than four times in the final verse relating that the fox is crushed by a stone coming from up the hill, sent down by the vizcacha. These facts seem to support the idea that *-ñah* is used to mark the culminating point of a story which also turns out to be a reversal of fortune. A reversal of fortune, however, may not always be detrimental to a character involved, although this is what is perceived in the texts about the fox. It might be that *-ñah* marks turning points[13] and/or culminating points in general and that these normally turn out to be a reversal of fortune.

In the Shausha *Juan del Oso* text there is what I have called a "turning point" midway in the story. The verses in this part make use of *-ñah* and might also in a detrimental way indicate a reversal of fortune for Juan del Oso. However, the story ends on a positive note for Juan del Oso but there are no uses of *-ñah* in this part of the text, which could imply that the use of *-ñah* indeed marks a reversal of fortune in the detrimental sense. However, there is not enough data to draw any certain conclusions in this

---

[13]The "turning points," according to my analysis, have occurred midway through the story. Hintz (1996), when explaining where *-ñah* occurs in the texts she has analyzed, for one of the texts, says that it occurs about midway through the story. She does not, however, make any claims in regards to "turning points" within the story.

respect. Nevertheless, the Coracora *Juan del Oso* story shows a parallel pattern midway through the story, in unit (20), that occurs in the very middle of what has been analyzed as a bridging scene, scene III. In chapter 6, triplet (20) was analyzed as a possible "turning point." This in an analogous way to the Shausha text is marked through the use of *-sqa*, the narrative past for this variety of Quechua.

In the longer Coracora texts the final rhetorical parts show similar patterns across texts. They often contain long monologues and the focus is longer on one participant at the time, noticed through the heavy use of the *ina-spa-* connective. I have discussed the nature of this particular section of the texts as containing a denouement and/or final suspense of the texts. In the case of most of the Shausha texts, these lack proper final suspenses due to the shortness of the texts and the fact that some of the profile patterns overlap in the concluding part of the stories. *Juan del Oso* has a final suspense which includes a longer monologue similar to what was observed in the Coracora texts, but this cannot be said to be a specific marker of the final suspense because longer monologues occur in other parts of the text as well.

In the Coracora texts the denouement/final suspense was normally followed by a conclusion. In the case of the Shawsha texts, the conclusions are sometimes followed by an author comment lacking *-shi*. In the case of one of the texts (found in appendix 7) the author comment and the conclusion fall together and also carry the reportative merged with another suffix to the form of *-sha:* 'RPT.THEN'.

7.3.3.4 In conclusion

Apart from the reportative, the connectives and also the changing of referent have played an important part in the artistic pattern formation in the texts from both varieties. In case of the changing of referent, it generally happens through the switch-reference markers in the Coracora texts (attached to the connective word) and through the rotation of subjects in the Shausha texts. The same connectives, switch-reference markers, or rotation of subject have also played an important role in the marking of the salience scheme and profile of the texts in both varieties concerned.

On higher levels, we have observed specific patternings in the forms of triplets and couplets (or some combination of the latter) forming scenes, which in turn have been forming acts. We have also noticed that the texts are structured according to a basic underlying principle of duality in the form of complementary halves in a mirror image. This principle of duality is perceived as operating on several levels in some of the texts.

8

Quechua Text Patterns and Their Implications

8.1 Preliminaries

In this final chapter I provide a summary of the results of the previous analyses of the texts, deal with various questions prompted by these analyses, and draw some tentative conclusions. The analyses reveal interesting issues in need of further investigation. These issues will only be dealt with briefly here because they would demand a separate study.

8.2 Structural patterns

8.2.1 Generalities

All the texts have been found to be patterned by verses forming couplet or triplet stanzas. In literary terms, the stanza consists in a "grouping of imagery" or a "logical division...in the thought or narrative" (Hamer 1966:6). In most texts a stanza corresponds to a little scene; in a couple of texts there are two or three stanzas to form scenes. The scenes in turn constitute acts. The acts and/or the whole texts (depending on length) are perceived as constituting complementary halves in a mirror image, which the graphic presentations of the texts clearly demonstrate.

The connectives, the evidential -*si*/-*shi*, the rotation of subject (marked through the switch-reference markers in Coracora and the underlying semantics in Shausha) each play a significant role in the artistic structuring of the texts. Moreover, these features also play specific roles in the information structuring of the text, indicating which events are considered main line events and which are not. In the following sections I will be discussing several factors related to these issues.

8.2.2 The function of the evidential

8.2.2.1 A formal marker of verse?

The basic unit in the artistic composition of the text is the verse. Minor questions have been raised about the definition and structure of the verse. The following discussion seeks to answer these questions.

The *verse* has been defined tentatively on the basis of (1) its constituency within a frame; for example, the triplet or couplet combinations forming stanzas in the texts, (2) its formal marking through the occurrence of the evidential -*si*/-*shi* RPT 'reportative, hearsay', and (3) the evidential's occurrence with the initial connectives in stanzas of episodic nature (*ina*- in Coracora, *chay-pita* in Shausha).[1]

In the Coracora and Shausha texts analyzed, the evidential -*si*/-*shi* 'RPT', with very few exceptions, occurs regularly in each structural unit defined as a verse. Normally it occurs on the initial element, which in the episodic units are usually the connectives.

In the Coracora texts, the connectives have typically been the *ina-pti-* and *ina-spa-* clauses. The *ina-spa-* clause has been analyzed as marking events of less acuity or of a subtly backgrounding nature, although they are events on the event line. According to Longacre's salience scheme they are marking secondary storyline. In a few instances the *ina-spa-* phrase lacks the formal marks of verse. My analysis here shows an apparent inconsistency, as I have analyzed the units introduced by these as either sub-lines or main lines according to the general pattern of the texts. In both *Watuchi* texts, these have been analyzed as sub-lines; this fits the overall pattern and strongly suggests that -*si* is indeed a marker of verse. However, in *Juan del Oso* the same connective clauses, lacking the evidential, have in certain parts been analyzed as marking a main verse line,

---

[1] Hornberger (1999:89) notes the use of the reportative. She says that in both texts that she analyzed (southern Peruvian Quechua) the reportative occurs as close to the beginning of the verse as possible, usually in the first word. However, she also notes that the use of the reportative in the two texts analyzed is different. In one of the texts, it "almost exclusively" occurs on the connective *hina*, while in the other text it occurs with other elements.

fitting into an otherwise consistent pattern. The lines marked in this way are in some intermediate position. Significant for all of them is that they occur in crucial parts of the texts, such as the climax, where, according to Longacre, deviations from the regular pattern is to be expected.

Moreover, in *Juan del Oso*, *-si* also occurs in some subordinate clauses or other clauses of a backgrounding nature. The function of *-si* in these seems to be that of marking sub-lines of a crucial nature.

In the Shausha texts, crucial parts of the texts also have similar sub-lines with *-shi* occurring in them. In *Juan del Oso*, at the climax, the order of elements is reversed, and *-shi* occurs with these elements in a final position (see appendix 8, scene VIII).

In sum, although the major function of the evidential in these texts may be that of formally marking the verse, the same evidential (or its absence) also has a specific rhetorical function in the marking of crucial parts of the texts. In the Coracora texts, the authors could have chosen between two different options in order to mark lines according to importance and still keep to the artistic pattern:

- by adding the evidential to subordinate events in order to raise the events to a higher level of importance in the information structure, or
- by leaving out the evidential but still using the event line marking connective, nonetheless suggesting an event of less acuity.

In the latter option, the events marked in this way conclude crucial episodic units, e.g. climactic episodes, suggesting a very close semantic tie to the preceding unit as elaborating or partly overlapping events, whether considered to be separate verses or sub-lines. The elaborations often create longer verses at climax.[2]

As I have indicated, the hearsay evidential can be used to demarcate a verse. Among other functions that Floyd (1999:135) ascribes to the hearsay evidential, is the function of being a grammaticalized marker of genre in Wanka Quechua, for folktales, legends, and myths. Although Floyd (p. 136) does not "deny the obvious connection between 'hearsay' and

---

[2]It may be significant that in many instances where *-si/-shi* occurs on clauses of subordinate nature there is a switch of focus, either a switch of participant or a switch of location, which might indicate that the evidential is a marker of focus of interest. However, as noted, switch of participant is marked through the use of the different-subject switch-reference markers in parts that are considered climactic in several texts. It could be that the different-subject switch-reference marker *-pti* and the reportative *-s(h)i*, together play a role of raising a subordinated event to a higher level in the information structure. That *-pti* has taken on such a discourse function is not strange considering that *-pti* together with the pro-verb *ina-* has been analyzed as marking main line or high acuity events. The suggested functions of *-pti* as a possible marker of climactic parts deserve further investigation.

folktales," he stresses that "the cognitive salience of the information source in the hearsay use has been bleached out of the folktale use" because "the original information source is lost." Although Floyd does not propose the evidential (-*shi* for Wanka Quechua) as a marker of verse, he still recognizes its formulaic nature in certain kinds of text.

The analysis shows that the verses form triplet or couplet combinations. In line with Hymes, the distinctive of a unit as a verse is its regular occurrence within a frame, not the regularity of parts (e.g. number of syllables) within the unit itself. This also suggests that the reportatives, although they occur with the verse, are not necessary in order to define the verse. The verse can be defined only in terms of its regular occurrence within a frame, that is, forming couplet and triplet stanzas. These in turn either equal or are part of forming scenes. However, this does not exclude the possibility of *-si/-shi* as a formal marker of verse.

The evidential's consistent co-occurrence with the connectives in the episodic units of the text also supports the idea of its function as a marker of verse. The connectives, apart from their cohesive functions in the texts, are obviously also of a formulaic nature. The structural units that they introduce normally occur in particular clusters of triplets and/or couplets. Their formulaic use is particularly obvious in the Coracora texts where the additional switch-reference markers also play an important role in the organization of the texts. The evidential is normally attached to the connectives. It is then natural to conclude that the evidential is also of formulaic nature when it occurs on its own in structural units of non-episodic nature.

The discussion above does not prove that *-si/-shi* is a marker of verse, but the patterns as outlined above and in previous chapters strongly suggest that it is. Nevertheless, the discussion above also indicates some overlapping functions of the evidential, and it is disconcerting that the verses are so different in structure and complexity.[3]

---

[3]The following information might be significant. Arnold (2004:158) says about Aymara songs that "Basic rhythmic cells and musical phrases are gradually extended and developed by the singers in ways that are homologous to the spinning out of a hank of fleece into long threads of sound," and that as a song develops (pp.164–165), the singer stretches certain musical cells "a little more in each verse, as if she were spinning out a hank of wool." She further mentions a song (p. 167) where a certain Aymara woman "as an older and more experienced singer, manages to interweave in a complex way a lyrical structure of couplets with a tripartite musical structure." As noted, my study does not consider patterns on lower levels which may include artistic patternings as of yet not recognized.

8.2.2.2 A marker of new information?

Weber (1989) noted for Huanuco Quechua that the evidentials play a part in the information structure of the sentence on discourse/text level, in the sense that the evidentials tend to occur with new information while the topic marker occurs on old or thematic information. The topic marker only occasionally occurs in our Coracora and Shausha texts.[4]

However, considering the use of the evidentials in the texts at hand, -*si*/-*shi* could certainly be said to occur in such a way as to mark or announce new information. For example, in the Coracora texts, the *ina*- connectives typically refer to previous events, that is, old information, while the added switch-reference markers tell whether the subject to come is the same or different from the one in the previous event. The additional -*si* 'RPT' could be announcing that what comes next in the sentence/verse is new information. It is also worth noticing that when a subordinate clause of any length occurs before the independent clause in the Shausha texts, the whole subordinate clause is considered the initial element and as such carries the evidential marker -*shi* on its final element. Most often the information given in the subordinate clause is a repetition or summary of previous events. Although the pattern does not create a theme-rheme profile of the sentence in the sense that it is perceived by Weber for the Huanuco variety where the topic marker -*qa* is involved, it is quite reasonable to think that the evidential is in fact announcing new information. This is only a strong tendency, as also Weber admits for the Huanuco variety. There are exceptions. Weber observed a basic pattern for the occurrences of the topic marker, the evidential, and the verb; he notes on the deviations from the pattern that "These deviations are not simply randomly distributed in a text, but constitute a rhetorical device for marking crucial points in a narrative" (1989:431).

Weber's findings seem to correspond well with mine. However, I suggest a slightly different interpretation for the use of -*si*/-*shi*: it marks the most basic information (including events, states, and background information) in the text, to be treated in the following discussion.

8.2.2.3 The evidential and skeletal structures

In the previous chapters we noted that the structural units called verses are extremely varied, both in length and structure. I believe that some of these units may also contain artistic features but, as stated earlier, a

---
[4]In the Ayacucho varieties -*qa* is used "to signal the topic or the theme..." (see Soto Ruiz 1976a:117); in Shausha the cognate suffix (-*ha*) occurs sporadically, glossed as 'topic', but its function is uncertain.

scrutiny of the verse is not part of this study. However, one is faced with the question of why there is such a difference between individual verses. Ralph Toliver (personal communication) suggested that the Quechua speaker operates with a kind of skeletal structure, though he did not elaborate on the nature of this structure. Toliver told me that one of his Quechua-speaking co-workers had given him the Juan del Oso story on two occasions; the first time in a very abbreviated form, at another time in a fuller form, filling in a lot of details.

The different graphic presentations of the texts analyzed may be indicative of different skeletal structures, which the author chooses for his particular story (maybe not consciously, although originally, in olden times it could have been so). Within the framework of these skeletal structures there is obviously room for much creativity at each telling. Much of this creativity presumably belongs to the past and has been passed down through the ages; the present tellers of the stories have learned both the skeletal patterns and much of the contents through multiple tellings by the older generations.

The basic unit in this skeletal structure is the verse, which at times consists of only one independent clause and at times includes various clauses of subordinate nature. The independent clause in the verse, introduced by an initial element containing the evidential -*si*/-*shi*, is required in the skeletal structure. When the independent clause is introduced by a connective in combination with -*si*/-*shi*, it plays a part in forming the episodic stanzas which move the story forward. Most detailed information or supportive material is given in a form subordinate to the independent clause, sometimes embedded within it in the form of nominal or adverbial clauses or direct quotations.

Based on study done on Pomabamba Quechua belonging to Quechua B, James Wroughton (1989) suggests that the indicative verb of the independent clause in Quechua forms a schematic thread of important events moving the story forward in a sequential order, but these events do not contain much in the form of sentiments, emotions, or other thematic information. The latter is all provided through various adverbial clauses as well as direct quotations. He includes stative verbs and verbs of cognition in his list of independent indicative verbs forming the schematic thread, but he does not include stage (setting) material. Wroughton's "schematic thread of important events" can be seen as an expanded version of what others have talked about in terms of main event line or foregrounded events. He does not propose any particular patterns for this schematic structure. He makes no mention of the connectives, the evidential, or the switch-reference markers in relation to this schematic structure. However, his insights in regards to the

8.2 Structural patterns

function of the independent clause as opposed to the subordinate clauses carry some significance for the present study as well.

In earlier literature dealing with information structure of texts, the main event line has often been defined in terms of temporal sequentiality (e.g. Payne, Hopper and Thompson). However, Chafe speaks in terms of "focus of interest" and also considers stage material and certain types of background information as part of the "backbone" of a narrative. It has also been noted that Kalmár stresses that languages have more than one means of expressing foreground and that sequentiality is only one of these means. He claims that quotes or dialogues belong to the foregrounded events. Quote-introducing verbs like 'say' and 'ask' do not carry much significance in and of themselves; we need to know what is being said. Moreover, Kalmár includes subordinate sentences as belonging to the foregrounded events but he does not include stage material. He is nonetheless concerned with the issue of "communicating essential information" rather than speaking about foreground in terms of sequentiality of the most important events.

Based on my analysis of the texts, I believe that the skeletal structure is formed by the independent clauses containing the most essential information or the most basic information. One could also conclude that all the basic information is marked through the use of -*si*/-*shi* since the evidential nearly always occurs right before the independent clause, either with the initial *ina-pti-*/*ina-spa-* connective clause or on some other initial element. I choose to call it the most basic information, in line with my findings and James Wroughton's (mentioned above). However, in line with Kalmár, I suggest that the direct quotations also belong to the most basic information. Normally, at least in the texts at hand, the quotation formula consisting of the verb *ni-* 'say' introducing a quote, also contains -*si*/-*shi*. Often a quote is both opened and ended through the use of the formula. In such cases it happens that both the beginning and ending formula contains -*si*/-*shi*. Considering the fact that Quechua tales often contain larger dialogic sections and may even be dialogic throughout, it seems necessary to consider the dialogues as belonging to the basic information structure. Another fact is that in several of the texts, *ni-* with the additional switch-reference marker functions as a connective to the previous quote in the sense of 'having said...'. In some varieties this form has developed into a regular connective, not necessarily referring back to a preceding quote.

Kalmár includes subordinate clauses in what he perceives as foregrounded material. I suggested earlier that -*si*/-*shi* on subordinate clauses in the texts have upgraded the clauses to a different level in the information structure. I suggest that in Quechua the information shared in subordinate clauses carrying the evidential are perceived as belonging to the basic information structure.

According to Olrik, a typical feature of folk narrative is that it is always "single-stranded"; that is, it uses dialogues to fill in details. This corresponds well with the findings of the present analysis. However, the single-strandedness in terms of basic information structures includes dialogues. I repeat a quote by Olrik here (in Dundes 1965:137): "With its single thread, folk narrative does not know the perspective of painting; it knows only the progressive series of basreliefs. Its composition is like that of sculpture and architecture; hence the strict subordination to number and other requirements." This view relates to Wallace's "figure and ground" perception in narration, where figure would stand for the sculptural part, the basrelief; the ground, corresponding to the perspective of painting, would not, according to Olrik, be of major importance in folk traditions. I believe this to be true of the Quechua narratives at hand too, although the narratives differ somewhat in respect to the "painting" or ground part. Some of the stories mainly consist of the basrelief—in my terms, the basic information—with very little additional information in terms of "painting." The lengthier Coracora *Juan del Oso* text is different, although the "painting" is often performed through elaborations added to the final verse of the triplets. These, which are introduced by the *ina-spa-n-si* connective, have been considered part of the basic information structure, according to my analysis of the evidential *-si* contained in the connective clause. Nevertheless, the *ina-spa-* verses have been analyzed as having a slightly backgrounding function or belonging to a secondary storyline, in Longacre's terms. If one carries the analogy of painting, figure, and ground further, a painting always shows "layers" of things at different distances in the perspective; so also does a narrative story. The means for showing this differs from language to language, as seen in the works of Longacre, Payne, and Jones and Jones referred to in chapter 3.

I conclude then that the evidential *-si/-shi* marks the basic information structure—an expanded basrelief, in terms of Olrik— rather than new information. How would the basic information structure relate to what has earlier been stated in regards to the initial connectives as (main) event line markers? I see two things going on at the same time; (1) the marking of basic information through the use of the evidential, and (2) the marking of main episodic events through the use of the connectives. In the episodic sections the two kinds of information usually overlap. A few lingering questions concerning the connectives as main event line markers will be dealt with in the next section.

8.2 Structural patterns

The graphic presentations of the various texts at hand also show the artistic nature of the basic information structures as these are organized into skeletal structures. The verse, in its most basic form consisting of an independent clause, is also the basic unit in this structure. It is not easy to decide whether the evidential marks the verse or the most basic information in the text, in terms of the independent clause (with the modifications referred to above; that is, the use of -si/-shi with subordinate clauses). It could indeed mark both.

It is tempting to conclude that the story itself imposes a skeletal structure in the form of verses and stanzas. From the point of view of the author, the basic information of the independent clause in the verse is obligatory; how much elaboration is given depends on factors like teller, audience, context, medium, and time restraints. In most cases the story would be known to the audience through repeated tellings in an oral setting. Maybe it is an art in itself to keep the story as short as possible without too much supportive information. Hymes (1981) suggests that among some North American Indian groups it seemed to be an art to be able to keep a story as short as possible.

I want to conclude by stating that the tentative definition as given earlier (section 5.3.1.3) of the evidential -si/-shi as a formal marker of verse in the texts at hand is indeed reasonable, although it cannot be conclusively defined as such, as the discussion above illustrates.

It is also to be expected that different varieties and maybe different authors have developed different systems and/or different ways of marking the information structures referred to above. In the Cusco[5] *Juan del Oso* (Manuelito, el Oso; see Loriot 1975) the evidential -si does not occur even once in the very lengthy text, although the suffix is otherwise used in the "hearsay" way, and also within folktales, according to Cusihuaman (1976:241). Why does it not occur in *Juan del Oso*? Was it considered to belong to a different genre in this variety of Quechua, or is it a missing feature due to the choice of the author? Or is it just not in the form of verse? These are questions that cannot be answered at this point.[6]

---

[5]Cusco Quechua is a neighboring variety of Ayacucho. Many Quechua speakers consider Cusco Quechua *the legitimate* Quechua.

[6]However, specifically based on the suffix -taq 'additive' occurring in units of episodic nature, certain groupings are perceived as forming patterns of a couplet plus a triplet to a scene. The suffix -taq seems to function in a similar way to that of *chay-pita* in the Shausha texts, in that it does not occur in the bridges. However, it often occurs with other connectives, e.g. *(h)ina*. Thus -taq could be a marker of verse of episodic nature or a marker of basic information in the scenes of episodic nature. As such it does not assume quite the same function as -si/-shi does in the other varieties considered so far. There also seems to be a specific interaction between the suffix -taq and the topic marker -qa which occur throughout the

8.2.3 Main event line

The discussion above suggests a difference between main event line, as traditionally recognized, and a basic information structure in the texts. In the preceding chapters I have talked also about the connectives as playing a crucial role in the marking of events of episodic nature, pushing the story forward, as well as constituting couplet and triplet stanzas. However, since it happens that the events forming stanzas are not necessarily in sequential order, I have proposed tentatively (chapter 5) in line with Chafe's view that it might be better to see the stanzas as "centers of interest" giving a story its forward motion. A "center of interest," according to Chafe, corresponds to a mental image. This would also be in line with the literary conception of a stanza as corresponding to a "grouping of imagery" or a "logical division" in a narrative (Hamer 1966:6). As stated earlier, this view of the stanza as moving the story forward is supported by the fact that many Quechua linguists perceive the clause and the paragraph, not the sentence, as intonational units in Quechua.[7] However, along with the events there is a consistent rotation of subject within the stanzas, that also provides for the sense of the forward motion of the story, in the underlying semantics in Shausha and marked in the surface structure through the switch-reference marker *-pti* 'different subject' in Coracora. In both cases this pattern is going hand in hand with the use of the connective. The two features interact in the main event line marking; however, there are a few additional factors to consider.

The stanzas have been analyzed as either corresponding to or playing a part in the forming of a scene. The bridging units typically occurring between scenes are also on the event line; but, these have been analyzed as having more of a subtle backgrounding function, in the sense of moving off and on scene, at the same time keeping the focus on the same subject (main participant). In Chafe's view these are events of less "acuity" or "resting places" (comparable with Longacre's secondary storyline) between "centers of interest" containing events of "high acuity" (focus of interest). One can conclude, then, that the connective in Coracora, occurring in both stanzas and bridges, marks all the events; while the switch of reference is what gives the story its forward motion, giving a feeling of rapid pace to the events. In the Shausha texts, on the other

---

text, in almost every sentence, comparable with Weber's theme-rheme structure of the sentence in relation to the evidential and the topic marker.

[7]In this respect, I have stated earlier that since I have worked on written (or at least transcribed) texts, I have not been able to check out whether the intonational paragraphs would correspond to the stanzas as they are perceived by me, although I suspect they would. This is an area of interest for a separate study.

8.2 Structural patterns

hand, the verse(s) in the interspersing "bridges" are typically not introduced by the connective *chay-pita,* unlike the verses in the triplet stanzas. This indicates that in Shausha, *chay-pita* normally marks main events.[8] *Juan del Oso* is an exception as the connective occurs only sporadically and the main events do not seem to be marked in any particular way. Could this have something to do with the evidential *-shi* playing a double function in an overlapping of basic information and event line information? This whole issue would be of interest for further research.

In conclusion, the different parts of the connective phrase play various functions in the text, although it is usually translated into Spanish as simply *entonces* 'then'. This is particularly evident in the Coracora text.

8.2.4 Which pattern gives rise to the other?

In the previous chapter (at the end of 7.3.2.3) the question was raised whether the connectives and the rotation of subject (possibly with switch-reference markers), creating the specific artistic pattern, give rise to the other functions that these features are perceived to have in the texts; for example, is the marking of the main event line a consequence of the artistic patterning and peculiar to the particular texts at hand? (As noted, there are other features, like the use of tense markers, that also play a role in this respect.) Weber, as noted earlier, thinks it is the other way round, that the sequence of events gives rise to the repeated connectives, and the rotation of subject antagonist, protagonist, naturally gives rise to the switch reference. I believe Weber has a point. The interaction of antagonist-protagonist would necessarily also cause rotation of subject and the use of the switch-reference marker *-pti* 'different subject' in Coracora. However, the specific groupings of these, as seen in the texts, do suggest that the pattern has been exploited for artistic reasons.

I studied *Juan del Oso* from other varieties of Quechua. In the text from North Junin, a neighboring variety of Shausha Quechua, I noticed a constant rotation of subject but not any consistent use of the connectives. I was not able to group the events in any nicely patterned stanzas. In Shausha from a slightly different variety from that quoted here, another *Juan del Oso* text shows a pretty constant switch of reference, normally going along with a constant use of the connective *chay-pita*. Irregularities are noticed at crucial points in the narrative.

This would support Weber's claim about the natural antagonist-protagonist rotation. But it would equally support my claim that the patterns are artistic in the way this rotation is grouped into neat triplet or couplet stanzas. Also, considering the bilingualism of the people of the

---
[8] Cf. Dooley and Levinsohn (2001:93–95) on what they call development markers.

area, there is a possibility that both the North Junin text and the Shausha text in their original forms had nicely patterned stanzas which have been lost in the course of time due to Spanish influence. In fact, in the Shausha text there are specific patterns in parts of the text that seem to be of artistic nature but which I have not yet been able to figure out.

The constant rotation of subject seems to be more than just a normal rotation of antagonist-protagonist. It looks as if the nature of the text (genre) demands such a pattern. Is there a possibility that the monologic texts are based on dialogic performances and turntaking and that the use of the evidential *-si/-shi* could also take on some other meaning than so far has been suggested for these particular kinds of text, e.g. more in terms of its basic meaning of 'hearsay'. As noted in section 4.1.2.2, Floyd says that the "hearsay prototype is characterized by short turns" but by "irregular marking" in more natural communication contexts. Whatever is the case, over time the evidential has developed into having a more formulaic nature, as also stated by Floyd; but does it have something to do with turn-taking? Certainly, the texts always also contain many dialogues, and Weber (1989:21–22) noted that some folktales are dialogic throughout, for which he provides a whole text as an example. I will not pursue this in detail here but leave the thought for further consideration.[9]

As has been mentioned many times, the consecutive initial connectives do not always suggest sequentiality of events in the texts; sometimes there are references to past events. This irregularity has been explained in terms of a need to conform to an artistic pattern. The stanzas have been analyzed in terms of centers of interest corresponding to a mental image. Although allowing information to occur from other centers of interest, e.g. in the form of flashbacks (cf. verse 33, appendix 1), this information would not necessarily fit into the grammatical pattern of the given center into which it is transposed. The verbal morphology of the additional information in the given stanzas in the texts shows that they are events prior to the other sequential ones in the stanza. Nonetheless, they adopt the connective implying sequentiality of events. In the Shausha *Juan del Oso* text a whole stanza, although it made use of the connective *chay-pita*,

---

[9]The concept of interchange between participants seems to be very prominent in the Quechua culture and applies to different verbal activities. For example, Gnerre (2004:371), as already mentioned, talks about riddles as a "dialogical enterprise." Lyons (2004:341) says about Ecuadorian Quichuas in the Province of Chimborazo that "Laborers harvesting barley...would sing in a call-and-response style known as *jaway*, as they advanced with their sickles across the field." According to an editorial note in the same publication (p.341) "these *jaway* harvest songs set the pace of the task of harvesting grain" and the highland Peruvian analogue is the *haylli*, a practice that stems from the time of the *Inca*. See article and footnote for more details with its references to other authors treating this theme. In conversation with a Quechua speaker a few years ago speaking the Junin variety, a neighboring variety to that of Shausha, he told me about this practice in the area that he came from.

otherwise showed a total lack of sequentiality of events. These facts would affirm that the connectives must also be of a formulaic nature in these texts. There is, of course, the possibility of seeing the connective as just a marker of events of episodic nature—even when these sometimes belong to a different center of interest.

Another Shausha text, *El burro perdido*, shows a consistent use of the connective *chay-pita* in nice groupings of triplet stanzas corresponding to scenes, but, it does not show consistent rotation of subject. This could be due to the nature of the text, as there is no obvious antagonist-protagonist interaction; rather it is a story about one man and the problems that arise around the disappearance of his donkey. If the irregularity is due to the nature of the text, this would support Weber's claim about the naturalness of the antagonist-protagonist rotation in the other texts. But even in this case, an original pattern of rotation of subject might have been lost, while the other patterns—perceived as artistic—persist (see my discussion in Bergli 2007).

8.2.5 Profiles of the texts

In the discussions above I have touched upon how the artistic patterns, as they are perceived, also function in marking certain parts of the profile of the text, that is, the plot structuring. I will not go into too many details here but share a few generalizations, as each text shows an individual structure. However, it needs to be stressed that although the texts are artistically arranged, they also comply with certain rules pertaining to the rhetorical plot pattern.

Most texts have an opening; often it overlaps with the stage. It has already been noticed that the rotation of subjects along with the specific connective patterns belongs to the episodic parts of the text. The stages typically lack a consistent use of these features and they typically keep the focus on just one participant. However, even the stages are perceived as verses contained in stanzas, marked by the evidential *-si/-shi*, and are often marked through the use of the narrative past tense markers: *-sqa* in Coracora, *-ñah* in Shausha. The stanzas containing the inciting moment typically have features of both stage and episodic development and moreover show features similar to those perceived at climax. It has also been noted that in the denouement and final suspense the focus is for a longer time on only one participant instead of the constant rotation in the previous units. This is manifested in the surface structure through the use of the *ina-spa-* connectives in the Coracora texts. In the case of the shorter Shausha texts, these typically lack final suspenses. The climax shows irregular stanzas through different connectives in the Coracora texts; additional elaborations creating lengthy verses occur in both varieties. In Shausha the subordinate clauses also contain the evidential, often in combination with the different-subject switch-reference marker, which otherwise is nearly non-existent in several of the texts. (It does, however occur with the inciting moment.) This is also evident in some of the Coracora texts, but elaborations also occur through additional *ina-spa-* clauses which lack the evidential, as was discussed in section 8.2.2.1. Moreover, the narrative past, *-sqa* in Coracora, *-ñah* in Shausha, tends to occur in climactic parts. One can indeed talk about a "bag of tricks," using Longacre's wording, for all the different devices available to mark the climactic parts. The texts also contain a conclusion, often an evaluating comment by the storyteller/author. In the shorter texts some of the specific parts mentioned above may overlap.

I have pointed out inconsistency in the use of the switch-reference markers. On occasion the different-subject switch-reference marker, *ina-pti-*, has been used when you would expect the same-subject switch-refernce marker *ina-spa-*. Stirling (1993) claims that such anomalies have to do with starting off a new rhetorical unit, indicating a switch in the spatio-temporal setting. My analyses show that the anomalies are rather due to rhetorical units or events perceived as crucial or climactic. It has also been noted that in many texts the different-subject switch-reference marker has occurred in subordinated clauses in such parts of the text, but complying with the underlying semantics of switch of referent. Considering all these facts, it is possible that the unexpected uses of the different-subject switch-reference marker do indeed occur because of the need to comply with an artistic pattern at the same time as it is a necessary rhetorical device to mark important events.[10]

It has also been noted that the same-subject switch-reference marker in the so-called "bridges" has been used when grammatically a different-subject switch-reference marker would be expected. In line with Stewart (1987) this usage has been explained in terms of keeping track of the main participant of the story.[11] It could, however, also be due to the need to keep to an artistic-rhetorical pattern creating a necessary division between triplets, as well as between scenes, announcing to the hearer the end of one scene and the beginning of a new, as has been discussed in detail in other chapters.

[10]Stirling, in general, does not talk about switch-reference markers in relation to poetic texts; she does, however, make reference to Woodbury (see below) and his perception of unexpected uses of the switch-reference markers in relation to rhetorical boundaries within texts that he conceives of as possibly texts of verbal art of some kind.

[11]This is also in line with Stirling's perceptions, although she explains it in somewhat different terms.

In Woodbury's study (1983), he makes note of one controlling independent verb with following (or maybe also preceding) appositional clauses where there is a tendency for surface structure (SS) marking, although there is a change of underlying referent at times. According to Woodbury these changes have to be explained in terms of new rhetorical units.

8.2.6 In conclusion

I am convinced that there is an interplay between grammatical and/or discourse features and an artistic text form, where both the rotation of subject, the connective, and the evidential play a role in the structuring of the texts. At times the storyteller is not able to coordinate the various patterns involved and as a consequence grammatical irregularities occur in order to comply with an artistic pattern of overriding importance. This seems to be most prevalent in the episodic parts of the texts. The layout of the texts, shown in the preceding chapters and in the appendices, as well as the graphic presentations of the texts, do show that there is a strict underlying artistic structure in them, manifested in the surface forms by the mechanics referred to above.

8.3 Artistic patterns once more

8.3.1 Parallelism

8.3.1.1 The concept of parallelism in literature

The previous section (8.2) summed up some of the most basic features related to the artistic structuring of the texts and also discussed specific issues related to these. In the present section I will discuss the structuring of the texts in relation to the concept of parallelism.

According to Jakobson, verse is defined by recurrent patterns on various linguistic levels "occurring in metrically or strophically corresponding positions" (1966:399). These recurrent or parallel patterns are typical within languages around the world, according to Jakobson as well as other literary scholars. Jakobson cites several scholars, among them Hopkins who said that "the structure of poetry is that of continuous parallelism" (1966:399). According to Hallberg (1992:122–123) parallelism and anaphoric repetition are both common structural elements in prose and poetry in old and modern verbal art. Parallelism had its own term already in the ancient Indic poetic descriptions.

Parallelism in literature normally refers to phonological, grammatical/morphological and semantic levels. Fabb (1997:137) defines parallelism in the following way: "Parallelism is a 'sameness' between two sections of a text, and can be structural or semantic." Structural parallelism he defines as "syntactic, morphological or phonological"; of these "syntactic parallelism" is the most common.[12] To date I have not seen any mention of structural parallelism beyond the level of syntactic structure. Although Fabb defines parallelism as "'sameness' between two sections of a text," his use of the term "section of a text" has to be understood as referring to the level of line and below in a poetic text; that is, the parallel patterns he gives examples of either hold between lines or clauses or phrases or words within the lines in a poetic text. Fabb gives examples and cites from studies done around the world but none of these venture beyond the syntactic level in respect to parallel structures.

Fabb defines parallelism as "'sameness' between *two* sections of a text" (italics mine), although he gives at least one example where 'sameness' holds between three different sections. According to Hallberg (1992:121) parallelism might correspond to multiple repetitions with variation of one theme encoded in similar structures. His definition reflects both semantic and structural parallelism at the same time.

I discussed in chapter 5 the triplet pattern in terms of parallelism and concluded that the parallelism between the individual verses is weak from a traditional point of view. The similarity of structure is only expressed through the repetitious connective clause. However, the repetitious clause is both anaphoric and cataphoric and as such creates an interesting pattern that can be perceived as parallelism (see 5.3.1.2). My conclusion is that parallelism is best perceived on the level between scenes, both through the consistent number of units to each scene and the function of these (verses and/or stanzas) within the scene. In the Coracora *Juan del Oso*, for example, the triplet stanza corresponds to a scene where the first verse creates a setting (a challenge, or question, etc.) to the action expressed in the second verse, while the last verse expresses an outcome. In *Watuchi II*, the three couplet stanzas to a scene function in a similar way. Similar patterns are perceived by Hymes in the Chinookan narratives, whose parts he refers to as *onset, ongoing, outcome,* although

---

[12]Fabb (1997:145) says that "At its simplest, syntactic parallelism involves structural identity between two sections of text in three simultaneous senses. First, each section of text contains the same classes of phrase and word. Second, corresponding phrases bear similar grammatical and thematic relations to the predicator. Third, the corresponding phrases and words are in the same order on both sections of text. In principle, each of these basic possibilities can be varied."

the verses are not so consistently marked through the same initial connectives as seen in most of the texts at hand. In 6.4.2 I claim that a pattern of parallelism, in terms of stage (or setting), action(s), outcome is perceived on various levels of the story (seen in figure 15). This type of underlying semantic pattern for the units concerned is probably universal in any narrative text, but the strict ordering of units to each level in the pattern is, I believe, artistically based, and the patterns perceived might be specific to the Quechua culture. As also noted in the previous section, the different graphs of the stories at hand show a variety of these artistically based (skeletal) structures. Typical of these is also duality, expressed in the form of complementary halves in a mirror-image which is most prevalent on the story or act level. I will return to this issue later.

8.3.1.2 Canonical parallelism

According to Fabb (1997:142) parallelism can hold for parts of a text or be "a basic principle of organization" and characteristic of a text as a whole. In the latter we have what is called CANONICAL PARALLELISM. Fabb sees canonical parallelism as similar to meter, for both are "organizing principles for a whole text." However, while parallelism typically groups the texts into line pairs, these do not match any "external template" as meter does. Fabb says "there are no reported kinds of 'syntactic meters'" (p. 143) and asks why it is so. Although Fabb over and over uses the term "section of a text," he does not consider the possibility of parallelism beyond the level of line pairs.

In the Quechua texts under study we have seen that parallelism operates on levels beyond that of sentences or line pairs, and the graphic presentations show strictly organized parallel patterns on other levels. I would claim that the different skeletal structures, as exemplified in the various graphs, correspond to external structural templates. Just as metrical texts match different external templates, so also do the structural patterns we have found in the texts we have studied, although on different levels.

It seems to me that not many literary scholars have moved beyond the lower structural levels in their scrutiny of artistic verbal patterns in languages. Hymes is one exception. There may be many artistic patterns as yet not discovered. Hymes claims that in some of the Chinookan narratives there is a text pattern showing an arch, which is exemplified in the analysis of the text "Seal and her younger brother lived there." "The scene-stanza ratio is 3:5:3" (that is, three, five, and three stanzas to each scene) for this text, according to Hymes (1981:331).[13] In the text analyzed by Hymes, I perceive the stanza in the very middle as implying a turning point in the story, in a way similar to what is perceived in the Quechua texts. Hymes, however, does not speak about this pattern in terms of parallelism.

According to Fabb, canonical parallelism in texts in many cultures may show "isolated non-parallel lines" at the end or the beginning of texts. He cites several examples from Jakobson (1966; also published in 1987) and says that the non-parallel lines can be interpreted "functionally" as "a way of marking the boundaries of the text..." (Fabb 1997:143). He also makes reference to a study by Hanson and Kiparsky (1997) that shows that non-parallel lines also may occur *within* a text to "mark moments of transition in the narrative" (p. 143).

If one considers the Quechua texts, some of these show irregular textual boundaries at the beginning and at the end as well as transitions within in the form of what I have been referring to as bridges, although otherwise they are patterned very consistently.

Fabb bases his work on the research done by various scholars on some eighty languages around the world; Quechua is not among them. However, neither Fabb nor any scholar he refers to considers parallel groupings on higher levels of text. I suspect that artistic patterns similar to those found in Quechua can be found in other languages as well.

8.3.1.3 Parallel structures and their artistic function

Fabb sees parallel structures as possibly having "three basic functions in verbal art" (1997:144):

- Parallelism is an "organizing principle" of text.
- The organized text constitutes "a formal object, revealing the structural principles of the language itself" and which would be recognized by the hearer. (Fabb makes reference to Jakobson's "poetic function" in this respect, which implies that the text is drawing attention to itself, not just as a message but as an artistic form.)
- "Parallelism is to express parallelisms in cultural thinking."

Concerning parallelism expressing cultural thinking, Fabb says that instead of the text revealing the structural principles of the language itself, it might be the other way round, that "parallelism in verbal behaviour,

---
[13] As alluded to earlier, Hornberger (1999) also makes note of a similar pattern in the Quechua texts that she analyzed.

8.3 Artistic patterns once more 203

and particularly in verbal art reflects a pervasive dualism underlying the principles of conceptual organization of a society." This brings up one of the questions raised earlier in this study: are the patterns as perceived in the texts based on underlying cultural patterns? Related to this question is also the question on how such patterns are kept in memory. A discussion on these issues follows.

8.3.2 Complementary halves and other patterns

8.3.2.1 Cultural pattern numbers

The graphic presentations of the texts show that on the highest levels, that of the story and the act, there is an obvious division into complementary halves. This division is based on both surface as well as underlying semantic structures indicating movement and/or turning points within the story. Is this structure of complementary halves in a mirror image based on some cultural pattern?

It has already been observed (chapters 4 and 6) that dualism was already important in the Inca empire, expressed, for example, in the layout of the city of Cusco, a city considered in the Inca empire as being the navel of the world. According to López-Baralt (1979) the principle of duality still plays a major role in both the social, ritual, and spatial organization of the Andean communities. This same principle of duality is also discussed by Rostworowski (1999). Rostworowski sees duality as the pervasive pattern in Andean society: all organization consists of multiples of "dual and quadripartite divisions." According to her, duality is seen both in the oppositions upper/lower and left/right.

López-Baralt, on the other hand, also makes notice of ternary structures seen in the lay-out of the city of Cusco. She sees the duality in an upper and lower half of the city of Cusco, each divided into two "barrios" which in turn are divided into three sections each. This pattern suggests a hierachical division that can be graphically presented in the following way, although it does not reflect the "upper" and "lower" division.

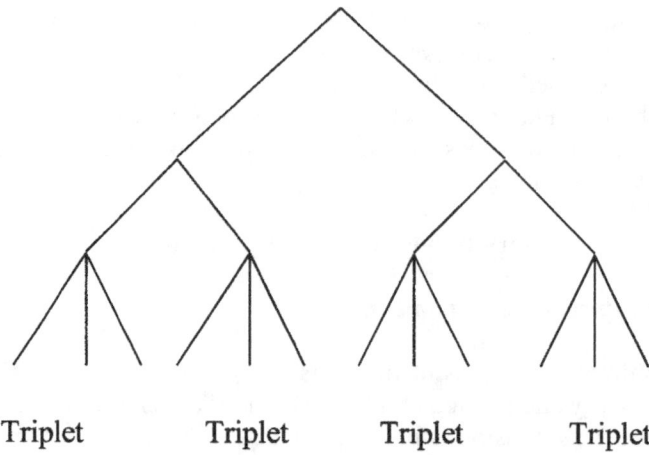

Figure 21: Hierarchical structure of the city of Cusco

The pattern shows duality only on the two upper levels and a ternary pattern at the bottom. If one considers the graphs of the texts analyzed, none of them exhibit a pattern that is the same as that in figure 21. The only text that could be said to demonstrate a similar pattern is *Watuchi II*, if one considers only the major episodic development as perceived in act II and act III (seen in figure 6). The second act of the Coracora *Juan del Oso* story also shows a similar pattern which would have been easier to see if the level of scene had also been shown in the graph of figure 10. Most texts also show a triplet pattern on the highest levels but, as has been discussed earlier and also referred to above, a dual pattern is perceived even in these, as the middle act or scene is always of a transitionary nature. However, duality in these cases is not so obvious in the surface structure.

Rostworowski sees the cultural numbers as only multiples of two, where the number eight is of great significance. Ternary patterns are never mentioned by her. A pattern possibly based on dual divisions on all levels is only found in the very first text presented in a graph form in figure 2. (See the discussion following the figure in 6.2.1.1.)

From what has been said so far it can be concluded that the patterns perceived in the texts do not exactly correspond to the cultural patterns as perceived by the ethnographers and ethnohistorians cited. However, in line with López-Baralt, both dual and triplet patterns are obvious. According to my analysis, duality is perceived in the dividing of the story and/or act into two more or less complementary halves in a mirror image. This pattern is obvious in many texts but quite subtle in others.

The cultural patterns referred to above have been noticed in relation to social and spatial organization. According to López-Baralt, the ternary pattern is also perceived in the Andean cosmic ordering; so, too, is the number five, the highest number perceived as significant for these purposes. In the level of acts, most texts studied show a total of three acts, while Coracora *Juan del Oso* shows a total of five acts. The largest number of scenes per act is also five. López-Baralt claims, however, that the most pervasive pattern is that of duality, a view in line with that of Rostworowski. A question is whether there are other cultural items showing duality. Another question is how the patterns in the texts are stored and retrieved in the minds of nonliterate Quechua speakers. The following section will look into these issues.

8.3.2.2 Textile patterns and text patterns

According to Arnold (1997) various studies compare weaving in the Andean cultures with other kinds of cultural activities and specific forms for social organization. Arnold herself compares the writing of text with the weaving of cloth as two gendered activities sharing many similarities in the Aymara culture—a culture coexisting with and very similar to that of the Quechuas in the Andean highlands of Bolivia and southern Peru. Arnold asserts that in the same way as men write their texts, the women "write" their designs into their "woven texts." Significant to the understanding of this is the fact that traditionally (before 1952 in Bolivia) boys had the opportunity to go to school while girls had their training in the works of the home, including weaving. Arnold moreover points to various similarities between the activity of weaving done by women and other cultural activities done my men, exemplified through the related vocabulary. For example, many weaving terms correspond to terms used by the men in relation to the agricultural work. (I do not know whether this is true in Quechua-speaking communities.)

Although Arnold's focus is not on the structural patterns of verbal text seen in relation to weaving patterns, she nevertheless mentions that "recent studies of the relationship between textile language and speech are beginning to suggest ways of understanding the linguistic parallels between the formal structure of textile designs and the syntax and discourse organization of spoken Andean languages (Arnold and Yapita 1992; Pärssinen 1992:104)" (1997:104). However, what she says further does not seem to have any significance as far as linguistic text structures are concerned; she continues the quote above by saying "For example, particular spatial configurations of textile layout may refer us analogically to the different levels of *ayllu* organization (a traditional Andean form for social organization), as they are perceived according to gender relations" (1997:104). Her article is mainly about gender relations and the related terminology as expressed in the activity of weaving. However, in a different section of her article she mentions how "certain weaving designs and their modes of repetitions in reflections, serial repeats, staggerings, and bilateral symmetries are repeated throughout distinct media" (1997:101), and mentions among these "dance choreography and the patterns of song verses."

As noted in chapter 2, Arnold and Yapita in another article (1999:245) state that even abstract thought in the Andean communities can be related to their textiles and the relation between parts and wholes in the textile patterns.

The comparison of verbal text to weaving is old. In chapter 2 I discussed the term "text" which etymologically derives from a Latin root meaning 'to weave'. Ong says that "Oral discourse has commonly been thought of even in oral milieus as weaving or stitching—*rhapsòdein*, to 'rhapsodize', basically means in Greek 'to stitch songs together'" (Ong 1982/97:13).

It is not unreasonable to think that in the oral "milieus" of the Quechuas—along with the Aymaras—people structure objects (songs, dances, etc.) in the same terms. The woven textile patterns could very well be reflected in the oral text creations; different textile patterns might also function as mnemonic devices for the structural patterns of text on higher levels. If the latter is not the case at the time being, it might originally have had such a function.

Another interesting feature is that in both Quechua and Aymara culture the men's ponchos and the women's mantas typically form two complementary parts (halves) in a mirror image. According to Weber (pers. comm.), the *mantas* and *ponchos* are usually woven as a single two-layered piece, folded at the left edge. When the cloth is unfolded there are two complementary halves in a mirror image. Sometimes they are woven in two parts and put together with a seam in the middle. The very middle stripe forms a transition between the two parts. On both sides of this middle stripe, there are broader stripes of various colours, often containing specific designs. Between the broader stripes there are thinner stripes marking the divisions. (If one carries the analogy further, the broader stripes could correspond to the scenic stanzas, interspersed by the bridges, manifested in the thinner stripes of the textile pattern.)

I present this idea as possibly meriting further research but even without the analogy I believe it has a value. I own a few Andean textiles which all display patterns of complementary halves in a mirror image. In one, made by an artisan I met in Ayacucho, the textile patterns show complementary halves in a mirror image in various directions, both vertically, horizontally, and diagonally (this is a weaving without a seam). This suggests that duality, perceived as complementary halves in a mirror image is a pattern that is of some significance in the Andean cultures. And why should it not be reflected in the patterns of the oral arts, as well as that of narrative composition? I also found it interesting that along with the specific weaving just mentioned, the artisan had made a written description of the woven textile, talking in terms of weaving as a form of text, into which people in the older times past wove their experiences. This strongly suggests a conscious awareness of the similar nature of weaving and storytelling/creation.

That people might be weaving their experiences into the textiles would also suggest that various cultural activities could be reflected in the organization of narrative text. A few thoughts in regards to this will be dealt with in the following section.

8.3.2.3 Text patterns and other cultural patterns

In chapter 5, in relation to Coracora *Juan del Oso*, I discussed how the form of the text, both the artistic patterns and the rhetorical structuring, may be metaphoric in respect to certain semantic plot features as well as specific cultural patterns. I made reference to de Beaugrande and Dressler, who say that "In poetic texts, the surface organization of the text is often motivated by special correspondences to the meaning and purposes of the whole communication..." (1981:56). I am suggesting that the developing conflict in *Juan del Oso* is emphasized by the constant change of subject in the *ina-pti-* triplets. On the other hand, the *ina-spa-* triplets with the focus on the same subject, occurring at the end of the story, underline a slowing down of the pace.

The feature of transitioning from location to location in the Coracora *Juan del Oso*, which is, by the way, a feature of all the texts, should be examined from a cultural perspective. Walking and moving from location to location is a significant aspect of Quechua culture from ancient times. The Quechua even today uses much of his time walking between his home and his pastures, between his home and his little fields spread around, and from field to field. Although the Inca empire is known for its advanced technical skills in many areas, to our knowledge there was no use of a wheel. Many roads were built throughout the empire, but only for walking or running. The messengers, the *chasquis*, ran with their messages, even with specific food items, throughout the enormous empire. One messenger would run to a specific place of rest, a *tambo* 'inn', where another would be waiting to take the message on to the next *tambo*.

The following analogy might be taken too far but it is possible to see the intervals of running reflected in the rapid pace of the *ina-pti-* triplets, and the place of rest reflected in the interspersing bridges. Moreover, some of the stories make a final conclusion in reference to getting home or not getting home. As noted in chapter 5, Weber (1989:314) says in reference to certain grammatical patterns that "Quechua seems to have an intense preoccupation with getting people to where they are going." This fact could be said to support the ideas above. However, the patterns as expressed in the texts, could only be reflecting general, universal cognitive patterns, in the way information structuring is conceived of by Chafe: the cluster of high acuity events in the triplets (corresponding to a "mental image") versus events of lesser acuity ("resting places") in the bridging units. Nevertheless, the original textual story patterns could have initially been constructed around such cultural events, subsequently taking on the form of specific artistic patterns as particular experiences were related in connection with weaving events. But it has to be stressed that this is mere speculation on my part.

However, other scholars have noted a metaphoric relation between the feature of walking and other cultural aspects, e.g. Schechter (1987) in regards to Quechua harp music and the musical genre called *sanjuán* in the northern Ecuadorian highlands. It is particularly the rhythmic aspect that is of interest. Schechter asserts that the "musicians are constrained *in their phrasing* by isorhythm,[14] not in their adherence to absolutely fixed melody" (p. 34). Schechter also says that "It comes as no surprise that the walking activity, vital to communication, to daily tasks, and to survival emerges in expressive culture" (p. 36). It is the balanced movement of walking that he sees reflected in the isorhythmic phrasing of the *sanjuán* music. Harrison, as noted in chapter 2, mentions an internal rhythm to the Ecuadorian Quechua song without talking about it in metaphorical terms. These insights come from Ecuadorian Quechua but may be just as significant in Quechua varieties farther south. I have also mentioned rhythm because the repeated initial connective gives a cadence to the text as a whole. There might be more to be discovered in this particular area with respect to the structural units referred to as verse.

Moreover, Schechter makes reference to other studies around the world that confirm an iconicity between music and various cultural aspects. Various studies of Quechua have shown the iconicity between sound and

---

[14]Isorhythm is a repeated rhythmic pattern, a periodic repetition or recurrence of rhythmic configurations in the *sanjuán*. The rhythm of the first half phrase is identically repeated in the second half.

8.3 Artistic patterns once more

language, both phonemic-lexical (de Reuse 1986) and lexical-grammatical (Nuckolls 1992 and 1996). It is quite reasonable to assume that iconicity occurs on higher structural levels as well, where the pace of locomotion is reflected in the pace of the text. The rhythmic movement in the texts could also be a reflection of the rhythmic movement of the shuttle during the process of weaving.

Regarding structural textual patterns in relation to other patterns in Quechua culture, one must ask: What textual patterns are specific to Quechua? The possible universality of many patterns will be looked at in more detail in the next section.

8.3.3 Textual patterns and universality

Olrik conceives of folktales and other folkloric genres as obeying epic laws. The most basic laws were presented in section 3.3.3. Olrik bases his laws on studies done mainly on European folk traditions but he also includes insights from a few other cultures, e.g. India. According to Dundes (1965:130), Olrik's laws need to be tested in other areas than Europe. Although this has not been a major enterprise of the present research, the analysis of the texts at hand shows that Olrik's principles, in general terms, also apply to the Quechua folktales. Though the folktales might be of European origin, some having arrived with the Spaniards as Mannheim (1991) claims, they still reflect Quechua rhetorical patterns.

The following "laws" are some of the most outstanding features seen in the Quechua texts: The stories have an opening and closing; they are single-stranded, discussed in some detail in section 8.2.2.3. They move from calm to excitement to calm (a final loosely attached episode); this is very noticeable in some of the Coracora texts. There are many rest-points in the longer narratives—the bridges. There are two characters to the scene. The stories have polarized characters as well as one leading character, as is very evident in *Juan del Oso*.

I do not find the law of repetition to be an outstanding feature in the texts except the repeated connectives and repeated verbal phrase in some of the most crucial parts of the Shausha texts. Olrik sees the law of repetition operating often with the pattern number three, which also applies to at least a couple of the examples just mentioned. The repeated connectives in the stanzas, I believe, is not the kind of repetition that Olrik's "law" refers to. However, three repetitions are prevalent in the pattern formation in many of the texts. Olrik, however, does not see the law of three in relation to artistic structuring of the narratives. Three as a pattern number in various respects is seen as pervasive in folk literature of

European origin. Olrik mentions that other cultures may operate with other pattern numbers and mentions Indic literature which is dominated by patterns based on the number four. Olrik sees this difference as connected to the religious conceptions of the people of India.

Dundes (1965) sees three as a pervasive pattern number in American culture of European origin, while Hymes (1981) sees other pattern numbers as being typical of various American Indian cultures. The typical pattern numbers of the Quechua culture have been discussed in some detail. Three is perceived as one of those pattern numbers, according to López-Baralt (1979) while Rostworowski (1999) claims that all structuring in Quechua culture is based on multiples of two. It is possible that the Inca culture operated with multiples of two, because both López-Baralt and Rostworowski claim that the most outstanding feature of Quechua religious and social organization is that of a pervasive dualism. Three as a cultural pattern number might have been introduced into Quechua culture through the arrival of European influence, both through the trinity of Christian thinking as well as through patterns directly related to narratives of European origin.

Fabb (1997:145) finds duality mentioned in studies by Bricker (1989) in Zinancateco and by Foster (1975, 1980) on Ancient Egyptian where cultural dualism is pervasive. Duality is also perceived as complementary halves in a mirror image basic to nature itself, e.g. the human body, the body of an animal, a leaf of a plant. I believe duality and also the number three is reflected in a myriad of ways in our own western cultures, whether American or European. A sense of symmetry is, I believe, basic to our humanness. (Tarasov made this claim in 1986). However, this might not be manifested to the same extent or in the same cultural expressions within different cultures.

Dualism found in the Quechua texts is likely to be found in other cultures if their texts are studied searching for it. It must be remembered that verbal art is highly formulaic in oral societies. Unfortunately, not many literary studies specifically mention duality or other patternings seen on the higher levels of the texts. Not many scholars seem to venture to these levels in text analysis. Hymes has had a wider perspective and found the pattern of an arch in the Chinookan texts. I have indicated that he also believes that all oral narrative, whether in literate or oral cultures, is organized in (verse) lines; but he admits that more studies are needed in this area in order to know to what extent patterns are universal. The research at hand, however, has had no pretentions of responding to the need for such a study. I doubt that all oral narrative is organized in lines, although I believe that there is some cyclic structuring in all narrative along the lines of repeated scenic units with an onset, ongoing, and outcome. I consider the strict organization of stories in verse lines, stanzas, etc., to be a feature specific to basically oral societies, at least when based on the charateristics that I have detected in Quechua. I am particularly thinking of the specific use of the connectives. Although formulaic features certainly have artistic value to the people concerned, they are also necessary as mnemonic devices. Moreover, as we have seen, formulaic features play very specific roles in the information structuring of the texts.

8.4 Final remarks

A final question concerns the conventionality of the patterns within and across varieties of Quechua.

Two varieties have been made the major focus of this research, one from each of the two major branches of Quechua. The stories analyzed are widely told by various authors or storytellers. One can conclude that there is considerable conventionality to the patterns observed both within and across varieties.

In regards to artistic structuring:

- Within the Coracora variety: although the patterns of higher structural levels differ, such as showing both triplet and couplet stanzas or a combination of these to the scene, they are based on the same features found on the syntactic/morphological level.
- Within Shausha the higher level patterns are simpler; the triplet pattern is pervasive on all levels and across texts. These are based on the same syntactic or morphological features and rotation of subject.
- Across Coracora and Shausha there is some difference in stanzas; couplets do not occur in any of the Shausha texts that we have, but the underlying patterns are much the same, both in the structure of a scene and in duality found in higher levels of the texts. Patterns are all based on the sentence-initial connective, the evidential, and the rotation of subject.

We found two identifiable patterns of information structuring:

- The event line markings follow a similar pattern both within and across the two varieties.

- The plot structuring is more varied, although the texts both within and across varieties show similar features to mark stages, climax, and final suspense.

I conclude by claiming that there is a surprising similarity in the patterns observed, both within and across the varieties considered. It is reasonable to assume that similar patterns can be found in other varieties of Quechua. It is also reasonable to assume that in certain areas the patterns are not so noticeable due to the influence of the Spanish language and the fact that more and more Quechuas are becoming bilingual as well as literate, basically in the Spanish language. However, an oral mode still coexists with a literate mode to a greater or lesser degree in different communities. The present research suggests that specific oral patterns are alive in many Quechua-speaking communities. Although the Coracora texts date a few decades back in time, the Shausha texts were collected much more recently.

In the tradition of Humboldt, many scholars "have demonstrated that different linguistic structures present different ways of perceiving the world..." (Sparing 1984:3). Sparing studied worldview as reflected in the German *Märchen,* though she does not pay particular attention to linguistic structures. Do the patterns of the texts at hand reflect both the dualism of the Andean worldview and the triadic of a European through the ternary structures? Do the ternary structures suggest a moving away from Andean dualism? I am not going to speculate more on this but leave the thought for further consideration. However, I believe it is important for any scholar of different cultures and languages to consider the relationship between worldview and linguistic structures. This applies specifically to text structures on higher levels, as the present study demonstrates.

Goody (1977) claims that literacy changes the cognitive processes of the oral mind. Others choose to think about changes in terms of changing worldviews (see Forstorp 1992). These are of course interrelated. In the Quechua texts we found that they may reflect pervasive cultural patterns and a specific worldview. Even if one does not consider worldview in relation to the textual patterns, the patterns still suggest a strong adherence to strict orderings, perceived on higher levels of the text, while features on lower levels play a crucial role.

I do not claim to have discovered all that is going on in the structuring of the texts at hand. My hope is that the present research will give some new insights and an impetus for further research in this area, particularly in other Quechua varieties. Of particular interest would be a study of

8.4 Final remarks

other kinds of text, e.g. personal narrative accounts, to see to what extent the formulaic patterns also play a role in these genres. Jakobson (1959) claims that patterns typical of formal texts have a tendency to carry over into more mundane texts rather than the other way round. Chafe (1982:49ff.) thinks that in oral cultures one can distinguish between language use typical of oral "literature" (e.g. that of rituals) versus that of a more mundane or colloquial kind. Havelock (1976:49) thinks in similar terms and says that even in oral cultures discourse is largely prosaic but that the "important and influential statement in any culture is the one that is preserved" and that the "conditions for preservation" involves mnemonic techniques like verbal or musical rhythm. The distinctions between various genres and forms for language use are issues that the present study has not dealt with but would be of crucial importance to a proper understanding of verbal communication in a basically oral culture.

Appendices

How to read the appendices

Although most of the information below has already been given at various points in my discussion of the texts, it may be a help to the reader to repeat it here with a few additional comments.

The arrangement of all the texts is my responsibility; line breaks and indentation show the artistic nature of the texts. Most of them display acts and scenes and the verses within (e.g. couplets or triplets of *ina-* verses). I have also arranged the texts in such a way as to suggest possible lines or minor poetic units within the verses; these are indented. The arrangement is mainly based on direct quotes, predicates, and subordinate clauses, but at times also on independent clauses (e.g. sub-units to the *ina-* verses); and in some cases also based on a few other features that seem to set a certain structural unit apart as a possible line or a poetic unit of some kind, as in the case of verse (2) in *Juan del Oso* in appendix 1, with two indented parts, both starting out with *ok* followed by a bisyllabic word with rhyming vowels. However, the nature of possible lines or other minor poetic units has not been in focus in this study, and many of the indented lines or minor units as shown in the text are often based on pure intuition on my part.

In the case of the Coracora version of *Juan del Oso* as displayed in appendix 1 and appendix 2, there are no indications as to possible acts or scenes; this is due to the way I have discussed the analysis of the texts. However, possible acts are indicated in chapter 6 through the displays of the text, namely figures 7–14. In the case of scenes these mainly correspond to the numbered artistic triplet stanzas. However, for a proper understanding of these the reader should also see the discussion of my analysis of these and the so-called "bridges" (chapter 5).

In general, for all the texts, the numbers in parentheses are the numbers of stanzas corresponding to scenes or "bridges." The numbers generally indicate verses and in a few cases possible sub-lines within the verses. There is an apparent inconsistency in the latter, as only a few sub-lines are indicated by numbers. Most of these have been treated as having some intermediate position, and some have also been discussed when analyzing the texts. In the case of *Juan del Oso* in appendix 1 and appendix 2, the numbers of the sentences occur as in the published text in Weber (1987).

On the right side of most of the texts, there is a chart indicating subject identification (SS for same subject as in previous sentences, DS for different subject from the one in the previous sentence), aspect (ASP), and tense (TENSE or TNS). This information has been added because it has played an important role in the analysis of the texts.

Appendix 1
Okumaripa Watuchin[1]

Velazco Yáñez Salomón

(1) 1 Chay okumare-s ka-sqa kallpa-sapa.
     This bear-RPT be-PRT strength-MUCH

   2 Tiya-sqa qaqa-p chawpi-pi.
     live-PRT rock-GEN middle-LOC

   3 Chawpi-n-ta-ña-taq   pasa-sqa mayo
     middle-3P-OBJ-NOW-EMPH   pass-PRT river

              mana chaki-q.
              not run.dry-AG

*1 That bear was very strong. 2 He lived in the middle of a hill (rock).
3 Through the middle of it passed a river that never went dry.*

(2) 4 Aypa ina-pti-n-ña-taq-si   chaka-nes-qa
     many do.like.this-ADVDS-3P-NOW-EMPH-RPT bridge-SIM-TOP

              ok lado chimpa-man
              one side bank-GOAL

              ok rako qeru-ta   chura-sqa.
              one big trunk-OBJ put-PRT

   4 Because of this they had put a big trunk across it.

---
[1]*Okumaripa Watuchin* 'Story about the bear' (*Juan del Oso*) from Weber (1987:169–180) is part of a collection by Lauriault (1957, 1958); morphological analysis is by David Weber and Conrad Phelps.

(3) 5 Chay   runa-s   ka-sqa apu   apu.
    this   man-RPT   be-PRT powerful powerful

       6 Y   miku-sqa   punchaw-nin-pi
         and   eat-PRT   day-3P-LOC

         ok   toru-ta-puni.
         One   bull-OBJ-CRT

    7 Y   chay qeru-nta-kama-s   apa-q
      and   this trunk-ALONG-LIM-RPT   bring-HAB

         chay   wañu-sqa   turu-ta   miku-na-n-paq.
         this   die-PRT   bull-OBJ   eat-NOM-3P-PUR

    8 Chay   machay-nin-pi-s   ka-sqa
      this   cave-3P-LOC-RPT   be-PRT

         ok   atu-n   perul   y   aypa   yanta-kuna
         one   big-3P   "pan"   and   much   firewood-PLUR

         chay-pi   timpu-chi-na-n-paq.
         this-LOC   boil-CAUS-NOM-3P-PUR

5 This man (bear) was very rich. 6 And he daily ate a bull. 7 And he carried this dead bull across this trunk in order to eat it. 8 In this cave was a big "pan" and a lot of firewood to make it boil.

(4) 9 Y   mana   pi-ta-pas   respeta-sqa-chu.
      and   not   who-OBJ-ALSO   respect-PRT-NEG

    10 Ok   llaqta-ta   ri-spa-n-ku-ña-taq-si
       one   village-OBJ   go-ADV-3-PL-NOW-EMPH-RPT

         may-man   yayku-spa-pas
         where-GOAL   enter-ADV-ALSO

         apu   runa-kuna-pa   ima-n-ta-pas
         owner   man-PLUR-GEN   what-3P-OBJ-ALSO

         lliw   aypu-rari-n   pobre-kuna-man.
         all   distribute-REPET-3   poor-PLUR-GOAL

9 And he didn't respect anybody. 10 When he went to a village, wherever he entered, the things of the rich men he distributed to the poor.

(5) 11 Warmi-n-ña-taq-si   ka-sqa   warma-cha-lla.
     woman-3P-NOW-EMPH-RPT   be-PRT   child-DIM-LIM

   12 Llaqta-manta-s   suwa-mu-sqa   chay   machay-nin-paq.
     village-ABL-RPT   rob-AFAR-PRT this   cave-3P-PUR

   13 Ina-spa-s   wawa-n   ka-sqa.
     do.like.this-ADV-RPT   son-3P   be-PRT

   11 There was also his very young wife. 12 He had stolen her from the village for (her to be in) his cave. 13 So he got to have a son.

(6) 14 Chay-lla-pi-s   llamka-sqa.
     this-LIM-LOC-RPT   work-PRT

   15 Ina-spa-n-si   chay-na   puri-sqa
     do.like.this-ADV-3P-RPT   this-SIM   walk-PRT

                runa-kuna-ta   wañu-chi-stin.
                man-PLUR-OBJ   die-CAUS-ADV

   14 He worked with nothing else than in this. 15 Like this he lived (walked), killing people.

(7) 16 Chay-ta-ña-taq-si   mana   muna-sqa-chu   warmi-n.
     this-OBJ-NOW-EMPH-RPT   no   want-PRT-NEG   woman-3P

   17 Ina-spa-s   wawa-n-ta   ni-n:
     do.like.this-ADV-RPT   son-3P-OBJ   say-3

                "Imayna-raq   iskapa-ru-ku-chwan?"   ni-spa.
                how-YET   escape-ASP-REF-12CND   say-ADV

   16 His wife didn't like (want) this. 17 Then she said to her son: "How do we escape?"

(8) 18 Ina-pti-n-ña-taq-si   chay   wawa-n   ni-n:
     do.like.this-ADVDS-3P-NOW-EMPH-RPT   this   baby-3P   say-3

                "Suya-yku-y   mama-y.
                wait-IN-2IMP   mother-VOC

             19 Ñoqa-m   tayta-y-ta   orma-yka-chi-saq
                I-DIR   father-1P-OBJ   fall-IN-CAUS-1FUT

                kay   qero-nta-kama   amu-chka-pti-n."
                this   trunk-ALONG-LIM   come-IMPRF-ADVDS-3P

20 Ina-pti-n-si   ok   vez   chay-na
   do.like.this-ADVDS-3P-RPT   one   time this-SIM

       torillo   tonto-ri-sqa
       bull   carry-ASP-PRT

       qero-ta   pasa-mu-chka-pti-n
       trunk-OBJ   pass-AFAR-IMPRF-ADVDS-3P

       qero-ta   moyo-rpari-chi-sqa.
       trunk-OBJ   move-MOMENT-CAUS-PRT

21 Ina-pti-n-si   mayo-man   pasa-yku-n.
   do.like.this-ADVDS-3P-RPT   river-GOAL pass-IN-3

18 And her son said: "Wait, mother! 19 I will make my father fall when he comes (walking) along the trunk." 20 And once when he was passing along the trunk, carrying the bull, he (the son) made the trunk move. 21 And he fell into the river.

(9) 22 Ina-spa-n   remolino-man   pasa-yku-n.
    do.like.this-ADV-3P   whirlpool-GOAL pass-IN-3

   23 Ina-spa-n-si   wañu-n.
      do.like.this-ADV-3P-RPT   die-3

   22 And he went into the whirlpool. 23 And he died.

(10) 24 Ina-pti-n-si   chay   wawa-n
     do.like.this-ADVDS-3P-RPT   this   baby-3P

         mama-n-ta   apa-ri-ku-spa-n
         mother-3P-OBJ   take-ASP-REF-ADV-3P

         ri-pu-n   llaqta-man.
         ir-BEN-3   village-GOAL

   25 Ina-pti-n-si   llaqta-pi
      do.like.this-ADVDS-3P-RPT   village-LOC

         mana   bautiza-sqa   ka-pti-n
         not   baptize-PRT   be-ADVDS-3P

         ok   kura-man   qo-yku-n
         one   priest-GOAL   give-IN-3

         bautiza-chi-na-n-paq.
         baptize-CAUS-NOM-3P-PUR

26 Ina-pti-n-si bautiza-ra-chi-spa
do.like.this-ADVDS-3P-RPT baptize-ASP-CAUS-ADV

yacha-y + wasi-man chura-n.
learn-INF + house-GOAL put-3

24 And his/her son, taking his mother along, went to the village. 25 And in the village, since he wasn't baptized, she gave him to the priest for him to baptize him (her son). 26 And after having baptized him, he/they put him in the school.

(11) 27 Ina-pti-n-si pichqa wata-yoq-ña.
do.like.this-ADVDS-3P-RPT five year-HAVE-NOW

28 Ina-pti-n-si barba-n wiña-ra-mu-n.
do.like.this-ADVDS-3P-RPT beard-3P grow-ASP-AFAR-3

29 Ina-pti-n-si chay-manta chuta-n
do.like.this-ADVDS-3P-RPT this-ABL pull-3

chay-pi waron-kuna.
this-LOC young.man-PLUR

27 And now he was five years old. 28 And his beard was growing. 29 And because of this the children pulled it (the beard).

(12) 30 Ina-spa-s
do.like.this-ADV-RPT

"Padreno-y,
godfather-VOC

kay warma-kuna-m bastidia-wa-n."
this child-PLUR-DIR bother-1O-3

30 Then (he said): "Godfather, these children are bothering me."

(13) 31 Ina-pti-n-si
do.like.this-ADVDS-3P-RPT

"ok taka-ta qo-y,
one fist.knock-OBJ give-2IMP

macho zonzo" ni-pti-n-si
big fool say-ADVDS-3P-RPT

taka-ta qo-n.
fist.knock-OBJ give-3

32 Ina-pti-n-si   wañu-rari-n.
   do.like.this-ADVDS-3P-RPT   die-REPET-3

33 Ina-pti-n-si   padreno-n-qa
   do.like.this-ADVDS-3P-RPT   godfather-3P-TOP

            sipi-na-n-paq   ni-sqa.
            kill-NOM-3P-PUR say-PRT

31 And as he said "give them a punch, you big fool," he gave them a punch. 32 And so many died. 33 And it was his godfather who had told him to kill.

(14) 34 Ina-pti-n-si
        do.like.this-ADVDS-3P-RPT

                  chay   sacristan-nin-wan
                  this   priest-3P-ACCOMP

                  atun   ochko-ta   ochku-ra-chi-n
                  big   hole-OBJ   make.hole-ASP-CAUS-3

                  pichqa negro-wan.
                  five   negro-ACCOMP

35 Ina-pti-n-si   chay   okumarí
   do.like.this-ADVDS-3P-RPT   this   bear

           chay   ochku-pa   pata-n-ta   pasa-chka-pti-n
           this   hole-GEN   edge-3P-OBJ   pass-IMPRF-ADVDS-3P

           tanqa-yku-rpari-sqa.
           push-IN-MOMENT-PRT

36 Ina-pti-n-si   pasa-yku-sqa.
   do.like.this-ADVDS-3P-RPT pass-IN-PRT

34 Then through his catechist he ordered to have a hole made by five negroes. 35 Then, when this bear passed along the edge of this hole, they pushed him into it. 36 Then he went (fell) into it.

(15) 37 Ina-spa-n-si   chay-manta-s   lloqsi-rpari-mu-n.
        do.like.this-ADV-3P-RPT this-ABL-RPT   leave-MOMENT-AFAR-3

    38 Ina-spa-n-si   chay   negro-kuna-ta
       do.like.this-ADV-3P-RPT   this   negro-PLUR-OBJ

           chay   uchku-pi   pampa-rpari-n.
           this   hole-LOC   bury-MOMENT-3

37 Then after this he left (jumped out) (of the hole). 38 Then he buried all the negroes in this hole.

(16) 39 Ina-spa-n-ña-taq-si   tayta-n-ina   kallpa-yoq.
        do.like.this-ADV-3P-NOW-EMPH-RPT   father-3P-SIM   strength-HAVE

     40 Chay-na-lla-ta-taq-si   miku-n-pas.
        this-SIM-LIM-OBJ-EMPH-RPT   eat-3-ALSO

39 And already he had the strength like his father. 40 Also he ate like him.

(17) 41 Ina-pti-n-si
        do.like.this-ADVDS-3P-RPT

              mana-ña   aguanta-y-ta   ati-spa-ña-taq-si
              not-NOW   handle-INF-OBJ   can-ADV-NOW-EMPH-RPT

              atu   atun   torre-man
              big   big   tower-GOAL

              chay   ayjado-n-ta   kacha-n
              this   godson-3P-OBJ   send-3

              campana   toca-mu-na-n-paq.
              bell   ring-AFAR-NOM-3P-PUR

        42 Chay   torre-pi-s   tawa   runa-kuna-ta   saya-ra-chi-mu-n,
           this   tower-LOC-RPT   four   man-PLUR-OBJ   wait-ASP-CAUS-AFAR-3

              chay-manta   tanqa-yka-mu-na-n-paq.
              this-GOAL   push-IN-AFAR-NOM-3P-PUR

     43 Ina-pti-n-si
        do.like.this-ADVDS-3P-RPT

              campana-ta   toca-chka-pti-n
              bell-OBJ   ring-IMPRF-ADVDS-3P

              tanqa-y-ta   muna-mu-n-ku.
              push-INF-OBJ want-AFAR-3-PL

     44 Ina-pti-n-si   mana   ati-n-cho.
        do.like.this-ADVDS-3P-RPT not   can-3-NEG

45 Aswan-si   chay runa-kuna-ta   tanqa-yka-ri-mu-n.
   si.no-RPT   this man-PLUR-OBJ   push-IN-ASP-AFAR-3

41 *And as he now couldn't stand him anymore, he (the priest) sent his godson to a tower to ring the bell. 42 In this tower he made four men wait for him in order to push him down (from there). 43 And while he was ringing the bell, they wanted to push him. 44 And they didn't manage (to do it). 45 Instead, he pushed down these men.*

(18) 46 Ina-spa-n-ña-taq-si   chay-pi   wañu-n chay runa-kuna.
        do.like.this-ADV-3P-NOW-EMPH-RPT   this-LOC die-3   this man-PLUR
     46 *Then these men died there.*

(19) 47 Ina-pti-n-ña-taq-si   padreno-n-qa
        do.like.this-ADVDS-3P-NOW-EMPH-RPT   godfather-3P-TOP

            lliw-ña   piña-ru-ku-n.
            all-NOW   annoy-ASP-REF-3

     48 Ina-spa-n-si   montaña-ta-ña-taq-si   kacha-rpari-n
        do.like.this-ADV-3P-RPT   the.woods-OBJ-NOW-EMPH-RPT   send-MOMENT-3

            chunka iskay-niyoq asno-ntin-ta   y
            ten   two-HAVE   mule-WITH-OBJ   and

            tawa vaca-ntin-ta.
            four cow-WITH-OBJ

     49 Ina-pti-n-si
        do.like.this-ADVDS-3P-RPT

            "Chay-pi   wañu-mu-chun"   ni-spa
            this-LOC   die-AFAR-3IMP   say-ADV

            chay montaña-man-ña-taq-si.
            this the.woods-GOAL-NOW-EMPH-RPT

47 *Then his godfather got very annoyed. 48 Then he sends him to the woods with twelve mules and four cows. 49 And saying "may he die there," he (the son) (goes) to the woods.*

(20) 50 Chay-pi-ña-taq-si   pone-rpari-sqa.
        this-LOC-NOW-EMPH-RPT   sleep-MOMENT-PRT

     51 Ina-spa-s   tota-manta
        do.like.this-ADV-RPT   morning-ABL

rikcha-ri-spa-n-ña-taq-si
look-ASP-ADV-3P-NOW-EMPH-RPT

qawa-kacha-ri-pti-n-ña-taq-si
look-HERE.AND.THERE-ASP-ADVDS-3P-NOW-EMPH-RPT

 lado-n-pi leon-kuna ka-chka-sqa.
 side-3P-LOC lion-PLUR be-IMPRF-PRT

52 Chay llapa asno-kuna
  this all mule-PLUR

apa-sqa-n-ña-taq-si,
take-REL-3P-NOW-EMPH-RPT

mana ka-sqa-chu.
not be-PRT-NEG

53 Ataka-n-kuna-lla-ña wischu+wischu ka-chka-sqa.
  bone-3P-PLUR-LIM-NOW spread.around be-IMPRF-PRT

50 And there (in the woods) he fell asleep. 51 When he woke up in the morning and looked around, there were lions at his side. 52 All the mules that he had taken along were not there. 53 Only the bones, spread around, were there.

(21) 54 Ina-pti-n-si   leyon-kuna-ta-qa
   do.like.this-ADVDS-3P-RPT lion-PLUR-OBJ-TOP

  chay okumari-qa ni-n:
  this bear-TOP say-3

  "May-pi chay asno-kuna vaca-y?"
  where-LOC this mule-PLUR cow-1P

  ni-spa.
  say-ADV

55 Ina-pti-n-ña-taq-si   leyon-kuna-qa
  do.like.this-ADVDS-3P-NOW-EMPH-RPT lion-PLUR-TOP

  pawa-yka-ri-n.
  fly-IN-ASP-3

56 Ina-pti-n-si   ok taka-wan   sapa
  do.like.this-ADVDS-3P-RPT one fist.knock-INSTRM only

leon pawa-yko-q-ta sipi-rari-n.
lion fly-IN-AG-OBJ kill-REPET-3

54 And this bear said to the lions: "Where are my mules and my cows?" 55 And the lions attacked (flew at) him. 56 And he killed with one punch only (various times, one punch for each) the lions that attacked him.

(22) 57 Ina-spa-s ka-q leon-kuna-ta ni-n:
do.like.this-ADV-RPT be-AG lion-PLUR-OBJ say-3

"Qam-kuna-m kunan yanta-ta carga-nki-chik
you-PLUR-DIR now firewood-OBJ carry-2-PL2

aqalli-ki-chik-wan-pas."
intestines-2P-PL2-INSTRM-ALSO

57 And to the other lions that were standing there, he said: "You will now carry the firewood even if it should be with your intestines."

(23) 58 Ina-pti-n-si
do.like.this-ADVDS-3P-RPT

chunka iskay-niyoq leon-pi carga-spa-n
ten two-HAVE lion-LOC carry-ADV-3P

ok-nin macho leon-pi-ña-taq-si echi-ri-ku-spa
one-3P big lion-LOC-NOW-EMPH-RPT mount-ASP-REF-ADV

pasa-n padreno-n-pa-ta.
pass-3 godfather-3P-GEN-OBJ

59 Ina-pti-n-si
do.like.this-ADVDS-3P-RPT

"Imayna-ña-mari kay-qa?
how-NOW-DIRSEC this-TOP

60 Leon-wan-pas carga-mu-n yanta-kuna-ta-pas.
lion-INSTRM-ALSO carry-AFAR-3 firewood-PLUR-OBJ-ALSO

61 Trampa chura-sqa-y-manta-pas iskapa-mu-n.
trap put-REL-1P-ABL-ALSO escape-AFAR-3

62 Ima-ña-ch kay-qa?"
how-NOW-CONJ this-TOP

ni-spa-n-si
say-ADV-3P-RPT

rima-pa-ku-n   padreno-n-qa.
talk-BEN-REF-3 godfather-3P-TOP

63 Ina-pti-n-si   kaq   padreno-n-qa   kacha-n
   do.like.this-ADVDS-3P-RPT again   godfather-3P-TOP send-3

"Kunan-mi   kaq   kuti-nki.
now-DIR   other.time return-2

64 Ina-spa-m   chay-manta   apa-mu-wa-nki
   do.like.this-ADV-DIR   this-ABL   take-AFAR-1O-2

raku qeru-kuna-ta   ima-pi-pas."
big   trunk-PLUR-OBJ   what-LOC-ALSO

58 And loading twelve lions, and mounting another big one, he goes to where his godfather lives. 59 And he (his godfather) says: "What is this? 60 Even with lions he carries firewood. 61 From the trap I made he also escapes. 62 Who is this one?," his godfather says to himself. And again his godfather sends him: "Now you return and come back with big trunks (bringing them) in/on whatever."

(24) 65 Ina-spa-s
     do.like.this-ADV-RPT

miku-na-n-paq
eat-NOM-3P-PUR

qo-n   soqta   vaca-ta.
give-3   six   cow-OBJ

66 Qati-ri-chi-n.
   follow-ASP-CAUS-3

65 And he gives him six cows to eat. 66 He makes them follow.

(25) 67 Ina-pti-n-si   pasa-n.
     do.like.this-ADVDS-3P-RPT   pass-3

68 Qati-ri-ku-spa   ri-chka-n.
   follow-ASP-REF-ADV   go-IMPRF-3

69 Ina-pti-n-si ok runa-wan tupa-rpari-n.
do.like.this-ADVDS-3P-RPT one man-ACCOMP meet-MOMENT-3

67 Then he leaves. 68 Following he goes. (Comment: this is a bit unclear to me as well as 66 above; probably the meaning is that he is shepherding the cows along/driving them ahead). 69 Then he meets (with) a man.

(26) 70 Ina-spa-n-ña-taq-si ni-n:
do.like.this-ADV-3P-NOW-EMPH-RPT say-3

"May-ta-m ri-nki,
where-OBJ-DIR go-2

ama ri-y-chu.
not go-2IMP-NEG

71 Si-chus ri-pti-ki-qa
if-DOUBT go-ADVDS-2P-TOP

mana-m yacha-ku-n-chu kuti-mu-yki"
not-DIR know-REF-3-NEG return-AFAR-1PRS2

ni-spa.
say-ADV

72 Ni-pti-n-si okumari-qa piña-kacha-ri-ko-n.
say-ADVDS-3P-RPT bear-TOP annoy-HERE.AND.THERE-ASP-REF-3

73 Ina-spa ni-n:
do.like.this-ADV say-3

"Ama amu-wa-y-chu.
not come-1O-2IMP-NEG

74 Ima-pas ni-q-niy yanqa-taq.
what-ALSO say-AG-1P in.vain-EMPH

75 Kay kay-pi sipi ima-ru-yki-man.
this this-LOC kill do-ASP-1PRS2-COND

76 Ina-pti-n qam aswan
do.like.this-ADVDS-3P you instead

mana tayta mama-yki-wan-pas
no father mother-2P-ACCOMP-ALSO

```
                    tupa-ra-pu-chka-waq-chu."
                    meet-ASP-BEN-IMPRF-2CND-NEG
```

70 And he said to him: "To where you are going, don't go! 71 If you go, it is not known how to return." 72 When he said this, the bear got angry. 73 And he said: "Don't come and (tell) me (this)! 74 What you are saying is in vain. 75 In this very place I might even kill you. 76 Then you instead won't meet your parents again."

(27) 77 Ina-spa-n-si   kaq   pasa-n.
     do.like.this-ADV-3P-RPT other.time   pass-3
77 And again he (the bear) leaves.

(28) 78 Tarde-ya-ru-pti-n-ña-taq-si
        late-VRBL-ASP-ADVDS-3P-NOW-EMPH-RPT

```
                chay    okumari-qa   ok    ni-n
                this    bear-TOP     one   say-3

                waka-n-ta-s        chay-pi
                cow-3P-OBJ-RPT     this-LOC

                miku-na-n-paq
                eat-NOM-3P-PUR

                sipi-chka-pti-n-si,
                kill-IMPRF-ADVDS-3P-RPT

                ok    yayan-nin      kusillo        amu-spa    ni-n:
                one   old.man-3P     little.devil   come-ADV   say-3

                "Imana-sqa-m         kay    animal+masi-ki-ta       sipi-nki?
                 what.do-PRT-DIR     this   animal+friend-2P-OBJ    kill-2

            79 Kunan-mi    qam-ta-pas        kay-na-ta       ruwa-ru-sqayki"
               now-DIR     you-OBJ-ALSO      this-SIM-OBJ    hacer-ASP-1FUT2

                ni-spa.
                say-ADV
```

80 Ni-pti-n-si   piña-ri-ku-n   okumari-qa.
   say-ADVDS-3P-RPT   annoy-ASP-REF-3   bear-TOP

81 Ina-spa
   do.like.this-ADV

```
                "Imana-sqa        mana   tayta-yki-ta
                 what.do-PRT      not    father-2P-OBJ
```

chay-na-ta   ni-mu-nki-chu?
this-SIM-OBJ say-AFAR-2-NEG

82 Ama   ñoqa-ta   qaspan-niy-ta   punki-chi-y-chu.
   not   I-OBJ   lung-1P-OBJ   swell.up-CAUS-2IMP-NEG

83 Yanqa-m   qam-ta-wan
   in.vain-DIR you-OBJ-ACCOMP

   qati-ra-chi-chka-yki-man"
   follow-ASP-CAUS-IMPRF-1PRS2-COND

   ni-spa.
   say-ADV

78 When it now had gotten late, and while this bear was killing one of his cows in order to eat, an old little devil is coming and says: "Why do you kill your animal-friend (your equal)? 79 Now I am going to do like this with you." 80 When he said this, the bear got angry. 81 And he said to him: "Why don't you talk like that to your father. 82 Don't make me enraged (make my lungs swell up). 83 In vain I would make you follow me."

(29) 84 Ni-pti-n-si   okumari
     say-ADVDS-3P-RPT   bear

     piña-kacha-ri-ku-spa
     annoy-HERE.AND.THERE-ASP-REF-ADV

     ok-ta   taka-ta   qo-n
     one-OBJ   fist.knock-OBJ give-3

     wañu-chi-q-lla-ña.
     die-CAUS-AG-LIM-NOW

85 Ina-pti-n-si   chay kusillo-qa   api-rpari-n.
   do.like.this-ADVDS-3P-RPT this little.devil-TOP grip-MOMENT-3

84 When he said this, the bear, being very angry, gave him a punch, as if to kill him. 85 Then this little devil grabbed him.

(30) 86 Ina-spa-n-si   qapi-rpari-n   qapari-npa-ri-n.
        do.like.this-ADV-3P-RPT strangle-MOMENT-3 scream-AFAR-ASP-3

     87 "Mana-ña-m   chayna-sqayki-ña-chu"
        not-NOW-DIR   do.this-1FUT2-NOW-NEG

ni-spa-n-si
say-ADV-3P-RPT

roqa-pa-rpari-ku-n.
beg-BEN-MOMENT-REF-3

88 Ina-spa-s
do.like.this-ADV-RPT

    (ina-spa-n-si)   chay vaca-kuna-ta-pas   qati-rpari-n.
    do.like.this-ADV-3P-RPT this COW-PLUR-OBJ-ALSO follow-MOMENT-3

89 Ina-spa-s   chay-pi deja-rpari-n.
   do.like.this-ADV-RPT this-LOC leave-MOMENT-3

86 Then he strangles; he screams. 87 And he begs (saying): "I am not going to do like this to you." 88 And his cows also he drives away. And he leaves him (the bear) there.

(31) 90 Ina-pti-n-si   chay okumari-qa llaki-sqa
    do.like.this-ADVDS-3P-RPT this bear-TOP   get.sad-PRT

    "Kay-cha   kay kay-pi   allin apu.
    this-DOUBT this this-LOC good owner

    91 Imana-saq-taq   kunan-qa?
    what.do-1FUT-QUEST now-TOP

    92 Imayna-taq kunan apa-saq   padreno-y-pa   ni-wa-sqa-n-ta?"
    how-QUEST   now   take-1FUT godfather-1P-GEN say-1O-REL-3P-OBJ

    ni-spa-s
    say-ADV-RPT

rima-pa-ku-n.
talk-BEN-REF-3

93 Chay-pi-s   yarqa-y-manta-pas   yaqa+yaqa-lla   wañu-n.
   this-LOC-RPT be.hungry-INF-ABL-ALSO almost+almost-LIM die-3

90 Then very sad, the bear says to himself: "This one here is very forceful. 91 What do I do now? How am I going to bring that what my godfather told me to." 93 In this place he almost dies from hunger.

(32) 94 Ina-spa-n-si   chay   ñawpa-q
       do.like.this-ADV-3P-RPT this   go.ahead-AG

              leon-kuna-wan   carga-mu-sqa-n-ta   maska-n.
              lion-PLUR-INSTRM   carry-AFAR-REL-3P-OBJ   seek-3

       95 Ina-spa-s   mana   tari-n-chu.
          do.like.this-ADV-RPT   not   find-3-NEG

       96 Ina-spa-s
          do.like.this-ADV-RPT

              kuti-na-n-paq
              return-NOM-3P-PUR

              ñaka+ñaka-y-ta   tari-ru-n
              suffer+suffer-INF-OBJ   find-ASP-3

              chay   ichi-sqa-n   leon-lla-ta.
              this   mount-REL-3P   lion-LIM-OBJ

94 And he looks for the lions (being ahead) on which he had (earlier) carried (his things). 95 And he doesn't find them. 96 And in order to return, suffering he finds this lion which he mounts.

(33) 97 Ina-spa-n-si
       do.like.this-ADV-3P-RPT

              chay   leon-pi   ichi-ri-ku-spa
              this   lion-LOC   mount-ASP-REF-ADV

              maska-n   ok-nin-kuna-ta.
              seek-3   one-3P-PLUR-OBJ

       98 Mana-s   tari-n-chu.
          not-RPT   find-3-NEG

       99 Aswan-si   chay kusillo-wan   topa-ro-n.
          instead-RPT this little.devil-ACCOMP   meet-ASP-3

       100 Ina-spa-s   mancha-ri-ku-n.
           do.like.this-ADV-RPT   get.afraid-ASP-REF-3

              101 Okumari-qa
                  bear-TOP

"Kunan-qa capaz-cha wañu-ra-chi-lla-wa-nqa-pas"
now-TOP almost-DOUBT die-ASP-CAUS-LIM-1O-3FUT-ALSO

ni-spa-s
say-ADV-RPT

mancha-ri-ku-n.
get.afraid-ASP-REF-3

102 Lomismu-lla-taq-si kusillo-pas mancha-ri-ku-n
the.same-LIM-EMPH-RPT little.devil-ALSO get.afraid-ASP-REF-3

"Kunan-qa wapu-ya-ru-n-ña-chiki.
now-TOP "strong"-VRBL-ASP-3-NOW-DOUBT

103 Chay-chiki kay atun leon-pi ichi-n"
this-DOUBT this big lion-LOC mount-3

ni-spa-n.
say-ADV-3P

104 Mancha-ri-sqa qawa-naku-n.
get.afraid-ASP-PRT look-RECIP-3

105 Ina-spa-n-si rima-paya-naku-y-ta ati-n-chu.
do.like.this-ADV-3P-RPT talk-BEN-RECIP-INF-OBJ can-3-NEG

106 Opalla-lla muyo-ri-spa-n
quietly-LIM turn-ASP-ADV-3P

ok-nin-pas ok-nin-pas pasa-mu-n-ku.
one-3P-ALSO one-3P-ALSO pass-AFAR-3-PL

97 And mounting this lion, he looks for the others. 98 He doesn't find them. 99 Instead he meets this little devil. 100 And he gets scared. 101 He gets scared and says: "Maybe he now will kill me." 102 In the same way the little devil also gets scared and says: "Maybe he has now become big, strong. 103 That is why he is sitting on this big lion." 104 Scared they look at each other. 105 Then (from fear) neither of them is able to talk to the other. 106 Quietly turning, both of them leave.

(34) 107 Chay-pi-s chay okumari-qa wañu-n yarqa-y-manta.
this-LOC-RPT this bear-TOP die-3 be.hungry-INF-ABL

108 Ina-spa-s mana-ña wasi-n-man chaya-n-chu.
do.like.this-ADV-RPT not-NOW house-3P-GOAL arrive-3-NEG

107 In this place the bear dies from hunger. 108 And he is not able to return home.

Appendix 2

Okumaripa Watuchin – Chart

			SS/DS	ASP	TENSE
(1)	1	Chay okumare-**s** ka-sqa			-sqa
	2	Tiya-sqa qaqa-pa chawpi-pi		(SS)	-sqa
	3	Chawpi-n-ta-ña-taq pasa-sqa mayo, mana chaki-q.		DS	-sqa
(2)	4	Aypa ina-pti-n-ña-taq-**si** chaka-nes-qa ok lado chimpa-man ok rako qeru-ta chura-sqa.		DS	-sqa
(3)	5	Chay runa-**s** ka-sqa apu apu.		DS	-sqa
	6	Y miku-sqa punchaw-nin-pi ok toru-ta-puni.		(SS)	-sqa
	7	Y chay qeru-n-ta-kama-**s** apa-q chay wañu-sqa turu-ta miku-na-n-paq.		SS	-q
	8	Chay machay-nin-pi-**s** ka-sqa ok atu-n perul y aypa yanta-kuna chay-pi timpu-chi-na-n-paq.		DS	-sqa

(4) 9 Y mana pi-ta-pas respeta-sqa-chu.   DS   -sqa

    10 Ok laqta-ta ri-spa-n-ku-ña-taq-**si**
         may-man yayku-spa-pas
         apu runa-kuna-pa ima-n-ta-pas
         lliw aypu-rari-n pobre-kuna-man.   SS   -rari -n

(5) 11 Warmi-n-ña-taq-**si** ka-sqa warma-cha-lla.   DS   -sqa

    12 Llaqta-manta-**s** suwa-mu-sqa   DS   -sqa
         chay machay-nin-paq.

    13 Ina-spa-**s** wawa-n ka-sqa.   DS   -sqa

(6) 14 Chay-lla-pi-**s** llamka-sqa.   DS   -sqa

    15 Ina-spa-n-**si** chay-na puri-sqa   SS?   -sqa
         runa-kuna-ta wañu-chi-stin.

(7) 16 Chay-ta-ña-taq-**si**
         mana muna-sqa-chu warmi-n.   DS   -sqa

    17 Ina-spa-**s** wawa-n-ta ni-n: SS   -n
         "Imayna-raq iskapa-ru-ku-chwan?"
         ni-spa.

(8) 18 Ina-pti-n-ña-taq-**si** chay wawa-n ni-n: DS   -n
         "Suya-yku-y mama-y.
         19 Ñoqa-m tayta-y-ta orma-yka-chi-saq
         kay qero-nta-kama amu-chka-pti-n."

    20 Ina-pti-n-**si** ok vez chay-na
         torillo tonto-ri-sqa
         qero-ta pasa-mu-chka-pti-n
         qero-ta moyo-rpari-chi-sqa.   DS?   -rpari -sqa

    21 Ina-pti-n-**si** mayo-man pasa-yku-n.   DS   -yku   -n

(9) 22 Ina-spa-n remolino-man pasa-yku-n.   SS   -yku   -n

    23 Ina-spa-n-**si** wañu-n.   SS   -n

(10) 24 Ina-pti-n-**si** chay wawa-n		
mama-n-ta apa-ri-ku-spa-n		
ri-pu-n llaqta-man.	DS	-n
25 Ina-pti-n-**si** llaqta-pi		
mana bautiza-sqa ka-pti-n		
ok priest-man qo-yku-n	DS -yku	-n
bautiza-chi-na-n-paq.		
26 Ina-pti-n-**si** bautiza-ra-chi-spa		
yacha-y + wasi-man chura-n.	DS	-n
(11) 27 Ina-pti-n-**si** pichqa wata-yoq-ña.	DS	?
28 Ina-pti-n-**si** barba-n wiña-ra-mu-n.	DS -ra	-n
29 Ina-pti-n-**si** chay-manta chuta-n	DS?	-n
chay-pi waron-kuna.		
(12) 30 Ina-spa-**s**	DS	?
"Paderno-y,		
kay warma-kuna-m bastidia-wa-n."		
(13) 31 "Ina-pti-n-**si**		
ok taka-ta qo-y,		
macho zonzo"		
ni-pti-n-si	(DS)	
taka-ta qo-n.	DS	-n
32 Ina-pti-n-**si** wañu-rari-n.	DS -rari	-n
33 Ina-pti-n-**si** padreno-n-qa		
sipi-na-n-paq ni-sqa.	DS	-sqa
(14) 34 Ina-pti-n-**si**		
chay sacristan-nin-wan		
atun ochko-ta ochku-ra-chi-n	DS -ru	-n
pichqa negro-wan.		
35 Ina-pti-n-**si** chay okumarí		
chay ochku-pa pata-n-ta		
pasa-chka-pti-n		
tanqa-yku-rpari-sqa.	DS -yu-rpari	-sqa
36 Ina-pti-n-**si** pasa-yku-sqa.	DS -yku	-sqa

(15) 37 Ina-spa-n-**si** chay-manta-s
    lloqsi-rpari-mu-n.   SS   -rpari -n

    38 Ina-spa-n-**si** chay negro-kuna-ta
    chay uchku-pi pampa-rpari-n.   SS   -rpari -n

(16) 39 Ina-spa-n-ña-taq-**si** tayta-n-ina
        kallpa-yoq.   SS   Ø
    40 Chay-na-lla-ta-taq-**si** miku-n-pas.   SS   -n

(17) 41 Ina-pti-n-**si**
        mana-ña aguanta-y-ta ati-spa-ña-taq-**si**
        atu atun torre-man
        chay ayjado-n-ta kacha-n   DS   -n
        campana toca-mu-na-n-paq.

    42 Chay torre-pi-**s** tawa runa-kuna-ta
        saya-ra-chi-mu-n,   DS   -ru   -n
        chay-manta tanqa-yka-mu-na-n-paq.

    43 Ina-pti-n-**si**
        campana-ta toca-chka-pti-n
        tanqa-y-ta muna-mu-n-ku.   DS   -n

    44 Ina-pti-n-**si** mana ati-n-cho.   DS   -n
    45 Aswan-**si** chay runa-kuna-ta
        tanqa-yka-ri-mu-n.   DS   -yku-ri -n

(18) 46 Ina-spa-n-ña-taq-**si** chay-pi
        wañu-n chay runa-kuna.   DS   -n

(19) 47 Ina-pti-n-ña-taq-**si** padreno-n-qa
        lliw-ña piña-ru-ku-n.   DS   -ru   -n

    48 Ina-spa-n-**si** montaña-ta-ña-taq-**si**
            kacha-rpari-n   SS   -rpari -n
        chunka iskay-niyoq asno-ntin-ta
        y tawa vaca-ntin-ta.

    49 Ina-pti-n-**si**
        "Chay-pi wañu-mu-chun" ni-spa
        chay montaña-man-ña-taq-**si**   DS   Ø

(20) 50 Chay-pi-ña-taq-**si** pone-rpari-sqa.   DS   -rpari -sqa

   51 Ina-spa-**s** tota-manta
         rikcha-ri-spa-n-ña-taq-**si**   (SS)
         qawa-kacha-ri-pti-n-ña-taq-**si**   (SS)
         lado-n-pi leon-kuna ka-chka-sqa.   DS   -chka -sqa

   52 Chay llapa asno-kuna
         apa-sqa-n-ña-taq-**si**,
         mana ka-sqa-chu.   DS   -sqa

      53 Ataka-n-kuna-lla-ña
            wischu + wischu ka-chka-sqa.   DS   -sqa

(21) 54 Ina-pti-n-**si** leyon-kuna-ta-qa
         chay okumari-qa ni-n: DS   -n
         "May-pi chay asno-kuna vaca-y?"
         ni-spa.

   55 Ina-pti-n-ña-taq-**si** leyon-kuna-qa
         pawa-yka-ri-n.   DS   -yka-ri-n

   56 Ina-pti-n-**si** ok taka-wan sapa
         leon pawa-yko-q-ta sipi-rari-n.   DS   -rari -n

(22) 57 Ina-spa-**s** ka-q leon-kuna-ta ni-n: SS   -n
         "Qam-kuna-m kunan yanta-ta
            carga-nki-chik
         aqalli-ki-chik-wan-pas."

(23) 58 Ina-pti-n-**si**
         chunka iskay-niyoq leon-pi
            carga-spa-n
         ok-nin macho leon-pi-ña-taq-si
            echi-ri-ku-spa
         pasa-n padreno-n-pa-ta.   DS (leon)? -n

   59 Ina-pti-n-**si**
         "Imayna-ña-mari kay-qa?
      60 Leon-wan-pas carga-mu-n
            yanta-kuna-ta-pas.
         61 Trampa chura-sqa-y-manta-pas
               iskapa-mu-n.
         62 Ima-ña-ch kay-qa?"
            ni-spa-n-**si**
         rima-pa-ku-n padreno-n-qa.   DS   -n

63 Ina-pti-n-**si** kaq padreno-n-qa kacha-n: DS? -n
   "Kunan-mi kaq kuti-nki.
64 Ina-spa-m chay-manta apa-mu-wa-nki
   raku qeru-kuna-ta ima-pi-pas."

(24) 65 Ina-spa-**s**
         miku-na-n-paq
         qo-n soqta vaca-ta. SS -n
    66 Qati-ri-chi-n. DS -ri -n

(25) 67 Ina-pti-n-**si** pasa-n. DS -n
    68 Qati-ri-ku-spa ri-chka-n. SS (DS)? -n

69 Ina-pti-n-**si** ok runa-wan tupa-rpari-n. DS? -rpari -n

(26) 70 Ina-spa-n-ña-taq-**si** ni-n: SS? -n
         "May-ta-m ri-nki,
         ama ri-y-chu.
    71 Si-chus ri-pti-ki-qa
         mana-m yacha-ku-n-chu kuti-mu-yki"
         ni-spa.

72 Ni-pti-n-**si** okumari-qa
         piña-kacha-ri-ko-n. DS -ri -n

73 Ina-spa ni-n: SS -n
    "Ama amu-wa-y-chu.
74 Ima-pas ni-q-niy yanqa-taq.
75 Kay kay-pi sipi ima-ru-yki-man.
76 Ina-pti-n qam aswan
    mana tayta mama-yki-wan-pas
    tupa-ra-pu-chka-waq-chu."

(27) 77 Ina-spa-n-**si** kaq pasa-n. SS -n

(28) 78 Tarde-ya-ru-pti-n-ña-taq-**si**
         chay okumari-qa,
         ok ni-n,
         waka-n-ta-**s** chay-pi
         miku-na-n-paq
         sipi-chka-pti-n-**si**, (DS)
         ok yayan-nin kusillo amu-spa
              ni-n: DS
         "Imana-sqa-m kay
              animal + masi-ki-ta sipi-nki?

Okumaripa Watuchin – Chart

       79 Kunan-mi qam-ta-pas kay-na-ta
           ruwa-ru-sqayki"
           ni-spa.
80 Ni-pti-n-**si** piña-ri-ku-n okumari-qa.   DS   -ri   -n

81 Ina-spa   SS   Ø
         "Imana-sqa mana tayta-yki-ta
         chay-na-ta ni-mu-nki-chu?
      82 Ama ñoqa-ta qaspan-niy-ta
         punki-chi-y-chu.
83 Yanqa-m qam-ta-wan
         qati-ra-chi-chka-yki-man"
         ni-spa.

(29) 84 Ni-pti-n-**si** okumari
         piña-kacha-ri-ku-spa
         ok-ta taka-ta qo-n   SS?   -n
         wañu-chi-q-lla-ña.
   85 Ina-pti-n-**si** chay kusillo-qa
         api-rpari-n.   DS   -rpari -n

(30) 86 Ina-spa-n-**si** qapi-rpari-n
         qapari-npa-ri-n. (two indep. verbs)   SS -rpari/-ri -n

        87 "Mana-ña-m chayna-sqayki-ña-chu"
         ni-spa-n-**si**
         roqa-pa-rpari-ku-n.   SS   -rpari -n

88 Ina-spa-**s**
         (ina-spa-n-si) chay vaca-kuna-ta-pas
         qati-rpari-n.   SS   -rpari -n

89 Ina-spa-**s** chay-pi deja-rpari-n.   SS   -rpari -n

(31) 90 Ina-pti-n-**si** chay okumari-qa llaki-sqa
         "Kay-cha kay kay-pi allin apu.
        91 Imana-saq-taq kunan-qa?
        92 Imayna-taq kunan apa-saq
         padreno-y-pa ni-wa-sqa-n-ta?"
             ni-spa-**s**,   (SS)
         rima-pa-ku-n.   DS   -n

93 Chay-pi-**s** yarqa-y-manta-pas
         yaqa + yaqa-lla wañu-n.   SS   -n

(32) 94 Ina-spa-n-**si** chay ñawpa-q
   leon-kuna-wan carga-mu-sqa-n-ta
     maska-n.   SS   -n

  95 Ina-spa-**s** mana tari-n-chu.   SS   -n

  96 Ina-spa-**s** kuti-na-n-paq
   ñaka+ñaka-y-ta tari-ru-n   SS -ru -n
   chay ichi-sqa-n leon-lla-ta.

(33) 97 Ina-spa-n-**si**
   chay leon-pi ichi-ri-ku-spa
   maska-n ok-nin-kuna-ta.   SS   -n
  98 Mana-**s** tari-n-chu.   SS   -n
  99 Aswan-**si** chay kusillo-wan topa-ro-n. SS -ru -n

100 Ina-spa-**s** mancha-ri-ku-n.   SS -ri -n
  101 Okumari-qa
   "Kunan-qa capaz-cha
   wañu-ra-chi-lla-wa-nqa-pas"
    ni-spa-**s**
   mancha-ri-ku-n.   SS -ri -n

  102 Lomismu-lla-taq-**si** kusillo-pas
   mancha-ri-ku-n   DS -ri -n
   "Kunan-qa wapu-ya-ru-n-ña-chiki.
  103 Chay-chiki kay atun leon-pi ichi-n
    ni-spa-n.
  104 Mancha-ri-sqa qawa-naku-n. DS (-ri) -n
105 Ina-spa-n-**si** rima-paya-naku-y-ta
   ati-n-chu.   SS   -n
106 Opalla-lla muyo-ri-spa-n
   ok-nin-pas ok-nin-pas pasa-mu-n-ku. SS   -n

(34) 107 Chay-pi-**s** chay okumari-qa
   wañu-n yarqa-y-manta.   DS   -n

  108 Ina-spa-**s** mana-ña wasi-n-man
   chaya-n-chu.   SS   -n

Appendix 3
Mankapa Cuenton[1]

Cuento de la Olla

Stage
Stanza I   SS/DS   ASP   TNS

1 Ok runas kasqa   -sqa
   Había dice un hombre que

2 Inaspañataqsi kasararukusqa ok warmiwan   SS   -ru   -sqa
   se casó con una mujer

3 Chayñataqsi chay runa kasqa   SS   -sqa
   ese hombre era viajero

Stanza II
4 Ok veztninpiñataqsi[2] karo ñanta richkasqa SS   -chka -sqa
   una vez se ausentó muy lejos

5 Ok samanaman chayaruspanñataqsi   SS
   y llegó a un lugar de alojamiento

         mankanta orqorimuspa
         en lo cual sacando su olla

---
[1]Lauriault (1958:62–63).
[2]The construction here seems strange, like several others in the original publication (this also applies to the following Coracora texts). Because of the unusual format of the first publication, certain errors/typos might also have been introduced through the later processing of the texts, for which I have to take responsibility. As for the Spanish, it is kept much like the original but missing accents have been added. The word order has sometimes been changed in order to better match with the Quechua line above (see also chapter 1).

chaypi lawakoq pasaykon   -yku   -n
comenzó a preparar una sopa

Scene I
Stanza III
6 Inaptinsi mana mankaqa timpuriyta atincho   DS   -n
　 y la olla no pudo hervir

7 Inaptinsi runaqa rimapakun: DS   -n
　 en lo que el hombre hablaba

　　　—imanantaq kay qanra mankataqa
　　　—que pasa con esta olla sucia

　　　chakuncho o chikichakuncho
　　　el mal olor o el que me va a venir

　　　icha waqllinchu,
　　　se pierde,

　　　kampas inapas kaypi ñotorparisaq—
　　　cuidado que voy a hacer en pedazos—

　　　nispa
　　　diciendo

Stanza IV
8 Niptinsi mankaqa rimarimparin kaynispa: DS   ri-rpari -n
　 cuando así hablaba la olla habló o contestó
　 en esta forma

　　　—warmikin waqllichakanqa
　　　—tu mujer estás perdiendo (en estos momentos)

　　　manam ñoqacho—
　　　y no digas que yo— ??

　　　nispa
　　　diciendo

9 Niptinsi
　 cuando le dijo así

　　　runaqa pensapakusqa   DS   -sqa
　　　el hombre pensado (pensó) pues

Scene II
Stanza V

        "kutiruni" nispa,   SS   -n
        regresaré, se dice entre sí

        kutin
        y regresó

10 Inaspa wasinman yaykurparin   SS   -rpari -n
   y entró a su casa

11 Inaptinsi okwan puñoch haqta tarirparin   DS/SS -rpari -n
   a la que encontró durmiendo con otro

Stanza VI
12 Inaspas mana rikuq
   y se hace que no vé

        tukuspa puriykachan   SS   -ykacha -n
        y comenzó a pasearse

13 Inachkaptillansi kaviton okuman pasaykuspa
   y ese hombre entró debajo de su catre

        pakarparikun   DS   -rpari -n
        donde se ocultó

Scene III
Stanza VII
14 Inaptinsi warmitaqa tapun somaqllata   DS   -n
   que después le preguntó a su mujer muy bonito

15 Inaptinsi warmiqa piñarirparikuspa
   a la que su mujer se molestó y

        allin mawa allinnintinta
        entre bien y mal

        rimayta kachaykuspa
        comenzó hablar con

        tratakun runallataqa   DS   -n
        lo que le resondró al hombre

Stanza VIII
16 Inaptin aswan piñarikuspa
   que mucho más se molestó (el hombre)

okta tanwanta apispa
agarrando su bastón

waqtarparin chay pakakuq runata omapi   DS   -rpari   -n
le pegó un golpe en la cabeza al hombre
que estaba oculto

17 Inaptinsi wañorparin   DS   -rpari   -n
lo que se quedó muerto

Conclusion
Stanza IX

18 Chay warmitaqsi qaway qawasqanmanta
y esa mujer de tanto mirar

quejakoq pasan: DS   -n
se fue a quejarse (diciendo)

—qosaymi runata sipirun—
—mi esposo ha matado a un hombre

nispa
diciendo

19 Inaptinsi qayachispa
y lo hizo llamar

tapuptinñaqsi chay runaqa:
cuando preguntó (respondió) aquel hombre
(que mató)

—mankan hochayoq
—la olla tiene la culpa

manka "warmiki waqllichkan"
a causa que la olla,
que tu mujer está perdida

niwaptinmi
me dijo

kay sipini—
por eso maté—

nispa nin   DS   -n
diciendo dice

Appendix 4

Watuchi I[1]

ACT I/STAGE SS/DS ASP TNS
Scene I
Stanza I
1 Condorse otoq compadreyoq kasqa   -sqa
   Había un cóndor que tenía compadre un zorro

2 Condorñataq risqa wasinta: SS   -sqa
   el cóndor había ido a su casa

   —Compadre akuchik loria misa uyarakamusun—
   —*Compadre vamos a la misa de gloria (oír)*—

Scene II
Stanza II
3 Inaspas oyakuq siqaykunku   SS   -yku -n
   y se fueron a oír

4 Inaspas chayaruptinkus   SS
   cuando llegaron

       5 chaypi aypa aypallaña condorpa ayllunkuna kasqa
          ahí había bastantes cóndores (familias)

       6 loria misata oyakusqa llapallan   DS   -sqa
          oyendo misa de la gloria todo

---
[1]Lauriault (1957:24–26).

247

Scene III
Stanza III
7 Atoqpa compadrenñataqsi chinkarparisqa   DS   -rpari -sqa
   el compadre del zorro ya también se perdió

8 Atoqñataqsi maskasqa   DS   -sqa
   el zorro también le buscó

   —qamchu compadrey kanki
   —*tu eres mi compadre?*

   qamchu compadrey kanki—
   tu eres mi compadre?—

   nispa
   diciendo

   manaña tarisqachu   -sqa
   no lo encontró

ACT II
Scene IV/Stage
Stanza IV
9 Niwña partapurukuspañataqsi
   cuando se equivocó del todo

   Diosman asuykusqa   SS   -sqa
   se acercó a Dios

10 Diosñataqsi nisqa: DS   -sqa
   el Dios también le dijo:

   —soqta piyarata kanchuta kanchurakamuy—
   —*6 piaros de sogas háztelo*—

Bridge
11 Inaspansi kanchuntin rin Diosman   DS   -n
   y se va con la soga ante Dios

Scene V
Stanza V
12 Oktawansi nin:
   volvió a decirle

   —qanchis piyaratawan kanchumuy—   DS   -n
   — *haga 7 piaros más*—

nispa
diciendo

13 Inaptinsi oktawan rin   DS   -n
cuando le dijo así volvió

kanchoq iskay piyaratawan
a hacer 2 piaros más

Scene VI
Stanza VI

14 Chaymanta kaq kutin Diosman   SS   -n
después otra vez volvió a Dios

nin: (SS)   -n
dice

—ñam com—
—*de la gloria*—

cinturamanta watarachikuspa
haciendo amarrar de la cintura

kachaykachikamun chay kanchuwan   SS   -yku   -n
se hizo soltar con esa soga

15 Chawpitañas kusa kusa
al medio ya grande grande (ya dice)

atenitañas amuykuchkan   SS   -yku-chka -n
está viniendo

Scene VII
Stanza VII

16 Coroñataqsi pasachkasqa altunta   DS   -chka -sqa
y un loro ya también (dice) estaba pasando por el aire

atoqñataq nisqa: DS   -sqa
al cual le dijo el zorro:

—weqro watoytañataq
—*loro cuidado*

kutuwaq—
que rompas mi soga—

17 Inaptinñataqsi kutirirparisqa
   por eso volviendo

        weqroqa kuturparisqa   DS   -rpari -sqa
   el loro lo rompió

18 Inaspa ormaykamusqa   DS   -yku   -sqa
   y que el zorro se cayó

19 Inaspa amusqa: SS   -sqa
   y vino

      —sacha awallamantaq
      —*encima de hierbas no más*

      paja awallamantaq—
      encima de paja no más—

         nispa
         diciendo

Scene VIII
Stanza VIII
20 Nichkaspansi atun waqcha rumiman ormaykusqa   SS   -yku   -sqa
   diciendo así, se cayó a una piedra afilada

21 Chaypis atoqpa akan cheqerparisqa   DS   -rpari -sqa
   ahí dice hasta se desparramó el caca de zorro

ACT III
Scene IX
Stanza IX
22 Inaptinñataqsi compadren chaypi kakaykachkaqta
                              tarirun   DS   -ru   -n
   y después su compadre lo encontró llorando

23 Inaspansi nin: DS   -n
   el cual (el zorro?) le dijo:

      —Imanasqam compadre
      — *por qué compadre*

      chay natapurini llullakuwanki.
      así mismo te has mentido

      Kunanmi anuyamuspay mikusqayki
      ahora sanándome te voy a comer

    mana chayqa wawqeymani nisaq
    o si no a mi hermano diré

Inaptinmi maypipas chaypipas
por eso en donde sea

        pan nichisunki,
        te hará decir pan

chayllatapas pensakacharispayki
pensando eso siquiera

kunan mikuyta aparamuway
ahora tráeme comida

o de no apaway mikunakaqman
o si no llévame donde se come

Qamqariki askamallamunki
tu si puedes ir a cualquier

    maykamapas riruwaq—
    sitio rápido—

Scene X
Stanza X

24 Inaptinsi condorqa nin: DS   -n
    el cóndor le dijo:

    —manam qamqa compadreychu
    —tu no eres mi compadre

kanki amigullaymi—
tu eres mi amigo no más—

        nispansi,
        diciendo

gloria misaman kaq pasakun   (SS)   -n
y lo volvió a la misa de gloria

—sichus tiempoy kanqa
—si voy a tener tiempo

inaptincha Diosta mañamusaq
pediré a Dios para que te

> mikunallan apachimusunaykipaq—
> *mande su comida—*

25 Inaspansi pasakun　　　　　　　　　　SS　　-n
　　y se fué

Bridge
26 Chaypis atoq compadrenqa quedarparin onqosqa　　DS　-rpari -n
　　ahí (dice) el zorro se quedó enfermo

Scene XI
Stanza XI
27 Inaptinsi ayllun tarirparin　　　　　　DS　-rpari -n
　　al cual lo encontró sus familias

> chay ranranrani　　　　　　　　　　DS
> *en pedregales*

> —anahachan anahachan—nispa
> *?? — cuando estaba—(delirando)*

> nichkaptin
> *cuando estaba diciendo así*

28 Inaspas nin:　　　　　　　　　　　　SS　　-n
　　y le dijo (que)

> —imanasunkim wawaqey akuchik
> *—tienes hermano*

> ripusun taytanchikmi
> *vamos a irnos, nuestro padre*

> maskakachaw achkanchik—
> *nos está buscando—*

Scene XII
Stanza XII
29 Inaspansi wawqenqa pasan　　　　　　SS　　-n
　　por eso (dice) se va su hermano

> qepirkuspa
> *cargándolo*

> chay onqosqa atoqa
> *el zorro enfermo*

30 Willakun kaymi sucedewan: DS   -n
    lo cuenta que le sucedió (diciendo)

  —compadrey condormi loria misawan
  —mi compadre cóndor llevándome a

      aparuwaspan
      la misa de la gloria

dejarparimuwaptin
cuando me dejó

ampuchkaptiy loroñataq
cuando me estuve viniendo el loro

waskayta kuturparimuy
yo también lo arrancó mi soga

tinurmaykamuni inaptinmi
por eso me caí (por eso)

chaypi onqochkarani compadrey amuspapas
(allá) estaba enfermo cuando vino mi compadre

manam riqsiwanchu,
también no me conoce

suyaylla suyaykuchunqa
nada más que se espera

      siminta yaykuspapas
      por la boca entrando

      ujitintam llogsiramusaq
      por el poto saldré

compadre kayta yacharashisaq
y le voy a enseñar ser compadre

kay ruwawasqanmanta—
de lo que me hizo así—

      nispankus
      diciendo

Conclusión
    chayanku wasinkuman   DS   -n
    y así (dice) llegaron a su casa

Appendix 5

Watuchi II[1]

ACT I/STAGE   SS/DS   ASP   TNS
Scene I
Stanza I
1   Orqopis atoq okuchawan tiyasqa   -sqa
     En el cerro (dice) vivían zorro con pericote

     2   Ninakusqaku: SS   -sqa
       y se decían

         —compadre kunanmi Santunchik—
         —compadre ahora es nuestro cumpleaños—

         nispa
         diciendo

    3   Atoqñataq nisqa: DS   -sqa
       el zorro le dijo:

         —compadre guitarrata tukamuchkay—
         —compadre vaya tocando la guitarra—

Stanza II
    4   Inaspañataqsi ninawan kañaykusqa   DS?   -sqa
       después lo quemó con candela

    5   Inaspansi ("cowite" nispansi) afanaykan atoqa   DS   -yka   -n
       y se afana creyendo que es un cohete el zorro

---
[1]Lauriault (1957:26–27).

ACT II
Scene II
Stanza III
   6 Okniñataqsi escaparparikun   DS   -rpari   -n
       el otro ya también se escapó

   7 Kaqñataqsi tuparparisqa mikuch kaqwan   DS   -rpari   -n
       volvió a encontrarse cuando estaba comiendo

        8 Inaspa:

            —compadre yarqaymantam kachkani
            —compadre, de hambre estoy

            mikurparisqayki—
            te voy a comer—

            nin atoq   -n
            le dijo el zorro

Stanza IV
   9 Inaptinsi
       y el otro le respondió

            —compadre, ama mikuwaychu—
            —compadre, no me comas—

                nispa nin okucha   DS   -n
                (diciendo) dice el ratón

  10 Inaptinsi okuchaqa pasaspan
      y el ratón yendose

           ñataqsi qallumpa puntachampi
           en su punta de la lengua

           apita aparamun   SS   -ru   -n
           trajo mazamorra

Stanza V
  11 Inaspansi malleykachin: SS   -yku   -n
      que le hizo probar

           —compadre kayta malleyku—
           —compadre prueba esto—

nispa
diciendo

—compadre, maymantataq kayta
—compadre, de dónde has traído esto

aparparimunki apariway
tráeme o llévame

api kaqman—
donde esa mazamorra—

nispa   DS
diciendo

12 okucha nisqa: DS   -sqa
   el ratón dijo:

—akuchikyari compadre—
—vamos pues compadre—

13 Inaspas pasanku   DS   -n
   y se fueron

Scene III
Stanza VI
14 Apita qawaykachispañataqsi qawah   DS   -n
   cuando lo hizo ver (la mazamorra) él ya también ve

15 Inaptinsi atoq mankaman omanta satirparisqa   SS? -rpari -sqa
   y el zorro puso o metió a la olla su cabeza

Stanza VII
16 Inaptinsi mankamanta mana oman lloqsiyta atisqachu DS   -sqa
   y de la olla no pudo salir su cabeza

17 Inaptinsi waqtakachakusqa kuchukunaman omanta   DS -chaku -sqa
   por eso se golpeaba a rincones su cabeza

Stanza VIII
18 Compadren okuchañataqsi pasakusqa   DS   -sqa
   el compadre ratón se fue

19 Inaspas atoq waqtarparin perqaman   DS -rpari -n
   y el zorro lo golpeó su cabeza a la pared

(Bridge)

Manas mallisqapaschu apita	SS -sqa
y no probó la mazamorra	

ACT III
Scene IV
Stanza IX
    20 Chaymantas atoq pasaspa condorwan
       de ahí yéndose el zorro con el cóndor

           toparparisqa   SS   -rpari -sqa
           se encontró

    21 Inaspas nisqa: SS   -sqa

           —compadre, yarqawanmi—
           —compadre, tengo hambre—

           nisqa atoq condorta   -sqa
           dijo el zorro al cóndor

Stanza X
    22 Condorñataqsi yanurusqa   DS   -ru   -sqa
       el cóndor ya también cocinó

           uchuy lluku mankachapi motita:
           en una ollita chicha maiz

           —compadre, kay motichatayari mikuyqa—
           —compadre, este motecito cómete—

           kay nisqa   (SS)   -sqa
           le dijo

    23 Atoqñataqsi mana mikuyta atisqachu   DS   -sqa
       el zorro ya también no podía comer

           atun omas kaptin
           porque su cabeza era grande

Stanza XI
    24 Atoqñataqsi nisqa: SS   -sqa
       el zorro ya también dijo:

           —mikuy ma ver qam compadre—
           —come tu compadre—

Watuchi II

mikusqa ratuchallas mikurparisqa *el cual comió rápido*	DS	-rpari	-sqa
25 Inaspa atoq nisqa: *por eso el zorro le dijo*	DS		-sqa

—compadre, mikurparisqayki,
—compadre, te comeré

manam aguantaniñachu yarqaymanta—
ya no puedo soportar este hambre—

—kay munduta apiykuchkay
—este mundo vaya agarrando

karnerukunata aparparimusqayki—
carneros te voy a traer—

(Bridge)
Manas compadrenqa amunchu   DS   -n
y no vino el compadre

Scene V
Stanza XII
26 Inaptinsi akampas toqyapaq mundo ñiterparisqa   DS   -rpari   -sqa
y el mundo lo apachurró hasta que reviente su cacana

27 Inaptinsi atoqqa chaypi
y el zorro allá

asnariytaña qallaykuchkasqa   DS   -yku-chka   -sqa
comenzó a pudrirse ya

Stanza XIII
28 Inaptinsi condorkuna muyuykarimusqa   DS   -yku-ri   -sqa
y los cóndores ?daban vueltas

chay atoq wañusqa mikunankupaq
para que coma ese zorro muerto

29 Inaptinsi chay amusqa   DS   -sqa
por eso vino aquel

chay atoqpa compadren
que era compadre de zorro

Stanza XIV
  30 Inaspansi nin ayllunkunata: SS   -n
     por eso le dice a sus familias

      —ama mikusunchu kay atoqtaqa
      —no vamos a comer este zorro

      ampi kasqampim wañun,
      ha muerto porque es zorro

      ampi yaruchwanmi ñoqanchikpas—
      podemos volvernos zorros también nosotros así —

         nispansi ninakunku   SS   -n
         se dijeron

  31 Inaspankus chaypi dejarparispankus
     por eso hay dejando

         pasakunku   SS   -n
         pasaron

ACT IV
Scene VI
Stanza XV
  32 Inaptinñataqsi compadren okuchañataq
     por eso (dice) su compadre ratón

         purikuchkaspan tuparparisqa   DS   -rpari   -sqa
         andando se encontró

  33 Inaspansi nin ó sapallan rimapakun: SS   -n
     y le dijo ó hablaba solo

      —compadreychus, inam wañurusqa,
      —(compadre) cómo mi compadre había muerto

      miki kara, chaykiki ampin apiptin
      era zonzo, por eso cuando agarró el zoncear

      wañukachachkan
      murió

      kaqllach kawsari muchkanqa
      volverá a (despertarse)

ampikaynin pasaraptin—
cuando le pase el zoncear—

    nispansi   SS   -n
    diciendo

    pasakun
    asi se fué

Stanza XVI
34 Inaptinñataqsi richkan richkan   SS   -chka   -n
  y yendo yendo

    inaptin kaqlla tuparparin chay wañusqata   SS   -rpari   -n
    volvió a encontrarle al muerto

35 Inaspas mancharikun   SS   -ri   -n
  por eso se asustó

Stanza XVII
36 Inaptinsi pelumpas sayaririrparinraq   DS   -ri-rpari -n
  por eso su pelo también se paró

37 Inaspas rimapakun ampikaspancha   DS   -n
  y hablaba y hablaba porque es zonzo

    purikuchkan kaypi wakpi   SS   -chka   -n
    estará andando por aquí por allá

(Conclusion)
Stanza XVIII
38 Inaspansi nin: SS   -n
  y le dijo

    —amaña compadre puriychu
    —no andes compadre

    manachu saykunki
    no te canses

    samakamuyña
    descánsate

    mana chaypachaqa Diospas
    de otro modo hasta Dios

castigashunkimanmi—
nos puede castigar —

   nispas nin   (SS)   -n
   así le dijo

39 inaspa pasakun   SS   -n
   y se fué

Appendix 6
El Zorro y la Vizcacha I[1]

(The Fox and the Vizcacha)

| | SS/DS | ASP | TNS |

Scene I

(1) 1 Chay-pita-sh ña-ta suk timpu-sh[2]
    that-ABL-RPT now-OBJ one time-RPT

        kitra-pa:ku-n
        open-PL-3

        biskacha-kah-wan   atuh-kahsi:kya-ta
        vizcacha-DEF-ACCOMP   fox-DEF channel-OBJ

  2 Chay-pita-sh hatun lumi-ta ami-chi-n
    that-ABL-RPT big stone-OBJ tip.over-CAUS-3

        atuh-kah-ta biskacha-kah.   DS   -n
        fox-DEF-OBJ vizcacha-DEF

  3 Chay-pita-shi pwidi-n-chu ni sulu-y-ta.   DS   -n
    that-ABL-RPT be.able-3-NEG (nor) take.out-INF-OBJ

        4 Palanka-ta ashi-ku-ya-lka-n
        crowbar-OBJ look.for-REF-IMPRF-PLIMPFR-3

---

[1] In Wroughton 1996:81–83.
[2] The jumping right into the story might be due to the fact that the story is one of a series of fox tales probably told by the same narrator.

	biskacha-kah atuh-kah		DS -ya	-n
	vizcacha-DEF fox-DEF			

1 Then once the vizcacha and the fox opened the gate of the (irrigation) channel. 2 Then the vizcacha made the fox tip a big stone. 3 Then the fox wasn't able to take it out. 4 And the fox and the vizcacha were looking for a crowbar.

Bridge

(2) 5 Fuyrsa-n-man   atinidu-sh.
     strength-3P-GOAL   concerned-RPT

      "ñuha kay-ta   kumsa-la-chi-ku-shah-tra:
      I   this-OBJ   push-OUT-CAUS-REF-1FUT-CONJ.THEN

      kay   lumi-kah"[3]
      this   stone-DEF

            ni-l   DS   -n
            say-ADVSS

    unku-ku-lu-n   pasah   trimpa-ku-yku-l
    carry-REF-OUT-3   much   kneel-REF-IN-ADVSS

5 He (the fox) was concerned about his strength. 6 "I'll make this stone move," he said kneeling down to be able to carry it.

Scene II

(3) 7 Chay-pita-sh   biskacha-kah
     that-ABL-RPT   vizcacha-DEF

      "palanka-man   li-lu-shah   u:yi,   kumpadre,"
      crowbar-GOAL   go-OUT-1FUT   listen 'compadre'

            ni-n   DS   -n
            say-3

      "Buynu, li-lu-y,   DS   Ø
      Well   go-OUT-INF

      ñuha unku-la-chka-shah-mi
      I   take-OUT-IMPRF-1FUT-DIR

---

[3]Note the absence of the *-ta* 'object number' here; it looks like the phrase is a postposed topic referring back to *kay-ta* (according to David Weber in personal conversation).

El Zorro y la Vizcacha I 265

        kay   lumi-kah-lla-ta-ha"
        this   stone-DEF-LIM-OBJ-TOP

8 Chay-pita-sh li-ku-n   biskacha-kah palanka ashi-h.   DS   -n
    that-ABL-RPT go-REF-3 vizcacha-DEF palanca look.for-AG

9 Chay-pita-sh altu-pa-ynin   pata-kah-man
    that-ABL-RPT up.above-ADV-3P ledge-DEF-GOAL

        yalku-lku-l
        ascend-ABOVE-ADVSS

        chay-traw-shi lika-pa:-mu-n   biskacha-kah   SS   -n
        that-LOC-RPT see-BEN-AFAR-3 vizcacha-DEF

        ishkaynin.
        'the.two.of.them'

7 Then the vizcacha said: "Listen 'compadre', I'll go for a crowbar." "OK, go! meanwhile I'll lift up this stone." 8 Then the vizcacha went for a crowbar. 9 Then, having arrived at the ledge, she looked at the other (the fox) from afar (or: 'They both looked at each other' (the addition of the final ishkaynin seems to give this meaning).

Bridge (with last part of verse above?)

(4) 10 "Ma: imana-ña-shi
     well.   what.do-NOW-RPT

        wik   pindihu atuh-kah?"
        that.there stupid fox-DEF

            ni-l   SS
            say-ADVSS

10 "Now...what is he doing that stupid fox," said the vizcacha.

Scene III

(5) 11 Chay-pita-sh tuh-kah
       that-ABL-RPT   fox-DEF

        unku-la-ya-n   nku-la-ya-n   DS -la-ya -n
        carry-DUR-IMPRF-3 carry-DUR-IMPRF-3

pasah trupa-lla-n-ta-pis
much tail-LIM-3P-OBJ-ALSO

wik-man kay-man hiwi-ya-l
that.there-GOAL this-GOAL move.rapidly-IMPRF-ADVSS

12 Chay-pita chay-pita
that-ABL that-ABL

mas-ta mas-ta
more-OBJ more-OBJ

katrkatrya:-ku-lpu-n.   SS   -lpu -n
tremble-REF-BELOW-3

Biskacha-kah asi-ku-lka-n.   DS   -n
vizcacha-DEF laugh-REF-PLIMPFR-3

13 Chay-pita-sh lumi-kah altu-pita sha-la-mu-ñah
that-ABL-RPT stone-DEF up.above-ABL come-OUT-AFAR-NARPST

pasah intiru-n-ta   DS   -ñah
much completely-3P-OBJ

aha-lu-ñah atuh-kah-ta.   SS   -ñah
crush-OUT-NARPST fox-DEF-OBJ

Pata-n patrya-lu-ñah   SS   -ñah
stomach-3P burst-OUT-NARPST

pasah wañu-ku-ñah.   DS   -ñah
much die-REF-NARPST

11 Then meanwhile the fox is carrying, carrying the stone, his tail moving rapidly from side to side. 12 Then suddenly he starts shaking more and more; the viszcacha laughs. 13 Then the stone came from above and completely crushed the fox. His stomach burst and he died.

Conclusion

(6) 14 Atuh-kah pasah pasah-shi hudiku-lu-n   SS   -lu -n
fox-DEF much much-RPT cheat-OUT-3

15 biskacha-kah-shi   ga:na-lu-n   pasah.   DS   -lu   -n
   vizcacha-DEF-RPT   win-OUT-3   much

14 The fox was completely "tricked." 15 —the vizcacha won.

Author comment:

Imay-traw-pis   ma: chay   pubri   atuh   pirdidu?
when-LOC-ALSO   well   that   poor   fox   lost

Now (well), when does the poor fox stop losing?

Appendix 7

El Zorro y la Vizcacha II[1]

(The Fox and the Vizcacha)

SS/DS ASP TNS

Scene I

(1) 1 Chay-pita   ña-ta   bagri-ta-sh   chaku-pa:ku-n
       that-ABL   now-OBJ   bagre-OBJ-RPT   catch-PL-3

             atuh-kah-wan   biskacha-kah[2]
             fox-DEF-ACCOMP   viszcacha-DEF

    2 Llapan bagri-ta   chaku-ya-pti-n-shi   DS   -lu   -n
       All   bagre-OBJ   catch-IMPRF-ADVDS-3P-RPT

             ana-lpu-lu-n   na-kah   biskacha-kah atuh-kah-man.
             go.down?-BELOW-OUT-3   thing-DEF vizcacha-DEF fox-DEF-GOAL

             "Ima-ta-ma: kay-traw   lula-nki   kumpadri?"
             what?-OBJ-DIR.THEN   this-LOC   do-2   'compadre'

                       ni-n.   DS   -n
                       say-3

    3 Chay-pita-sh,
       that-ABL-RPT

---

[1] Wroughton (1996:83–86).
[2] The jumping into the story might be due to the fact that the story is one of a series about the fox, probably narrated by the same person.

269

	"Kay-traw ma: bagri-ha Siñur zurru."	SS	-n
	this-LOC well bagre-TOP señor fox		
	ni-n biskacha-kah atuh-kah-ta.		
	say-3 vizcacha-DEF fox-DEF-OBJ		

(Bridge?)

	"Ma: yanapa:-shayki palla-y-ta,"	SS	-n
	well help-1FUT2 catch-INF-OBJ		
	ni-n		
	say-3		
	"Ali!" ni-n.	DS	-n
	OK! say-3		

1 Then the fox and the vizcacha catch fish (bagre). 2 While the fox was catching lots of fish, the vizcacha went down to the fox "What are you doing, compadre?" said (the vizcacha). 3 Then "Well, let's see the fish here, Mister fox." "Well...I will help you gather them." "OK," he says.

??Scene II/background information

(2)	4	Pahcha-kah-ta-sh witrha-la-:li-ñah	DS	-lu	-ñah
		waterfall-DEF-OBJ-RPT close-OUT-PLDIR-NARPST			
		biskacha-kah altu-traw.			
		vizcacha-DEF up.above-LOC			
	5	Hatun lumi utrku-man-shi ana-ku-yku-l			
		Big stone hole-GOAL-RPT ?-REF-IN-ADVSS			
		chay-traw-shi palla-ya-n	SS/DS? -ya	-n	
		that-LOC-RPT catch-IMPRF-3			
		bagri-kah-ta biskacha-kah.			
		bagre-DEF-OBJ vizcacha-DEF			
	6	Atuh-kah mas luli-man-shi yayku-lu-n	DS	-lu	-n
		fox-DEF more inside-GOAL-RPT enter-OUT-3			
		lumi-kah siki-n-man bagri chaku-h.			
		stone-DEF foot.of.stone-3P-GOAL bagre catch-AG			

4 The vizcachas had shut up the waterfall above. 5 Descending into the large hole in the stone, the vizcacha was fishing bagres.

6 *The fox went even further (into the hole) at the foot of the rock to fish 'bagres'.*

Scene III

(3) 7 Chay-pita-sh biskacha-kah li-ku-n altu-ta.   DS   -n
       that-ABL-RPT viszcacha-DEF go-REF-3 up.above-OBJ

       "Ma:, lika-la-mu-shah
       well... see-OUT-AFAR-1FUT

       yaku-kah hunta-la-mu-n-man, karahu."
       water-DEF fill-OUT-AFAR-3-COND 'caramba'

           ni-l li-ku-n.   (SS   -n)
           say-ADVSS go-REF-3

8 Chay-pita-sh
   that-ABL-RPT

       "Altu-pita-m wishya-mu-shayki
       up.above-ABL-DIR whistle-AFAR-1FUT2

       ña llapa-ya:-mu-pti-n-ha
       thing to.complete-IMPRF-AFAR-ADVDS-3P-TOP

       wishya-mu-shayki-m
       whistle-AFAR-1FUT2-DIR

       u:yi, kumpadri!"
       listen 'compadre'

           ni-n biskacha-kah atuh-kah-ta   SS   -n
           say-3 vizcacha-DEF fox-DEF-OBJ

9 Atuh-kah chay-pita-sh
   fox-DEF that-ABL-RPT

       lumi-kah-man ushtu-ku-yku-l
       stone-DEF-GOAL get.underneath-REF-IN-ADVSS

       palla-ku-n trankilu-sh   DS   -n
       catch-REF-3 peaceful-RPT

latash lunku-n-man bagri-ta.
'cloth' little.bag-3P-GOAL bagre-OBJ

7 *Then the vizcacha walks uphill: "Now (well)...I'm going to see that the water from above doesn't surprise us, 'caramba'!" she says, leaving.* 8 *Then: "From above I'll call you when it is getting full, do you hear, compadre!" the vizcacha says to the fox.* 9 *The fox then, getting under the stone, peacefully catches fish to put in his little bag.*

Scene IV

(4) 10 Chay-pita chay-pita chay-pita-shi
    that-ABL   that-ABL   that-ABL-RPT

        wishya-la-mu-n   biskacha-kah altu-pita.   DS   -lu -n
        whistle-OUT-AFAR-3 vizcacha-DEF up.above-ABL

        "Falta   muchu,
        missing much

        imay   u:ra-tra:
        when   hour-CONJ.THEN

        kay   hunta-mu-nha yaku-kah   panay-lan,"
        this   fill-AFAR-3FUT water-DEF   gradually-YET

          ni-n.
          say-3

11 Chay-pita-sh trankilu
  that-ABL-RPT peaceful

        atuh-kah pasah   miku-lku-l
        fox-DEF   much   eat-ABOVE-ADVSS

        miku-lku-l
        eat-ABOVE-ADVSS

        palla-ku-n gulusu   atuh.   DS   -n
        catch-REF-3 gluttonous fox

12 Chay-pita-sh biskacha pindihu-kah
   that-ABL-RPT   vizcacha   sly-DEF

        katra-lpa-la-mu-ñah   yaku-kah-ta   DS -lu ñah
        send-BELOW-OUT-AFAR-NARPST water-DEF-OBJ

pasah diripinti   kitra-yka-la-mu-ñah.   SS -lu -ñah
much all.of.a.sudden open-IN-OUT-AFAR-NARPST

Atuh pubri-kah-ta pasah dyunavis
fox poor-DEF-OBJ much at.once

ñiti-lu-ñah   lumi-kah luli-   traw DS -lu -ñah
crush-OUT-NARPST   stone-DEF inside-LOC   (stone)

pasah diyunavis wañu-ku-ñah.   DS -lu -ñah
much at.once   die-REF-NARPST

Atuh-kah illa-li-ku-n.   SS -li -n
fox-DEF   disappear-PNT-REF-3

10 *Then the vizcacha whistles from above: "Who knows when this water is going to fill up," she says. 11 Then peacefully the fox eats and eats—the gluttonous fox. 12 Then the sly vizcacha sent the water down—all of a sudden opened up (some hindrance for the water to flow downhill). The stone completely crushed the poor fox (well toward the inside of the hole); he died at once and the fox disappeared.*

Conclusion/Author comment

(5)   Chay-lah-sha: ga:na-lu-ñah   biskacha-kah atuh-kah-ta
       that-YET-RPT.THEN win-OUT-NARPST   vizcacha-DEF fox-DEF-OBJ

       pasah ima-traw-pis   chay-ta
       much what?-LOC-ALSO   that-OBJ

       chay kwintu antigwu willa-ku-n.
       that story old   tell-REF-3

The vizcacha always beats the fox; so says the old story.

Appendix 8

Hwan Usu[1]

Felipe Inga
Shausha Quechua

	SS/DS	ASP	TNS

ACT I
Intro

1 Sala-ta-s   kwida-ya:-ñah   -ya: -ñah
  corn-OBJ-ALSO care-IMPRF-NARPST

   suk siñura muntaña-kah-traw.
   one señora hill-DEF-LOC

1 A woman was guarding the corn in the hills.

Scene I/Stage

2 Sala kwida-h-ta-sh   DS   -lu   -n
  corn care-AG-OBJ-RPT

   Hwan Usu tra-lu-n.
   Juan bear arrive-OUT-3

3 Hwan Usu-sh apa-ku-n   matray-nin-man   SS   -n
  Juan bear-RPT take-REF-3 cave-3P-GOAL

4 Matray-nin-traw-shi ka-chi-ku-n.   SS   -n
  cave-3P-LOC-RPT   be-CAUS-REF-3

[1] Weber (1987:161–167).

5 Hatun palta laha lumi-wan   witrha-lu-n   SS   -n
   big   plane stone stone-INSTRM close-OUT-3

   pwirta-n-ta   siñurita-kah-ta.
   door-3P-OBJ   señorita-DEF-OBJ

2 While she was guarding the corn Juan Oso arrived. 3 Juan Oso took her to his cave. 4 He made her stay in his cave. 5 He closed the señorita up with a big stone at the door.

Scene II

 6 Chay-pita-sh chuli-n-ta   watra-ku-lu-n   DS -lu -n
   this-ABL-RPT son-3P-OBJ   give.birth-REF-OUT-3

   Hwan Usu-pa-ta.
   Juan bear-GEN-OBJ

 7 Chay-pita-sh u:chu a:ñu-man tra-lu-ñah   DS -lu -ñah
   this-ABL-RPT eight year-GOAL arrive-OUT-NARPST

   siñura-kah-pa   wawi-n
   señora-DEF-GEN   son.of.woman-3P

   Hwan Usu-pa   chuli-n
   Juan bear-GEN son-3P

 8 Chay-pita-sh chay-lla mash sirvi-ya-n   DS -ya -n
   this-ABL-RPT this-LIM more serve-IMPRF-3

   llapan pubrisa-kah-ta:
   all   poverty-DEF-OBJ

   charki, asikumu nuvillu,   wa:ka,
   jerky   like.this young.bull cow

   llapan lliw-ta yanu-ku-na-n-pah   matray-kah
   all   all-OBJ cook-REF-NOM-3P-PUR   cave-DEF

   luli-lla-man.
   inside-LIM-GOAL

6 Then she gave birth to the son of Juan Oso. 7 Then the son of the woman and Juan Oso turned eight years old. 8 Then there he (Juan Oso) "served" them more poverty: jerky like young bulls—all to cook inside the cave.

Scene III

9 U:chu a:ñu-man tra-lu-pti-n-shi
   Eight year-GOAL arrive-OUT-ADVDS-3P-RPT

        tra-lu-l-shi   kimsa-ta
        arrive-OUT-ADVSS-RPT three-OBJ

        ñaka-lu-n   kumsa-y-ta.   DS -lu -n
        suffer-OUT-3 push-INF-OBJ

10 Yapa-traw   kimsa-kah-traw-shi
    Once.more-LOC three-DEF-LOC-RPT

        tikla-la-chi-n   lumi-kah-ta.   SS -lu -n
        turn.over-OUT-CAUS-3 stone-DEF-OBJ

11 Pusha-ku-n   distritu-kah-ta-sh   DS   -n
    take.along-REF-3 district-DEF-OBJ-RPT

        iskwila-man trula-h.
        school-GOAL put-PRMC

9 When he had turned eight years old, trying three times, he was not able to make the rock move. 10 Again, the third time he was able to turn over the stone. 11 He was taken to the district (town) to place him in school.

Bridge

12 Hwan Usu-pa   siñura-n
    Juan bear-GEN señora-3P

        distritu-kah-man pusha-ku-l-shi
        district-DEF-GOAL take-REF-ADVSS-RPT

        trula-mu-n iskwila-man.   SS   -n
        put-AFAR-3 school-GOAL

12 The wife of Juan Oso, after taking him (the son) to the district, put him in school.

ACT II
Scene IV

13 Iskwila-man   trula-mu-pti-n-shi
    school-GOAL   put-AFAR-ADVDS-3P-RPT

llapan uru-n-ta
all   youth-3P-OBJ

[?] suk tinka-y-lla-wan   wañu-chi-n.   DS   -n
one   give.punch-INF-LIM-WITH   die-CAUS-3

Sukkah-ta   waha-chi-n.
another-OBJ   cry-CAUS-3

Sukkah-ta   waha-chi-n.
another-OBJ   cry-CAUS-3

14 Chay-pita-sh llapan uru-kah-pa   tayta-n
   this-ABL-RPT all   youth-DEF-GEN   father-3P

           lika-li-la-:li-mu-n.   DS   -li-lu   -n
           see-PNT-OUT-PLDIR-AFAR-3

15a Baha-ku-n-shi   chay siñura-kah-pa   wawi-n-shi.[2]   DS/SS?   -n
    descend-REF-3-RPT   this señora-DEF-GEN son.of.woman-3P-RPT

           15b "Imayna-kah-man   uru-m-aa   chay,
               now.when-DEF-GOAL   youth-DIR-THEN   this

               uchuk   uru-lla-m
               small   youth-LIM-DIR

               waha-ku-n   llapan uru-kah-ta?"[3]
               cry-REF-3   all   youth-DEF-OBJ

                       ni-l-shi
                       say-ADVSS-RPT

           kiha-ka-la-:li-n   ña   siñura-kah-ta.   DS/SS?   -lu -n
           complain-REF-OUT-PLDIR-3   now   señora-DEF-OBJ

13 Having put him in school, he killed the children with a single slap; others he caused to cry; others he caused to cry. 14 Then all the fathers of the children saw this. 15a The son of the señora descended (unclear). 15b "How long is this child going to make all the children cry?" (saying) they complained to the woman.

---

[2]According to David Weber (personal conversation) the final word of (15a) could have been *wayinmanshi*, in which case the sentence would mean "They (the parents) descended to the mother's house". This would give the sentence better sense.

[3]According to David Weber (personal conversation) the final suffix might be -ta(q) 'emphatic'.

Scene V

16 Chay-pita-sh ña   suk   timpu-traw
   this-ABL-RPT now   one   time-LOC

                maña-paku-li-ñah   walaka-ta.   DS   -li   -ñah
                ask.for-INSTL-PNT-NARPST sling-OBJ

17 Walaka-kah-wan-shi   tu:rri-kah-ta-ña
   sling-DEF-INSTRM-RPT tower-DEF-OBJ-NOW

                walaka-li-ñah   SS   -li   -ñah
                throw.with.sling-PNT-NARPST

18 [?]   kimsa   walaka-y-traw-shi
          tres   throw.with.sling-INF-LOC-RPT

                tikla-la-chi-n   tu:rri-kah-ta,   SS   -lu   -n
                turn.over-OUT-CAUS-3 tower-DEF-OBJ

                chay distritu   iskwila-traw ka-sha-n-traw.
                this   district   school-LOC   be-REL-3P-LOC

*16 Then another time he had asked for a sling. 17 With this sling
he made sling shots against the tower. 18 After three times he
made the tower there in the district school turn over.*

Scene VI

19 Chay-pita-sh   ña   kumunidad-kah-kuna   akurda-la-:li-n
   this-ABL-RPT now people.of.community-DEF-PLUR acordar-OUT-PLDIR-3

                "Mihur-ta   icha   uru-kah-ta
                better-ADV yes.or.no youth-DEF-OBJ

                sulu-ku-chun
                take.away-REF-3IMP

                Chay   siñura-kah   llapan
                this   señora-DEF   all

                tu:rri-nchik-ta-pis   distruy-lu-ñah.
                tower-12P-OBJ-ALSO ruin-OUT-NARPST

                Imayna-kah-man chay uru-m?
                how-DEF-GOAL   this youth-DIR

Pi-pa-m   ma: chay uru?
who-GEN-DIR then this youth

Sulu-ku-chun   mihur-ta"
take.away-REF-3IMP better-ADV

    ni-l-shi
    say-ADVSS-RPT

        ni-n.   DS -lu -n
        say-3

20 Ni-pti-n-shi   waha-ku-n Hwan Usu-pa   walmi-n.
   say-ADVDS-3P-RPT cry-REF-3 Juan   bear-GEN mujer-3P

    "Kay   uru-:,
    this   youth-1P

    chawrah   sulu-ku-ya:-shah-mi.
    then   take.away-REF-IMPRF-1FUT-DIR

    li-ku-shah-mi.
    go-REF-1FUT-DIR

    Chawrah kapital-man   li-ku-shah"
    then   capital-GOAL go-REF-1FUT

        ni-n.   DS   n
        say-3

21 Kapital-man   li-ya-pti-n-shi
   capital-GOAL go-IMPRF-ADVDS-3P-RPT

    yalu-na-ya-pti-n-shi
    leave-DES-IMPRF-ADVDS-3P-RPT

        ni-n
        say-3

    li-ya-pti-n-shi
    go-IMPRF-ADVDS-3P-RPT

    Hwan Usu alkansa-lu-n.   DS -lu -n
    Juan bear overtake-OUT-3

22 "Toma tu pasaje y llévate a la capital.
　 Take your ticket and go to the city

　 Con este te ganarás buscarás tu suerte."
　 With this you'll gain and seek your luck

19 Then the people in the community agreed: "It's better that you take your son away. This señora? (unclear) ruined all our towers. What other thing is this youngster going to do? It's better that you take him away," they said. 20 When they said this, the woman of Juan Oso cried "My son, I'll take him away. We'll go. Then to the city we'll go," she said. 21 As they were going to the city, Juan Oso overtook them and said: 22 "Take your ticket and go to the city; with this you'll find and seek your luck."

Bridge

23 Chinay-pa-sh　　　hu-yku-lu-n,
　 like.this-ADV-RPT　give-IN-OUT-3

　　　　"[?] swirti-ki-ta　kay　hillay-kah-wan"
　　　　　　luck-2P-OBJ　this　money-DEF-INSTRM

　　　　ni-l-shi
　　　　say-ADVSS-RPT

　　　　katra-lu-n　　walmi-n-ta　　chuli-n-ta.　　　SS　-lu　-n
　　　　send-OUT-3　woman-3P-OBJ　son-3P-OBJ

23 Like this he gave, saying: look for (your) luck with this money; and he sent away his son and woman.

ACT III
Scene VII

24 Chay-pita-sh　kapital-kah-man　tra-lu-n.　　　　DS　-lu　-n
　 this-ABL-RPT　capital-DEF-GOAL　arrive-OUT-3

25 Kapital-kah-man　yayku-na-n-pah-shi　　(iglisya-wan)
　 capital-DEF-GOAL　enter-NOM-3P-PUR-RPT　church-ACCOMP

　　　　iglisya-pita　yala-mu-ñah　　　　　　　　DS　　-ñah
　　　　church-ABL　leave-AFAR-NARPST

　　　　ku:ra-kah.
　　　　priest-DEF

26 Ku:ra-kah-wan   tinku-naka-la-:li-n   DS (recip) -lu-n)
priest-DEF-ACCOMP meet-RECIP-OUT-PLDIR-3

Hwan Usu-kah y siñura-pa mama-ntin
Juan bear-DEF and señora-GEN mother-WITH

27 Chay-pita-sh ni-n: DS   -n
this-ABL-RPT say-3

"Buynu, Hwan Usu-kah
well Juan bear-DEF

ñaka-la-chi-ma-n tuta na-kah-wan
suffer-OUT-CAUS-1O-3 night thing-DEF-ACCOMP

Kundinadu-kah-mi ñaka-la-chi-ma-n tuta
condemned-DEF-DIR suffer-OUT-CAUS-1O-3 night

Dun Hwan.
Don Juan

Yaku fwirsa achka ka-pti-n-ha
water power much be-ADVDS-3P-TOP

kundinadu-kah-ta wañu-ya-lla-chi-y.
condemned-DEF-OBJ die-IN-LIM-CAUS-INF

Chawraha pa:ga-lu-shayki llapan ri:kisa-:-ta
then pay-OUT-1FUT2 all riches-1P-OBJ

llapan mu:la-:-ta, wa:ka-:-ta,
all mule-1P-OBJ cow-1P-OBJ

uysh-ni:-ta, kawallu-:-ta,
sheep-1P-OBJ horse-1P-OBJ

pa:tu-:-ta, kuchi-:-ta,
duck-1P-OBJ pig-1P-OBJ

paluma-:-ta, pa:vu-:-ta.
dove-1P-OBJ turkey-1P-OBJ

Lliw-ta-m rigala-lu-shayki
all-OBJ-DIR give-OUT-1FUT2

Dun Hwansitu.
Don Juancito

Wañu-la-chi-pti-k-ha
die-OUT-CAUS-ADVDS-2P-TOP

lliw-ta-m   asinda-:-ta   rigala-lu-shayki.
all-OBJ-DIR   hacienda-1P-OBJ give-OUT-1FUT2

Kay   lliw-ta-m   hu-shayki: kwartu.
this all-OBJ-DIR   give-1FUT2   room

Llapan implimintu-:-ta-m   hu-shayki
all   furniture-1P-OBJ-DIR   give-1FUT2

Dun Hwansitu.
Don Juancito

Wañu-la-chi-nki   kundinadu-kah-ta.
die-OUT-CAUS-2FUT   condemned-DEF-OBJ

Wañu-la-chi-pti-k-ha   hu-yku-lu-shayki-m.
die-OUT-CAUS-ADVDS-2P-TOP   give-IN-OUT-1FUT2-DIR

Kunstansya-ta   lula-pa-lu-shayki"
document-OBJ   make-BEN-OUT-1FUT2

ni-l-shi   ni-n.
say-ADVSS-RPT   say-3

24 *Then they arrived in the capital. 25 As they were arriving in the capital, a priest was leaving the church. 26 Juan Oso and his mother, the señora, met the priest. 27 Then he (the priest) said: "Well, Juan Oso, this thing makes me suffer in the nights. The comdemned makes me suffer in the night, don Juan. Since you have much 'strength of water' (meaning unclear), kill the condemned! Then I will pay you with my riches: all my mules, cows, sheep, horses, ducks, pigs, doves, turkeys —everything/all I'm going to give you, don Juan. If you kill him, my whole hacienda I'll give you. All this I'll give you: rooms; all my furniture I'll give you, don Juan. You'll kill the condemned. If you kill him, I'll give you this. I'll make you a document (of proof)" (saying, he said).*

Scene VIII

28 Ku:ra-kah lima-pa-lu-pti-n-shi   DS   -n
   priest-DEF talk-BEN-OUT-ADVDS-3P-RPT

      Hwan (ka-sha-n) [?] walachi-n.
      Juan be-REL-3P   dawn-3

29 Wañu-la-chi-n Hwan.   DS -lu -n
   die-OUT-CAUS-3 Juan

      Wañu-la-chi-n   kundinadu-kah-ta
      die-OUT-CAUS-3 condemned-DEF-OBJ

      barrita-kah-wan   wipya-y-ta
      bar/rod-DEF-INSTRM beat-INF-OBJ

      pacha wala-mu-pti-n-shi.
      space dawn-AFAR-ADVDS-3P-RPT

30 Puhi-lu-sha   lika-li-lu-n   DS -li-lu -n
   beat.to.pieces-OUT-PRT see-PNT-OUT-3

      kundinadu-kah chay-pita-sh.
      condemned-DEF this-ABL-RPT

28 When the priest said this, Juan stayed all night. 29 Juan kills him; he kills the condemned, beating him with the rod until it dawns. 30 The condemned then is left in pieces.

Scene IX

31 Chay u:ra-lla-sh   tra-lu-n   ku:ra-kah.   DS -lu -n
   This hour-LIM-RPT arrive-OUT-3 priest-DEF

      "Kay-ha wañu-la-chi-:   tayta ku:ra   DS   ?
      this-TOP die-OUT-CAUS-1 father priest   (Juan)

      kundinadu-kah-ta
      condemned-DEF-OBJ

      Kay-ha lik   tullu-n-pis
      this-TOP onomatopoeia bone-3P-ALSO

      kay-ta   sita-y[?] kundinadu-kah-pa."
      this-OBJ throw-INF condemned-DEF-GEN

32 Ni-pti-n-shi   ku:ra-kah ni-n: DS   -n
   say-ADVDS-3P-RPT   priest-DEF say-3

   "Buynu, lula-pa-lu-shayki.
   Well   make-BEN-OUT-1FUT2

   Kanan kunstansya-wan   kanan
   Now   document-INSTRM   now

   kay asinda-:-ta-m   lula-pa-lu-shayki
   this hacienda-1P-OBJ-DIR   make-BEN-OUT-1FUT2

   Y   kay   llapan ri:kisa-:-ta-m   hu-yku-lu-shayki,
   And   this all   riches-1P-OBJ-DIR   give-IN-OUT-1FUT2

              Dun   Hwansitu.
              Don   Juancito

   Salva-la-ma-nki ham
   save-OUT-1O-2   you

   kay   kundinadu-kah   mika-la-ma:-na-n-pita-m.
   This condemned-DEF   eat-OUT-1O-NOM-3P-ABL-DIR

              Grasyas.
              thank you

   Salva-la-ma-nki   vi:da-:-ta-m.
   save-OUT-1O-2   life-1P-OBJ-DIR

   Kanan lliw-ta-m   rigala-lu-shayki.
   now   all-OBJ-DIR   give-OUT-1FUT2

   Kay   ri:kisa-ta   ham-pa [?]
   this riches-OBJ   you-GEN

              Hwansitu.
              Juancito

   Pichha-m (ham) ñuha-pa asinda-:-mi.
   five-DIR you   I-GEN   hacienda-1P-DIR

   Trusku-kah-wan   ka-shah.
   four-DEF-ACCOMP   be-1FUT

                Sukkah-ta   hu-yku-lu-shayki"
                other-OBJ   give-IN-OUT-1FUT2

                ni-l-shi
                say-ADVSS-RPT

      hu-yku-lu-n   Hwan-kah-ta.   (SS -lu   -n)
      give-IN-OUT-3   Juan-DEF-OBJ

   33 Hwan-kah-shi   ri:ku.   DS   ∅
      Juan-DEF-RPT   rich

31 At this hour the priest is arriving. "Here I have killed the condemned, father priest. Throw away these bones of the condemned!" (Juan Oso says) 32 When he said this the priest said: "Well, I'll make you (it). Now with the document I'll make my hacienda yours. And all my riches I'll give you, Don Juan. You have saved me from being devoured by the condemned! Thank you! You have saved my life. Now I'm going to give you all. These riches are yours, Juan. I have five haciendas. I'll keep four and the other I'll give to you," (saying) he gives it to Juan. 33 Juan was now rich.

Conclusion
(The conclusion is a bit confusing—see translation below)

(Scene X?)

      34 Huya-pa   pacha wala-mu-na-n-pah
         early-ADV   space dawn-AFAR-NOM-3P-PUR

                     mama-n-ta   lika-la-chi-n,   SS   -lu   -n
                     mother-3P-OBJ   see-OUT-CAUS-3[4]

      35 "Kay-mi   asinda-yki.
         this-DIR   hacienda-2P

                     Kay-wan-mi   ka-ku-nki"
                     this-ACCOMP-DIR be-REF-2

                            ni-l-shi
                            say-ADVSS-RPT

---

[4]It could be that this "verse", which lacks the evidential, is a sub-line to the previous verse, verse 33, although the verse indicates a lapse of time. It might still be within a "center of interest."

lika-la-chi-n	na	DS -lu	-n
see-OUT-CAUS-3	thing		

ku:ra-kah Hwan Usu-kah-ta.
priest-DEF Juan bear-DEF-OBJ

34 Early, as it is dawning, he shows his mother. 35 "This is your hacienda. This one is for you (with this you are left)," saying, the priest shows it to Juan.

Author comment

36 Fwirsa-lla-n-wan chay-ta ga:na-lu-n!
strength-LIM-3P-INSTRM this-OBJ win-OUT-3

36 With his strength alone he gained all this!

Bibliography

Adelaar, Willem F. H. 2004. Linguistic peculiarities of Quechua song texts. In Delgado-P. and Schechter, 61–75.

Arnold, Denise Y. 1997. Making men in her own image. In Howard-Malverde 1997a, 99–131.

Arnold, Denise Y. 2004. Midwife singers: *Llama*-human obstetrics in some songs to the animals by Andean women. In Delgado-P. and Schechter, 145–179.

Arnold, Denise Y., and Juan de Dios Yapita. 1992. Fox talk: Addressing the wild beasts in the southern Andes. *Latin American Indian Literatures Journal* 8(1):9–37.

Arnold, Denise Y., and Juan de Dios Yapita. 1999. Las canciones de los animales en un ayllu andino: Hacia la arquitectónica textil de un texto oral. In Godenzzi, 229–271.

Aviram, Amittai F. 1994. *Telling rhythm: Body and meaning in poetry.* Ann Arbor: The University of Michigan Press.

Becker, Alton. 1982. The poetics and noetics of a Javanese poem. In Tannen 1982a, 217–238.

Benson, Janice. 1996. El aspecto perfectivo en la narrativa del quechua de Huamalíes. In Parker, 5–26.

Bergli, Ågot, ed. 1990. *Educación intercultural.* Comunidades y Culturas Peruanas 23. Pucallpa, Perú: Instituto Lingüístico de Verano

Bergli, Ågot, ed. 1996. *Estudios lingüísticos de textos de la Amazonia Peruana.* Pucallpa, Perú: Instituto Lingüístico de Verano.

Bergli, Ågot. 2000. Patrones más altos de organización y su función en textos folklóricos del quechua de Ayacucho. In *Actas - I Congreso de Lenguas Indígenas de Sudamérica* II:63–77. Presented in 1999 at the I Congreso de Lenguas Indígenas de Sudamérica. Lima: Universidad Ricardo Palma.

Bergli, Ågot. 2002. *Higher organizational patterns and their function in Quechua oral legendary texts*. Dr. art thesis. Norges Teknisk-Naturvitenskapelige Universitet.

Bergli, Ågot. 2007. Cambio de referencia y sus funciones extendidas. Published on CD, *Comunicaciones. V Congreso Nacional de Investigaciones Lingüistico-Filológicas*. Lima: Biblioteca Nacional del Perú.

Berlin, Brent, and Paul Kay. 1969. *Basic color terms: Their universality and evolution*. Berkeley: University of California Press.

Bernardo, Robert. 1980. Subjecthood and consciousness. In Chafe 1980a, 275–299.

Beyersdorf, Margot. 1986. Voice of the Runa, Quechua substratum in the narrative of José María Arguedas. *Latin American Indian Literatures Journal* 2(1):28–48.

Blakemore, Diane. 1992. *Understanding utterances*. Oxford: Blackwell.

Blass, Regina. 1990. *Relevance relations in discourse*. Cambridge: Cambridge University Press.

Börtnes, Jostein. 1980. *Episke problemer*. Oslo: Solum Forlag A/S.

Brend, Ruth M., ed. 1974. *Advances in Tagmemics*. Amsterdam: North-Holland Publishing.

Brice Heath, Shirley. 1982. Protean shapes in literacy events: Ever-shifting oral and literate traditions. In Tannen 1982a, 91–117.

Bricker, V. R. 1989. The ethnographic context of some traditional Mayan speech genres. In R. Bauman and J. Sherzer (eds.), *Explorations in the ethnography of speaking*, 368–388. Cambridge: Cambridge University Press.

Briggs, Lucy T. 1994. El k"arik" ari en dos textos de lengua aymara: análisis morfosintáctico y del discurso. In Margot Beyersdorf and Sabine Dedenbach-Salazar Sáenz (eds.), *Andean Oral Traditions: Discourse and Literature/Tradiciones Orales Andinas: Discurso y Literatura*, 161–197. (Bonner Amerikanistische Studien/Estudios Americanistas de Bonn, 24) Bonn: Holos.

Bright, William. 1982. Poetic structure in oral narrative. In Tannen 1982a, 171–184.

Bright, William. 1984. *American Indian linguistics and literature*. Amsterdam: Mouton.

Brody, Jill. 1986. Repetition as a rhetorical and conversational device in Tojolabal (Mayan). *International Journal of American Linguistics*, 52(3):255–274.
Brown, Gillian, and George Yule. 1983. *Discourse analysis*. Cambridge: Cambridge University Press.
Brown, Gillian, Kirsten Malmkjær, Alastair Pollitt, and John Williams, eds. 1994. *Language and understanding*. Oxford: Oxford University Press.
Burns, Donald H., and Pablo Alcócer Hinostrosa. 1975. *Un análisis preliminar del discurso en quechua: Estudio lexico y gramatical del cuento* Taklluscha y Benedicto *en el quechua de Ayacucho*. Documento de Trabajo 6. Pucallpa, Peru: Instituto Lingüístico de Verano.
Campbell, Barbara. 1986. Repetition in Jamamadí discourse. In Joseph E. Grimes (ed.), *Sentence initial devices, 171–185*. Summer Institute of Linguistics and The University of Texas at Arlington Publications in Linguistics 75. Dallas.
Carpenter, Lawrence K. 1985. Lowland Quichua ethnopoetics. *Latin American Indian Literatures Journal* 1(1):47–62.
Cerrón-Palomino, Rodolfo. 1987. *Lingüística quechua*. Cusco, Peru: Centro de Estudios Rurales Andinos "Bartolomé de Las Casas".
Chafe, Wallace L. 1976. Givenness, contrastiveness, definiteness, subjects, topics, and point of view. In Li, 25–55.
Chafe, Wallace L. ed. 1980a. *The pear stories*. Norwood, N. J.: Ablex.
Chafe, Wallace L. 1980b. The deployment of consciousness in the production of a narrative. In Chafe 1980a, 9–50.
Chafe, Wallace L. 1982. Integration and involvement. In Tannen 1982a, 35–53.
Chafe, Wallace L. 1984. How people use adverbial clauses. *Berkeley Linguistic Society* 10:437–449.
Chafe, Wallace, and Johanna Nichols, eds. 1986. *Evidentiality: The linguistic coding of epistemology*. Advances in Discourse Processes XX. Norwood, N.J.: Ablex.
Cusihuaman, Antonio G. 1976. *Gramática quechua: Cuzco – Collao*. Lima: Ministerio de Educación.
de Beaugrande, Robert-Alain, and Wolfgang Ulrich Dressler. 1981. *Introduction to Text Linguistics*. New York: Longman.
Dedenbach-Salazar Sáenz, Sabine. 1999. Jichhaxa sikuyay pikt'itasma, kayñarak pikt'itasma...[Un aporte al análisis textual aymara]. In Godenzzi, 187–228.

Delgado-P., Guillermo. 2004. *¡Katari, Jatariy!* Una revisita al mesianismo y tres canciones-memoria. In Delgado-P. and Schechter, 183–235.

Delgado-P., Guillermo, and John M. Schechter. 2004. *Quechua verbal artistry: The inscription of Andean voices.* Bonn: Bonn Americanist Studies/BAS. Volume 38.

Dimter, Matthias. 1985. On text classification. In van Dijk 1985e, 215–230.

Dixon, R. M. W. 1994. *Ergativity.* Cambridge Studies in Linguistics 69. Cambridge: Cambridge University Press.

Dooley, Robert A., and Stephen H. Levinsohn. 2001. *Analyzing discourse: A manual of basic concepts.* Dallas: SIL International.

Dundes, Alan, ed. 1965. *The study of folklore.* Englewood Cliffs, N. J.: Prentice-Hall.

Dundes, Alan. 1980. *Interpreting folklore.* Bloomington: Indiana University Press.

Enkvist, Nils Erik. 1985a. Introduction: Stylistics, text linguistics, and composition. *Text* 5(4):251–267.

Enkvist, Nils Erik. 1985e. Text and discourse linguistics, rhetoric, and stylistics. In van Dijk 1985e, 11–38.

Escobar, Anna Maria. 1987. *Types and stages of bilingual behavior: A sociopragmatic analysis of Peruvian bilingual Spanish.* Ann Arbor: University Microfilms International.

Fabb, Nigel. 1997. *Linguistics and literature.* Oxford: Blackwell.

Faigley, Lester, and Paul Meyer. 1983. Rhetorical theory and readers' classifications of text types. *Text* 3(4):305–325.

Ferrara, Alessandro. 1985. Pragmatics. In van Dijk 1985f, 137–157.

Finnegan, Ruth. 1973. Literacy vs. non-literacy: The great divide? Some comments on the significance of 'literature' in non-literate cultures. In Robin Horton and Ruth Finnegan (eds.), *Modes of thought: Essays on thinking in Western and non-Western societies,* 112–144. London: Faber and Faber.

Floyd, Rick. 1999. *The structure of evidential categories in Wanka Quechua.* Summer Institute of Linguistics and The University of Texas at Arlington Publications in Linguistics 131. Dallas.

Forstorp, Per-Anders. 1992. Orality–och literacybegreppen hos Ong: En kritisk granskning. In Jan Erik Lindström and Berit Sahlström (eds.), *Talspråk, skriftspråk, bildspråk.* Sweden: Universitetet i Linköping.

Foster, J. L. 1975. Thought couplets in Khety's 'Hymn to the inundation'. *Journal of Near Eastern Studies* 34(1):1–29.

Foster, J. L. 1980. Sinuhe: the ancient Egyptian genre of narrative verse. *Journal of Near Eastern Studies* 39(2):89–117.

Fretheim, Thorstein. 2000. Constraining explicit and implicit content by means of a Norwegian scalar particle. *Nordic Journal of Linguistics* 23:2.
Galin, Anne. 1981. Semantics and structure: An analysis of two trickster tales. *Text* 1(3):241–268.
Gentili, Bruno. 1997. Muntlighet og skriftbruk i Hellas. In Mario Vegetti, 29–51.
Givón, Talmy. 1984. *Syntax: A functional-typological introduction* 1. Amsterdam: John Benjamins.
Givón, Talmy. 1990. *Syntax: A functional-typological introduction* 2. Amsterdam: John Benjamins.
Godenzzi, Juan Carlos, ed. 1999. *Tradición oral andina y amazónica. Métodos de análisis e interpretación de textos.* Cusco: CBC Centro de Estudios Regionales Andinos "Bartolomé de Las Casas" and PROEIB-ANDES. Programa de Formación en Educación Intercultural Bilingüe para los Países Andinos.
Goody, Jack. 1977. *The domestication of the savage mind.* Cambridge: Cambridge University Press.
Goody, Jack. 1987. *The interface between the written and the oral.* Cambridge: Cambridge University Press.
Goody, Jack. 1995. *The East in the West.* Cambridge: Cambridge University Press.
Goody, Jack. 2000. *The power of the written tradition.* Washington, D.C.: Smithsonian Institution Press.
Gnerre, Maurizio. 2004. Sound symbolism in southern Peruvian Quechua riddling. In Delgado-P. and Schechter, 367–395.
Greenberg, Joseph E. 1956. The general classification of Central and South American languages. In Anthony Wallace (ed.), *Men and cultures: Selected papers of the Fifth International Congress of Anthropological and Ethnological Sciences,* 791–794. Philadelphia: University of Pennsylvania Press.
Greenberg, Joseph E. 1987. *Language in the Americas.* Stanford: Stanford University Press.
Grimes, Joseph E. 1972. Outlines and overlays. *Language* 48(3):513–524.
Grimes, Joseph E. 1975. *The thread of discourse.* The Hague: Mouton.
Grimes, Joseph E., and Naomi Glock. 1970. A Saramaccan narrative pattern. *Language* 46(2)(Part 1):408–425.
Guaman Poma de Ayala, Felipe. 1980. *El primer nueva corónica y buen gobierno,* 3 vols. Edited by J. V. Murra and R. Adorno; translated by J. I. Urioste. Mexico, D.F.: Siglo Veintiuno.

Gumperz, John J., and Dell Hymes, eds. 1986. *Directions in sociolinguistics: The ethnography of communication*, second edition. New York: Basil Blackwell.
Gülich, Elisabeth, and Uta M. Quasthoff. 1985. Narrative analysis. In van Dijk 1985f, 169–197. London: Academic Press.
Haiman, John, and Pamela Munro, eds. 1983. *Switch-reference and universal grammar*. Amsterdam/Philadelphia: John Benjamins.
Hallberg, Peter. 1992. *Litterär teori och stilistik*. Goteborg: Akademiförlaget.
Hamer, Enid. 1966. *The metres of English poetry*. London: Methuen.
Hanson, Kristen, and Paul Kiparsky. 1997. The nature of verse and its consequences for the mixed form. In J. Harris and K. Reichl (eds.), *Prosimetrum: Cross-cultural perspectives on narrative verse and prose*. Cambridge: D. S. Brewer.
Harrison, Regina. 1989. *Signs, songs, and memory in the Andes; Translating Quechua language and culture*. Austin: University of Texas Press.
Havelock, Eric A. 1963. *Preface to Plato*. Cambridge, Mass.: Belknap Press of Harvard University Press.
Havelock, Eric A. 1976. *Origins of Western literacy*. Toronto: The Ontario Institute for Studies in Education.
Headland, Thomas N., Kenneth L. Pike, and Marvin Harris, eds. 1990. *Emics and etics: The insider/outsider debate*. Frontiers Of Anthropology 7. Sage Publications.
Heath, Shirley Brice. 1982. Protean shapes in literacy events: Ever-shifting oral and literate traditions. In Tannen, 91–117.
Heitzman, Allene. 1991. Tiempo y lugar en la narrativa del ashéninca pajonalino. *Revista Latinoamericana de Estudios Etnolingüísticos* 6:113–132.
Hermon, Gabriella. 1985. *Modularity in Syntax: Evidence from Quechua and other languages*. Dordrecht: Foris Publications.
Hintz, Diane M. 1996. Tiempo y plano de prominencia discursivo en el quechua de Corongo. In Parker, 233–271.
Hodge, Robert. 1985. Song. In van Dijk 1985a, 121–135.
Hodge, Robert. 1990. *Literature as discourse*. Baltimore: The Johns Hopkins University Press.
Hopper, Paul. 1979. Aspect and foregrounding in discourse. In Givón (ed.), *Syntax and semantics* 12, 213–241. New York: Academic Press.
Hopper, Paul J., ed. 1982a. *Tense-aspect: Between semantics and pragmatics*. Amsterdam: John Benjamins.
Hopper, Paul J. 1982b. Aspect between discourse and grammar: An introductory essay for the volume. In Hopper 1982a, 3–18.

Hopper, Paul J., and Sandra A. Thompson. 1980. Transitivity in grammar and discourse. *Language* 56(2):251–299.
Hopper, Paul J., and Sandra A. Thompson, eds. 1982. Introduction. *Syntax and Semantics 15: Studies in Transitivity*, 1–5. New York: Academic Press.
Hornberger, Nancy H. 1999. Función y forma poética en "El cóndor y la pastora". In Godenzzi, 81–147.
Howard-Malverde, Rosaleen. 1986. The achkay, the cacique and the neighbor: Oral tradition and talk in San Pedro de Pariarca. Bulletin de l'Institut Francais d'Etudes Andines XV(3–4).
Howard-Malverde, Rosaleen. 1989. Storytelling strategies in Quechua narrative performance. *Journal of Latin American Lore* 15(1):3–71.
Howard-Malverde, Rosaleen, ed. 1997a. *Creating context in Andean cultures*. New York: Oxford University Press.
Howard-Malverde, Rosaleen. 1997b. Introduction: Between text and context in the evocation of culture. In Howard-Malverde 1997a, 3–18.
Hrushovski, Benjamin. 1960. On free rhythms in modern poetry. In Sebeok, 173–190.
Huanca L., Tomás. 1989. *El yatiri en la communidad aymara*. La Paz: Ediciones CADA.
Hymes, Dell. 1979. How to talk like a bear in Takelma. *International Journal of American Linguistics* 45(2):101–106.
Hymes, Dell. 1980. Verse analysis of a Wasco text: Hiram Smith's "Atúnaqa". *International Journal of American Linguistics* 46(2):65–77.
Hymes, Dell. 1981. *In vain I tried to tell you*. Philadelphia: University of Pennsylvania Press.
Hymes, Dell. 1984. The earliest Clackamas text. *International Journal of American Linguistics* 50(4):358–383.
Hymes, Dell. 1986. Models of the interaction of language and social life. In Gumperz and D. Hymes, 35–71.
Hymes, Dell. 1992. Helen Sekaquaptewa's "Coyote and the Birds": Rhetorical analysis of a Hopi coyote story. *Anthropological Linguistics*, 34(1–4)45–72.
Hymes, Dell. 1996. *Ethnography, linguistics, narrative inequality*. London: Taylor and Francis.
Hymes, Dell. 2002. Translation of oral narratives. *Anthropology News* May 2002.

Hymes, Dell. 2003. Emic analysis of oral narrative: A native American example. In Mary Ruth Wise, Thomas N. Headland, and Ruth M. Brend (eds.), *Language and Life: Essays in Memory of Kenneth L. Pike*, 185–200. SIL International and the University of Texas at Arlington Publications in Linguistics 139. Dallas.

Hymes, Virginia, and Hazel Suppah. 1992. How long ago we got lost: A Warm Springs Sahaptin narrative. *Anthropological Linguistics* 34(1–4):73–83.

Isbell, Billie Jean. 2004. Protest arts from Ayacucho, Peru: Song and visual artworks as validation of experience." In Delgado-P. and Schechter, 237–262.

Jakobsen, Alfred. 1952. *Norskhet i språket hos Petter Dass*. Svorkmo: Svorkmo Prenteverk.

Jakobson, Roman. 1959. Linguistics and poetics. Concluding statement at the Conference on Style, Indiana University, April 1958. Revised and expanded at the Center for Advanced Study in the Behavioral Sciences, 1959.

Jakobson, Roman. 1960. Concluding statement: Linguistics and poetics. In T. A. Sebeok, 350–77.

Jakobson, Roman. 1966. Grammatical parallelism and its Russian facet. *Language* 42(2):399–429.

Jakobson, Roman. 1968. Poetry of grammar and grammar of poetry. *Lingua* 21:597–609.

Jones, Larry B., and Linda K. Jones. 1979. Multiple levels of information in discourse. In L. Jones (ed.), *Discourse studies in Mesoamerican languages*, 3–27. Summer Institute of Linguistics and University of Texas at Arlington Publications in Linguistics 58. Dallas.

Kalmár, Ivan. 1982. Transitivity in a Czech folk tale. In Sandra A. Hopper and Paul J. Thompson, 241–259.

Kempson, Ruth. 1988. Grammar and conversational principles. In F. Newmeyer (ed.), *Linguistics: The Cambridge survey*. Vol 2: *Linguistic theory: Extensions and implications*. Cambridge: Cambridge University Press.

Kindberg, Eric, and Mary Lynn Kindberg. 1996. Una gramática del quechua de Cailloma. Información de Campo 726 (ms.). Lima: Instituto Lingüístico de Verano.

Kittang, Atle, and Asbjørn Aarseth. 1993. *Lyriske strukturer*. Innføring i diktanalyse. Universitetsforlaget Oslo.

Kruckenberg, Anita Boström. 1979. *Roman Jakobsons poetik: Studier i dess teori och praktik.* Uppsala: Lundequistska.

Labov, W., and J. Waletzky. 1967. Narrative analysis: Oral versions of personal experience. In J. Helm (ed.), *Essays on the verbal and visual arts*, 12–42. Proceedings of the 1966 Annual Spring Meeting of the American Ethnological Society. Seattle: University of Washington Press.

Lagerroth, Erland. 1980. *Literaturvetenskapen vid en korsväg.* Rabén & Sjögren.

Lakoff, George. 1987. *Women, fire, and dangerous things.* Chicago and London: The University of Chicago Press.

Lakoff, George, and Mark Johnson. 1980. *Metaphors we live by.* Chicago: The University of Chicago Press.

Lakoff, Robin Tolmach. 1982. Some of my favorite writers are literate: The mingling of oral and literate strategies in written communication. In Tannen, 239–260.

Lambrecht, Knud. 1994/98. *Information structure and sentence form: Topic, focus, and the mental representations of discourse referents.* Cambridge: Cambridge University Press.

Landerman, Peter N. 1991. *Quechua dialects and their classification.* Ph.D. dissertation. University of California, Los Angeles.

Langacker, Ronald W. 1987. *Foundations of cognitive grammar, vol. 1: Theoretical prerequisites.* Stanford: Stanford University Press.

Langacker, Ronald W. 1988. A view of linguistic semantics. In B. Rudzka-Ostyn (ed.), *Topics in Cognitive Linguistics*, 50–90. Amsterdam: John Benjamins.

Larsen, Helen. 1974. Some grammatical features of legendary narrative in Ancash Quechua. In Brend, 419–440.

Larson, Mildred L. 1978. *The functions of reported speech in discourse.* Summer Institute of Linguistics and University of Texas at Arlington Publications in Linguistics 59. Dallas.

Lauriault, Jaime. 1957. Textos quechuas de la zona de Coracora, Depto. de Ayacucho. *Tradición. Revista Peruana de Cultura* 19–20:92–146.

Lauriault, Jaime. 1958. Textos quechuas de la zona de Coracora, Depto. de Ayacucho. *Tradición. Revista Peruana de Cultura* 21:90–153.

Leech, Geoffrey N. 1969/73. *A linguistic guide to English poetry.* London: Longman.

Leech, Geoffrey. 1985. Stylistics. In van Dijk 1985e, 39–57.

Levinsohn, S. H. 1975. Functional sentence perspective in Inga (Quechuan) discourse. *Journal of Linguistics* 11:13–37.

Levinsohn, S. H. 1976. Progression and digression in Inga (Quechuan) discourse. *Forum Linguisticum* 1:122–147.

Levinsohn, S. H. 1991. Variations in tense-aspect markers among Inga (Quechuan) dialects. In Mary Ritchie Key (ed.), *Language change in South American Indian languages*, 145–165. Philadelphia: University of Pennsylvania Press.
Li, Charles N. 1976. *Subject and Topic*. New York: Academic Press.
Longo, Oddone. 1997. Informasjon og kommunikasjon i antikken. In Mario Vegetti (ed.), *Nytt lys på antikkens litteratura*, 7–27. Cappelen Akademisk Forlay as.
Longacre, Robert E. 1974. Narrative versus other discourse genre. In Brend, 357–376.
Longacre, Robert E. 1976. *An anatomy of speech notions*. Lisse: Peter de Ridder Press.
Longacre, Robert E. 1983. *The grammar of discourse*. New York: Plenum Press.
Longacre, Robert E. 1985. Interpreting biblical stories. In van Dijk 1985e, 170–171.
Longacre, Robert E. 1996. *The grammar of discourse*. Second edition. New York: Plenum Press.
López-Baralt, Mercedes. 1979. La persistencia de las estructuras simbólicas andinas en los dibujos de Guamán Poma de Ayala. *Journal of Latin American Lore* 5(1):83–116.
López-Baralt, Mercedes. 1980. The Quechua elegy to the all-powerful Inca Atawallpa: A literary rendition of the Inkarri myth. *Latin American Indian Literatures* 4(2):79–86.
Lord, Albert B. 1965. Yugoslav epic folk poetry. In Alan Dundes, 265–268.
Loriot [Lauriault], James. 1975. *Notás sobre referencia en un texto quechua de Cuzco*. Datos Etno-Lingüísticos 15 (microfiche). Lima: Instituto Lingüístico de Verano
Lyons, Barry J. 2004. The landowner inside Mount Tungurahua: A Quichua song and a fieldwork story. In Delgado-P. and Schechter, 337–366.
Manes, Joan. 1987. Derivational relationships and lexical analysis: An examination of Quechua speech act verbs. In Jef Verschueren (ed.), *Linguistic action: Some empirical-conceptual studies*, 27–44. Norwood, N. J.: Ablex.
Mann, W., and S. Thompson. 1986. Relational propositions in discourse. *Discourse Processes* 9:57–90.
Mannheim, Bruce. 1986. Popular song and popular grammar and metalanguage. *Word* 37(1–2):45–75.
Mannheim, Bruce. 1991. *The language of the Inka since the European invasion*. Austin: University of Texas Press.

Mannheim, Bruce. 1999. Hacia una mitografía andina. In Godenzzi, 47–79.
Maranda, Pierre. 1985. Myths: Theologies and theoretical physics. In van Dijk 1985e, 187–197.
Maynard, Senko Kumiya. 1982. Hiroshima folktales: Text-typology from the perspective of structure and discourse modality. *Text* 2(4):375–393.
Morote Best, Efraín. 1987. Introducción. In Weber, 7–12.
Mukarovský, J. 1958. Standard language and poetic language. In Garvin (ed.), *A Prague school reader on esthetics, literary structure, and style*, 18–30. Washington D.C.: Georgetown University Press.
Muysken, Pieter. 2004. Two languages in two countries: The use of Spanish and Quechua songs and poems from Peru and Ecuador. In Delgado P. and Schechter, 35–60.
Nuckolls, Janis B. 1992. Sound symbolic involvement. *Journal of Linguistic Anthropology* 2(1):51–80.
Nuckolls, Janis B. 1996. *Sounds like life: Sound-symbolic grammar, performance, and cognition in Pastaza Quechua.* Oxford: Oxford University Press.
Ohtsuka, Keisuke and William F. Brewer. 1992. Discourse organization in the comprehension of temporal order in narrative texts. *Discourse Prosesses* 15(3):317–336.
Olrik, Axel. 1965. Epic laws of folk narrative. In Dundes, 29–141.
Ong, Walter J. 1982/97. *Orality and literacy.* N.Y.: Methuen & Co.
Öyslebö, Olaf. 1978. *Stil- og språkanalyse.* Oslo/Bergen/Tromsø: Universitetsforlaget.
Palmer, Gary B. 1996. *Toward a theory of cultural linguistics.* Austin: University of Texas Press.
Parker, Gary. 1963. La clasificación genética de los dialectos quechuas. *Revista del Museo Nacional* 32:241–252.
Parker, Stephen, ed. 1996. *Estudios Etno-Lingüísticos III.* Documento de Trabajo 31. Pucallpa, Peru: Instituto Lingüístico de Verano.
Parry, Adam. 1971. Introduction and footnotes, *passim.* In Adam Parry (ed.), *The making of homeric verse: The collected papers of Milman Parry,* ix–xlii. Oxford: Clarendon Press.
Pärssinen, Martti. 1992. *Tawantinsuyu: The Inka state and its political organization.* Helsinki: SHS.
Pavel, Thomas G. 1985. Literary narratives. In van Dijk 1985e, 83–103.
Payne, Doris L. 1992a. Narrative discontinuity versus continuity in Yagua. *Discourse Processes* 15(3):375–394.

Payne, Doris L. 1992b. Introduction. In Doris L. Payne (ed.), *Pragmatics of word order flexibility*, 1–13. Amsterdam: John Benjamin.
Payne, Thomas E. 1996. Estatividad y movimiento. In Bergli, 221–268.
Pilkington, Adrian. 2000. *Poetic effects: A Relevance Theory perspective.* Amsterdam/Philadelpia: John Benjamins.
Pike, Kenneth L. 1967. *Language in relation to a unified theory of the structure of human behavior.* The Hague: Mouton & Co.
Pike, Kenneth L. 1990. On the emics and etics of Pike and Harris. In Thomas N. Headland, Kenneth L. Pike, and Marvin Harris, 28–47.
Plett, Heinrich F. 1985. Rhetoric. In van Dijk 1985e, 59–84.
Powlison, Paul S. 1969. *Yagua mythology and its epic tendencies.* Ph.D. dissertation. Bloomington: Indiana University.
Powlison, Paul S. 1985. *Yagua mythology: Epic tendencies in a new world mythology.* Dallas: International Museum of Cultures.
Powlison, Paul S. 1993. *La mitología yagua: Tendencias épicas en una mitología del nuevo mundo.* Pucallpa, Peru: Instituto Lingüístico de Verano.
Propp, Vládimir. 1958. *Morphology of the folktale.* Translated by Laurence Scott from 1928 original. Indiana University Publications in Anthropology, Folklore, and Linguistics 10. 1968/1977, rev. ed., University of Texas Press.
de Reuse, Willem J. 1986. The lexicalization of sound symbolism in Santiago del Estero Quechua. *International Journal American Linguistics* 52(1):54–64.
Roberts, John R. 1988a. Amele switch-reference and the theory of grammar. *Linguistic Inquiry* 19(1):45–63.
Roberts, John R. 1988b. Switch-reference in Papuan languages: A syntactic or extrasyntactic device? *Australian Journal of Linguistics* 8:75–117.
Rørvik, Harald. 1968. *Innføring i pedagogisk psykologi.* Oslo/Bergen/Tromsø: Universitetsforlaget.
Rostworowski de Diez Canseco, María. 1999. *History of the Inca realm.* Cambridge: Cambridge University Press.
Schechter, John M. 1987. Quechua Sanjuán in Northern Highland Ecuador: Harp music as structural metaphor on Purina. *Journal of Latin American Lore* 13(1):27–46.
Schechter, John M., and Guillermo Delgado-P., eds. 2004. *Quechua verbal artistry: The inscription of Andean voices.* Bonn Americanist Studies/BAS 38.
Schottelndreyer, Mareike, and S. H. Levinsohn. 1976. The Catio folktale as a play in acts and scenes. *Poetics* 5:247–280.

Scollon, Ron, and Suzanne Scollon. 1981. Narrative, literacy and face in interethnic communication. In Roy Freedle (ed.), *Advances in discourse processes* 7. Norwood, N.J.: Ablex.

Sebeok, Thomas A., ed. 1960. *Style in language.* Cambridge, Mass.: MIT Press.

Shaver, Dwight A. 1996. Análisis gramatical de un texto en el quechua de Lambayeque. In Parker, 70–101.

Sherzer, Joel. 1990. *Verbal art in San Blas: Kuna culture through its discourse.* Cambridge Studies in Oral and Literate Culture 21. Cambridge University Press.

Slobin, Dan I. 1991. Learning to think for speaking: Native language, cognition, and rhetorical style. *Pragmatics* 1(1):7–25.

Soto Ruiz, Clodoaldo. 1976a. *Gramática quechua: Ayacucho-Chanca.* Lima: Ministerio de Educación/Instituto de Estudios Peruanos.

Soto Ruiz, Clodoaldo. 1976b. *Diccionario quechua: Ayacucho-Chanca.* Lima: Ministerio de Educación/Instituto de Estudios Peruanos.

Sparing, Margarethe Wilma. 1984. *The perception of reality in the Volksmärchen of Schleswig-Holstein.* Lanham, Md.: University Press of America.

Sperber, Dan, and Deidre Wilson. 1995. *Relevance: Communication and cognition.* Oxford: Blackwell.

Stankiewicz, Edward. 1960. Linguistics and the study of poetic language. In Sebeok, 69–81.

Stewart, Anne M. 1984. Why *-ski*? A study of verbal aspect in Conchucos Quechua. In Arnold M. Zwicky and Rex E. Wallace (eds.), *Ohio State University Working Papers in Linguistics* 29:70–104.

Stewart, Anne M. 1987. *Clause-combining in Conchucos Quechua discourse.* Ph.D. dissertation. University of California, Los Angeles.

Stirling, Lesley. 1993. *Switch-reference and discourse representation.* Cambridge Studies in Linguistics 63. Cambridge University Press.

Strahm, Ester. 1978. Cohesion Markers in Jirel Narrative. In Joseph E. Grimes (ed.), *Papers on Discourse,* 342–348. Dallas: Summer Institute of Linguistics.

Svensen, Åsfrid. 1985/1991. *Tekstens mönstre. Innföring i litterær analyse.* Oslo: Universitetsforlaget.

Szemiński, Jan. 1997. *Wira Quchan y sus obras: Teología andina y lenguaje, 1550–1662.* Lima: IEP/BCRP.

Talmy, Leonard. 1987. The relation of grammar to cognition. In B. Ruczka-Ostyn (ed.), *Topics on cognitive linguistics,* 165–205. Amsterdam: John Benjamin.

Tannen, Deborah, ed. 1982a. *Spoken and written language: Exploring orality and literacy.* Norwood, N.J.: Ablex.

Tannen, Deborah. 1982b. The oral/literate continuum in discourse. In Tannen 1982b, 1–16.

Tarasov, L. 1986. *This amazingly symmetrical world.* Moscow: MIR Publishers.

Thompson, Stith. 1977. *The folktale.* Los Angeles: University of California Press.

Torero, Alfredo. 1964. Los dialectos quechuas. *Anales Científicos* 2(4):445–478.

Torvik, Arne. 1994. *Litteraturteori, Litteraturlesing og Litteraturformidling.* TANO.

Urban, Greg. 1987. Style in South American Indian languages. Paper presented at the Amazonian Languages Conference, Eugene, Oregon, August 4, 1987.

van Dijk, Teun A. 1972. *Some aspects of text grammars.* The Hague: Mouton.

van Dijk, Teun A. 1985a. *Handbook of discourse analysis 1.* London: Academic Press.

van Dijk, Teun A. 1985b. Introduction: Discourse analysis as a new cross-discipline. In van Dijk 1985a, 1:1–9.

van Dijk, Teun A. 1985c. Introduction: Levels and dimensions of discourse analysis." In van Dijk 1985f, 2:1–11.

van Dijk, Teun A. 1985d. Semantic discourse analysis. In van Dijk 1985f, 2:103–136.

van Dijk, Teun A. 1985e. *Discourse and literature.* Amsterdam: John Benjamins.

van Dijk, Teun A. 1985f. *Handbook of discourse analysis 2.* London: Academic Press.

Vázquez, Juan Adolfo. 1977. The field of Latin American Indian literatures. *Latin American Indian Literatures* 1(1):1–33.

Vegetti, Mario, ed. 1997. *Nytt lys på antikkens litteratur.* Norwegian edition: Trond Berg Eriksen, Håkon Harket, Eivind Tjønneland. *Cappelens upopulære skrifter.* Cappelen Akademisk Forlag as.

Verschueren, Jef, ed. 1987. *Linguistic action: Some empirical-conceptual studies.* Advances in Discourse Processes 23. Norwood, N.J.: Ablex.

Wallace, Stephen. 1982. Figure and ground: The interrelationships of linguistic categories. In Paul J. Hopper, 201–223.

Weber, David John. 1986. Information perspective, profile, and patterns in Quechua. In Wallace Chafe and Johanna Nichols, 137–155.

Weber, David John, ed. 1987. *Juan del Oso*. Serie Lingüística Peruana 26. Pucallpa, Peru: Instituto Lingüístico de Verano.
Weber, David John. 1989. *A grammar of Huallaga (Huanuco) Quechua*. Los Angeles: University of California Press.
Weber, David, and Elke Meier, eds. 2008. *Achkay: Mito vigente en el mundo quechua*. Serie Lingüística Peruana 54. Lima: Instituto Lingüístico de Verano.
Weiss, Gerald. 1977. Rhetoric in Campa narrative. *Journal of Latin American Lore* 3(2):169–182.
Wells, Rulon. 1960. Nominal and verbal style. In Sebeok, 213–220.
Wendland, Ernst R. 2004. *Translating the literature of Scripture: A literary-rhetorical approach to Bible translation*. Publications in Translation and Textlinguistics 1. Dallas: SIL International.
Wiget, Andrew O. 1980. Aztec lyrics: Poetry in a world of continually perishing flowers. *Latin American Indian Literatures* 4(1):1–11.
Wilson, Deidre. 1994. Relevance and understanding. In Gillian Brown, Kirsten Malmkjær, Alastair Pollitt, and John Williams (eds.) *Language and understanding*. Oxford Applied Linguistics.
Wise, Mary Ruth. 1971. *Identification of participants in discourse: A study of aspects of form and meaning in Nomatsiguenga*. Publications in Linguistics and Related Fields 28. Norman: Summer Institute of Linguistics of the University of Oklahoma.
Wise, Mary Ruth. 1974. Social roles, plot roles, and focal roles in a Nomatsiguenga Campa myth. In Brend, 389–418.
Wise, Mary Ruth. 1989. Language typology in relation to narrative texts of indigenous languages of Latin America. In Shin Ja J. Hwang and William R. Merrifield (eds.), *Language in context: Essays for Robert E. Longacre*, 137–153. Dallas: Summer Institute of Linguistics.
Wise, Mary Ruth. 1990. Lo tradicional y lo moderno en la literatura indígena. In Bergli (ed.), 141–149.
Wise, Mary Ruth. 1993. Nuevas tendencias en la clasificación genealógica de lenguas amazónicas peruanas. *Signo y Seña* 3:73–91.
Wise, Mary Ruth, and Ivan Lowe. 1996. Grupos de permutación en el discurso. In Bergli, 105–128. (Previously published in 1972 as Permutation groups in discourse, in *Languages and Linguistic Working Papers* 4:12–34. Washington: Georgetown University Press.)
Wise, Mary Ruth, Thomas N. Headland, Ruth M. Brend, eds. 2003. *Language and life: Essays in memory of Kenneth L. Pike*. Dallas: SIL International and the University of Texas at Arlington.
Wolfson, Nessa. 1979. The conversational historical present alternation. *Language* 55(1):168–182.

Woodbury, Anthony C. 1983. Switch-reference, syntactic organization, and rhetorical structure in Central Yup'ik Eskimo. In Haiman and Munro, 291–325.

Worton, Michael, and Judith Still, eds. 1990. *Intertextuality: Theories and practices*. Manchester University Press.

Wroughton, James F. 1989. Tema en *usya*, narrativa del quechua de Pomabamba Ancash, desde los puntos de vista de las referencias a los participantes y la relación entre los diferentes tipos de verbos. Paper given at VIII Congreso Peruano del Hombre y la Cultura Andina, Trujillo, Perú. Published in 2008 as Usya, texto narrativo del quechua de Pomabamba. In Heidi Coombs and Ågot Bergli (eds.), *Estudios quechuas II*, 148–158. Serie Lingüística Peruana 55. Lima: Instituto Lingüístico de Verano.

Wroughton, John R. 1996. *Gramática y textos del quechua shausha huanca*. Documento de Trabajo 30. Pucallpa, Peru: Instituto Lingüístico de Verano.

Young, E. Richard, Alton L. Becker, and Kenneth L. Pike. 1970. *Rhetoric: Discovery and change*. New York: Harcourt, Brace & World.

www.ingramcontent.com/pod-product-compliance
Lightning Source LLC
Chambersburg PA
CBHW070015010526
44117CB00011B/1580